D1200938

International Manual on Collective Bargaining for Public Employees

edited by
Seymour P. Kaye
Arthur Marsh
foreword by
Theodore W. Kheel

The Praeger Special Studies program—
utilizing the most modern and efficient book
production techniques and a selective
worldwide distribution network—makes
available to the academic, government, and
business communities significant, timely
research in U.S. and international economic, social, and political development.

International Manual on Collective Bargaining for Public Employees

PRAEGER SPECIAL STUDIES IN INTERNATIONAL POLITICS AND GOVERNMENT

Praeger Publishers   New York   Washington   London

PRAEGER PUBLISHERS
111 Fourth Avenue, New York, N.Y. 10003, U.S.A.
5, Cromwell Place, London S.W.7, England

Published in the United States of America in 1973
by Praeger Publishers, Inc.

Library of Congress Catalog Card Number: 71-130530

Printed in the United States of America

To Melanie, Lauren, and James Kaye

FOREWORD
Theodore W. Kheel

Public employment grows in significance each day, as governments at every level undertake new programs to supply additional services for the public good. The expansion is worldwide, posing accelerated problems of the greatest magnitude and the utmost urgency. The vast dimension of the public sector is graphically apparent, for example, in the State of New York, where the public payroll comprises nearly 800,000 public employees. These men and women work for some 8,600 state and local authorities.

Across the U.S. continent, there are more than 12 million public workers, the majority of whom work for state and local governments. It is anticipated that these numbers will swell by two-thirds by the early 1980s. This same expansion is occurring in Europe and elsewhere. As public responsibility and government activity have reached into new areas, public employees have followed the example of workers in the private sector and have organized for their mutual benefit.

This organizational growth has been accompanied by increasing resort to strikes--by teachers in scores of cities, by policemen and firemen, by social workers, by amusement park attendants and zoo keepers, and in Sweden by even the military. The strike fever is contagious; leapfrogging demands and multiplying disputes leave government hesitant and defensive and distracted from the other unresolved social, economic, and political problems of domestic crisis.

These internationally related developments have confronted the country with one of the most difficult questions, perhaps the most important challenge, of our time: how to prevent strikes that imperil the public interest while providing millions of employees with the opportunity to participate in the process of determining the conditions of their work. Our response to this challenge will be measured no less than will the capacity of our government to serve the public welfare and the ability of our people to live together in a society of overlapping claims.

The dilemma of balancing individual rights with the public interest poses questions like the following:

1. Does a legal prohibition of all strikes by public workers most effectively prevent disruption of services?

2. How best can a law contribute to the creation of a climate conducive to settlement of disputes by the parties?

3. How best can a law or machinery established by law give proper weight to the critical human element in labor relations and to the skill and responsibility of negotiators and third-party interveners?

4. If strikes are prohibited, can equitable treatment for employees be achieved without resort to outside authority for the ultimate determination? Is there any legal obstacle to third-party determination? What is the most effective way to frame the issue or issues? Can government fairly insist that public employees be compelled to work and not strike and not also insist that taxpayers be compelled to accept the decision of a third party?

5. In those areas where strikes are prohibited, can a system of penalties be devised effectively to discourage unlawful conduct?

6. If joint determination is to be pursued, what machinery is most effective? Should the same procedures for resolving disputes be applied to all groups of public employees? Should a third-party intervener have the obligation to make public recommendations or the power to decide whether or not to make recommendations?

7. If a settlement is not reached with the assistance of a third party, how should the deadlock be resolved?

8. What can be done generally to improve the atmosphere of labor-management relations in the public as well as the private sector?

These are but a few of the questions. We are now in the stages of infancy in public employment relations. There may be no conclusive answers, but I do see some underlying principles and some avenues of further inquiry and possible change. The giant steps toward constructive change lie in the insight inherent in this book--with this kind of necessary forum and scholarship, with the exposure and understanding of experience from country to country.

Seymour P. Kaye, Arthur I. Marsh, and their colleagues have, by their discussion and analysis, stimulated and steered thinking, bringing us closer to the objective of developing techniques that will secure the rights of employees without disrupting essential services. Through these and similar efforts, we can make collective bargaining work more effectively in public employment.

This international symposium serves to create an environment for more harmonious labor relations in which disputes are resolved without resort to strikes because the parties have a basic trust and a fundamental sense of their mutual goals and mutual understanding. Only if the pragmatic lawyers, judges, professors, and officials aid in achieving that climate can we meet our objectives--to provide continuity of community services while affording equitable treatment to public employees.

"Come now, and let us reason together . . ."
The Bible: The Book of the prophet Isaiah,
1:17-18

Rather than mirror secular modes and manners
of public employee labor relations and in order to
penetrate rather than reflect images and postures,
this international forum views comparative study as
a window to the world of ideas and innovation.

By fusing information and insight into a co-
herent vision of reality, comparative intelligence
restores a wholeness to understanding that partisan
experience atomizes. The problems of burgeoning
public employment are worldwide, for we are irrevo-
cably involved in a network of peoples and affairs
that girdles the globe. "No man is an island, entire of itself; every man is a piece of the Continent, a part of the main . . . involved in mankind."[1]

By bridging the generation gap, separating the
eras of unilateral state authority and bilateral
collective bargaining, the wisdom of interrelationship offers not only light to the people of one
country but also hope to the world for greater ac-
cord and less travail. As man shoots celestially
for the heavens above and the stars beyond, he
leaves a wake of terrestrial problems of peace, of
ecology, and, in general, of organizing life on this
planet. With the prospect of one in every five persons manning public jobs that are necessary and
essential for adequate education, transportation,
health, welfare, and safety, earthmen have their
priorities marked big and bold.

---

[1]John Donne, "XVII, Meditation," The Complete
Poetry and Selected Prose of John Donne, ed. Charles
Coffin (New York: Modern Library, 1952).

Much of today's frustration is caused by a surplus of simple answers, coupled with a shortage of
simple problems, causing a relative drought of understanding about the roots and routes of change.
Change in the public establishment is linked to
change in the concept of authority. The fiefdom of
public service, with the obedient servant pledged
to prince and nation, has been liberated. New traditions and changed relationships arise as the sovereign state becomes the consulting employer, as
homage becomes protest, as allegiance becomes agreement, and as fiat becomes consensus.

Such emerging mood and movement are a developing universal life style requiring innovated, not
recycled, ideas. Thus, the enervated public sector
finds comparison, counterpart, and challenge between
the United States, Belgium, Great Britain, the Federal Republic of Germany, Italy, Sweden, and Norway.

Profiling U.S. bargaining, sketched from over
60,000 disputes, William E. Simkin, former director
of the Federal Mediation and Conciliation Service,
outlines its characteristics as follows:

> The first is that there are few things
> about bargaining that are static.
> Change is everywhere.
>
> The second is that the process is highly
> adaptable in a very diverse economy
> where adaptability is essential to sur-
> vival and growth.
>
> The third is that its process stimulates
> imagination and innovation. It embodies
> important elements of creation.[2]

Finally, as Simkin notes, with special emphasis,
"one very obvious and serious problem area is bargaining in the public service."[3]

---

[2] William E. Simkin, <u>Collective Bargaining--
a Prognosis</u> (Washington, D.C.: U.S. Information
Service, 1969), p. 3.

[3] <u>Ibid</u>.

The dimension of this problem area changes with the size and shape of population and protest from country to country, but the "mod" look is basically the same: burgeoning public employment, services, and unionism; spiraling costs; and surging disputes. For the United States alone, there is a projected public employment population explosion of 13 million employees by 1975. Such growth has spawned fiery strikes and expansive issues, cradled in a collective negotiation process that is challenged to reconcile two natural urges: employee pressure for job security and advancement and employer resistance to collective encroachment upon government's right to provide stable, continuous services. Such a contest breeds decisions conceived "in heat" and delivered amid pains of militant strikes disabling the body politic.

Maturity seems distant as the public sector is nurtured on conflict and controversy, but the impact of its growing pains is immediate and immense. The sounds of fury, composed of employee aspirations clashing with legal restraints, echo dissension and disorder. The resultant clamor lends itself to drama and distortion. Hence, local government is popularly described as a case of governing the ungovernable in which, says The New York Times, "there may be no villains, but there are an awful lot of victims . . . everyone's got muscle but the people."

So, all is not quiet on the western front. Escalation of unrest by the aroused sleeping giant of public unionism rallies reaction and resistance in the face of drawn and locked bridges, jammed highways, mounting mail, piled garbage, vacant classrooms, stalled trains, and restricted police and fire calls. Brinksmanship and gamesmanship tend to ignite the immediate wrath of the press, which deplores alleged reckless transference of sovereignty and surrender to power tactics. In turn, the ire of the citizenry, thinly disguised by a veneer of hard nonchalance, quickly flares up.

Particularly polarized are urban centers, which are impacted by balkanized competition between unions, especially uniformed services' unions, vying for recognition and reward. The plight of the city, emphasizes New York City's mayor, is on the bargaining table, where decision-making ricochets in the cross fire of budgetary controls, shrinking tax bases, legal restraints, and rising expectations.

The crescendo of charge and countercharge, heard in this internecine civic warfare, drowns out rational response to such vital questions as the following:

1. Is there a right to strike by the public sector for enhanced job security without jeopardizing the public interest manifest in uninterrupted, effectively regulated services and benefits?
2. Are strike bans workable and in what form and shape?
3. Are there alternatives for harmonizing seemingly conflicting goals and interests within or without collective bargaining?
4. What are the criteria and content for workable collective bargaining machinery adequately safeguarding the taxpayer, governmental executives, and the public workers?

This symposium was spurred by Seymour P. Kaye's experience as general counsel of the New York City Mayor's Office of Labor Relations, which governs the labor relations of over 250,000 public employees, and was accelerated by his intense European exposure and residence as director of industrial relations for International Telephone and Telegraph--Europe, where he supervised that company's labor relations in over 12 countries.

With the help of Professor Arthur I. Marsh of Oxford University as coeditor, the forum was fortunate to enlist subsequently the scholarship and experience of the following contributors: Theodore W. Kheel, a foremost U.S. public mediator; Arvid Anderson, chairman of the New York City Office of Collective Bargaining; Marc Somerhausen, Belgian jurist and educator; Dieter Gaul, a German jurist and educator; Paolo G. Pisano, Rome resident partner of an international law firm; and Steven D. Anderman, a law professor at Warwick University in England.

Drawing from their wide areas of expertise, these commentators endeavor to portray the public scene graphically, blending experience with insight

and separating shadows from light, in order to reveal the shape and substance of the following issues:

1. Freedom to form and join representative organizations grounded in policy and practice
2. Status, in membership and role, of employee
and employer associations
3. Policy and practice, de jure and de facto,
regarding representation, negotiation, and implementation
4. Scope of representation relating to normal
and critical issues
5. Right to strike in terms of legality, sanctions, and incidence
6. Techniques and tactics of impasse resolution.

As pundits rather than prophets and not to
oversimplify and overstate but to communicate and
clarify, these international commentators have
pooled their experience for the following common
purposes:

1. Focusing the dimension of public unions in
size and shape
2. Identifying critical issues and policies
and assessing their present and future impact
3. Composing and clarifying common and uncommon policies and procedures
4. Describing and defining the role of associations, government, community, citizens, and the
press in the whole context of public employment
5. Synthesizing developments and patterns into
discernible trends
6. Furnishing a frame of reference for legislation, advocacy, and understanding.

The flood of current problems in public employee labor relations portends the wave of the
future. In quiet desperation one could succumb to
its crosscurrents with the air of poetic resignation contained in one of Langston Hughes' poems:

```
        I could tell you
           if I wanted to
        what makes me
           what I am;
        but I don't
           really want to--
        and you don't
           give a damn.
```

But, instead, as is the aim of this study, one could
devote energy and resources toward communicating information and creating understanding. In such pur-
suit comparative study can best search and suggest,
discover and dispel, by heeding the words of Henry
Thoreau: "Probe the earth to see where your roots
run."

Seymour P. Kaye

ACKNOWLEDGMENTS

For invaluable source and reference material acknowledgment is due such institutions and individuals as P. Tofahrn, general secretary, Public Services International; the Netherlands Ministry of Home Affairs; Sven-Wilhem Beckman, Bitradande director, Svenska Arbetsgivareforeningen; Jack Oates, formerly of the British Ministry of Labour; Herbert Haber, director of the New York City Office of Labor Relations; Professor Herman Bloch, St. Johns University, New York; Professor John Ulmann, Hofstra University, New York; and Axel Kaufman and Victor Malka, Copenhagen.

Necessary liaison and interchange with various countries were generously provided by the following: International Telephone and Telegraph colleagues such as Corbin McNeill, Campbell MacArthur, Jeff Noble, John Lewandoski, Donovan Conlon, Jakob Eldon, A. J. Skipp, and Klaus Troester; and friends and mentors such as David Crombie, Ugo Galassi, and Theodore W. Kheel.

Secretarial assistance beyond the call of duty came from Janine Halain, Kathy O'Neill, Susan Borelli, and the legal staff of Rains, Pogrebin, and Scher.

For warmth and inspiration special tribute is due Paul R. Hays, justive of the United States Court of Appeals, Second Circuit, who introduced the author to labor law at Columbia University School of Law; Judge Royal S. Radin, Alexander Jaffee, Marvin Weiselberg, and their respective wives, for their faith and friendship; Bertha Kassewitz and Gloria Kaye, for their support; and Harry Rains and the law colleagues of Seymour P. Kaye, for their assistance.

Finally, lighting the way were Melanie, Lauren, and James Kaye, who made the book a common cause, and Eveline Portnoy Hunt, who made it a joint venture.

CONTENTS

LIST OF TABLES AND FIGURES

International Manual on Collective Bargaining for Public Employees

1

THE UNITED STATES
Arvid Anderson
Seymour P. Kaye

Collective bargaining in the public service is
changing the establishment of government at all
levels. The growth of public employee unions and
the development of public employee labor relations
in the United States has had and is having a profound effect on governmental institutions. Some 40
states have enacted laws governing the employment
relationship for some or all of their employees.
Less than 20 of these state laws are comprehensive
in their coverage, but the trend to full-scale bargaining laws is clear.[1] Bargaining laws have covered employees at all levels of government--federal,
state, and local.

The 1960s marked a period when public employee
unions and collective bargaining established a very
firm foothold throughout the country. Although the
extension of collective bargaining is far from complete, with respect to all governmental units and
jurisdictions and categories of employees, the
trend at the end of the decade was so firmly established as to be irreversible.

GROWTH OF PUBLIC UNIONISM

In the United States today approximately one
out of every six and shortly one out of every five
employees will be on a public payroll at either the
state, local, or federal level, working in education,

health, transportation, housing, sanitation, police, fire, and other services.[2] It is anticipated that the nearly 12 million employees of government will swell to 15 million by 1975.[3]

Public employee organizations have capitalized on the aspirations of public servants to receive the same gains and benefits achieved by their counterparts in private employment. Thus, the decade of the 1960s marked a "catch-up" period in economic benefits for public employees.

Public employee unions--particularly those representing skilled tradesmen, fire fighters, public utility workers, and certain white-collar classifications--have existed for a considerable period of time. Many were formed during the period of the growth of collective bargaining in the private sector in the mid- and late 1930s.

The period of rapid growth of public employee unions commenced in the late 1950s, taking on impressive dimension by the early 1960s. The enactment of the Wisconsin statute for municipal employees in 1959, President John F. Kennedy's Executive Order 10988 for federal employees in 1962, and Mayor Robert Wagner's Executive Order for employees of New York City in 1958 all encouraged the growth of public employee unions.

These early laws were followed by the enactment of a more comprehensive statute by Wisconsin in 1962 providing for full-scale collective bargaining by local employees. That act was followed by municipal bargaining statutes in Connecticut, Michigan, Massachusetts, Rhode Island, and other states; and the New York City Collective Bargaining Law in 1967.

The enactment of the Taylor Law* in New York State marked another period of broad extension of collective bargaining rights to public employees. This growth also witnessed a change in the character

---

*New York State Public Employees' Fair Employment Act, Ch. 392, Sec. 210(f), New York Laws 1102(1967).

of public employee organizations. Employee associations took on the characteristics of militant
trade unions. Tables 1-4 and Figure 1 indicate the
very large growth in public employee unions, as
well as their distribution by state and union.

HISTORY OF PUBLIC UNIONISM

The history of public employee relations can be
divided into three periods: before 1946, 1946-59,
and after 1959. Before the early 1920s the federal
government and many state government payrolls were
stamped with patronage hallmarks accompanied by
totally inconsistent and irregular hiring, classification, retirement, promotion, and pay practices.
Such practices spurred the advent of civil service
systems at the state and federal level and also
created the demands for public employee unions.

The letter carriers, as early as 1868, organized a campaign for an eight-hour day. In 1912
the Lloyd-LaFollette Act granted rights to federal
civil service employees to petition Congress collectively and to affiliate with organizations as
long as they did not advocate the right to strike.
In 1919 the Boston police strike occurred, and
Calvin Coolidge made his famous statement that
"there is no right to strike against the public
safety by anyone, anywhere, anytime."[4]

In 1926 Justice Louis Brandeis wrote in Dorchy
v. Kansas that "neither the common law nor the
Fourteenth Amendment confers the absolute right to
strike."[5] But limitations and prohibitions on
strikes by courts and legislatures did not discourage the growth of public employee unions. In 1940
the U.S. Civil Service Commission required all governmental agencies to establish grievance procedures and to consult with their employees.[6]

Although the period of the New Deal firmly
established and protected the process of collective
bargaining for private-sector employees, public-
sector employees were specifically excluded from
coverage. It was during the New Deal that Franklin
D. Roosevelt, secularizing the Wagner Act, declared
the following:

TABLE 1

Union Membership by Sector, United States, 1956-68

Year	Total* (thousands)	Manufacturing Number (thousands)	Percent	Nonmanufacturing Number (thousands)	Percent	Government Number (thousands)	Percent
1956	18,104	8,839	48.8	8,350	46.1	915	5.1
1958	17,968	8,359	46.5	8,574	47.7	1,035	5.8
1960	18,036	8,591	47.6	8,375	46.4	1,070	5.9
1962	17,564	8,050	45.8	8,289	47.2	1,225	7.0
1964	17,920	8,342	46.6	8,125	45.3	1,453	8.1
1966	19,126	8,769	45.8	8,640	45.2	1,717	9.0
1968	20,210	9,218	45.6	8,837	43.7	2,155	10.7
Absolute Change							
1956-60	-68	-248		-25		155	
1960-68	2,174	627		462		1,085	
1956-68	2,106	379		487		1,240	
Percentage Change							
1956-60	-0.4		-2.8		-0.4		16.9
1960-68	12.1		7.4		5.5		101.4
1956-68	11.6		4.3		5.8		135.5

*Includes membership outside United States.

Source: Harry P. Cohany and Lucretia M. Dewey, "Union Membership Among Government Employees," Monthly Labor Review, July 1970, p. 16.

> A strike of public employees mani-
> fests nothing less than an intent on
> their part to prevent or obstruct the
> operations of government until their
> demands are satisfied. Such action,
> looking toward the paralysis of gov-
> ernment by those who have sworn to
> support it, is unthinkable and in-
> tolerable.[7]

That declaration and that of President Coolidge
symbolized the public attitude toward the question
of governmental strikes and public employee unionism. The general public attitude still urges the
prohibition of the right to strike by public employees, especially in the areas of safety, essential services, and even convenience. Nevertheless,
public employee unionism and collective bargaining,
both de jure and de facto, have continued to grow.
During the post-World War II period of 1946-59
several state legislatures enacted strike bans.
Perhaps the best known are New York State's Condon-
Wadlin Act and the strike ban for federal employees
in the Taft-Hartley Act.[8] The Condon-Wadlin Act
(1947) provided for no collective bargaining between the public employer and its employees but did
prohibit strikes, defined as follows:

> the failure to report for duty, the
> willful abstinence from one's posi-
> tion, the stoppage of work, or the
> abstinence in whole or in part from
> the full, faithful and proper per-
> formance of the duties of employment
> for the purpose of inducing, influenc-
> ing or coercing a change in the con-
> ditions or compensation, or the rights,
> privileges or obligations of employ-
> ment.

Under its sanctions, a striking employee was subject to immediate dismissal, with full reinstate-
ment contingent upon five years of probation and
three years of fixed, static compensation.

TABLE 2

Total Membership of Selected Unions with Major Proportion
(at least 50 percent) of Membership in Public
Service, United States, 1952-68

Union	1952	1954	1956
UNIONS OF FEDERAL EMPLOYEES			
Total	452,242	526,033	533,43
ASCS County Office Employees, National Association of (Ind.)*			
Federal Employees Association (Ind.)	90,000	99,000	98,00
Government Employees, American Federation of	48,000	62,000	64,00
Government Employees, National Association of (Ind.)			
Internal Revenue Association (Ind.)			
Letter Carriers, National Association of	95,000	103,000	108,00
Letter Carriers, National Rural Association of (Ind.)	34,570	36,355	35,90
Messengers, National Association of Special Delivery	2,000	2,000	2,00
Post Office Clerks[b]	95,000	101,576	97,05
Post Office Craftsmen[b]		40,000	40,10
Post Office and General Services Maintenance Employees (Ind.)	10,000	7,549	7,70
Post Office Mail Handlers, Watchmen, Messengers, and Leaders; National Association of[c]	2,000	6,000	9,00
Post Office Motor Vehicle Employees, National Federation of	6,172	6,274	6,95
Postal and Federal Employees, National Alliance of (Ind.)		19,000	18,00
Postal Supervisors, National Association of (Ind.)	16,500	19,479	19,92
Postal Transport Association[d]	27,000	23,800	26,80
Postal Union, National (Ind.)			
Postmasters, National Association of (Ind.)			
Postmasters, National League of (Ind.)	26,000		
UNIONS OF STATE AND LOCAL EMPLOYEES			
Total	211,000	226,468	285,00
Firefighters, International Association of	76,000	85,000	85,00
State, County, and Municipal Employees; American Federation of	85,000	96,328	150,00
Teachers, American Federation of	50,000	45,140	50,00

*Agricultural Stabilization and Conservative Society.

[a]Where 1956 figures are not shown, base period is first subsequent year for which figures are shown.

[b]Post Office Clerks and Post Office Craftsmen merged to form United Federation of Postal Clerks (AFL-CIO) on July 1, 1961.

1958	1960	1962	1964	1966	1968	Percent Change, 1956–68[a]
545,709	535,277	667,021	793,458	933,035	1,100,087	106.2
		12,888	14,098	14,300	14,130	8.6
90,000	53,000	49,500	40,000	80,000	95,000	− 3.1
60,000	70,322	106,042	138,642	199,823	294,725	360.5
			15,000			
		27,125	27,000	24,130	26,360	− 2.8
110,000	138,000	150,114	167,913	189,628	210,000	94.4
36,723	38,321	35,852	42,300	40,340	41,192	14.7
1,987	2,000	1,500	1,500	2,073	2,605	30.3
100,000	135,000	145,000	139,000	143,146	166,000	71.0
38,500						
7,700	7,400	8,000	8,424	9,237	13,175	71.1
5,500	4,000	14,000	29,000	32,000	24,000	166.7
5,000	5,000	5,000	6,200	8,141	8,000	15.0
18,000	18,000	25,000	26,000	37,000	45,000	250.0
21,808	19,250	26,000	28,000	31,700	33,000	65.6
25,491						
25,000	32,000	43,000	62,000	70,000	80,000	220.0
			33,881	32,717	28,900	−14.7
	12,984	14,400	14,500	18,000	18,000	38.6
343,772	361,156	399,856	450,197	521,277	662,120	132.3
93,000	95,000	109,035	115,358	115,000	132,634	56.0
200,000	210,000	220,000	234,839	281,277	364,486	143.0
50,772	56,156	70,821	100,000	125,000	165,000	230.0

[c]Post Office Mail Handlers merged with Laborers' International Union of North America (AFL–CIO) on April 20, 1968.

[d]Postal Transport Association merged with United Federation of Postal Clerks (AFL–CIO) on July 1, 1961.

Source: Harry P. Cohany and Lucretia M. Dewey, "Union Membership Among Government Employees," Monthly Labor Review, July 1970, p. 17.

TABLE 3

Proportion of Government Employees Organized, United States, 1956-68

Year	Government Total Employment	Government Percent Organized	Federal Government Total Employment	Federal Government Percent Organized	State and Local Government Total Employment	State and Local Government Percent Organized
1956	7,277	12.6	2,209	--	5,069	--
1960	8,353	12.8	2,270	--	6,083	--
1964	9,596	15.1	2,348	38.2	7,248	7.7
1966	10,792	15.9	2.564	41.8	8,227	7.8
1968	11,846	18.2	2,737	49.4	9,109	8.8

Note: Dashes indicate data not available.

Source: Harry P. Cohany and Lucretia M. Dewey, "Union Membership Among Government Employees," Monthly Labor Review, July 1970, p. 18.

FIGURE 1

Distribution of 2,550,000 Organized U.S. State and Local Public Service Employees, 1969

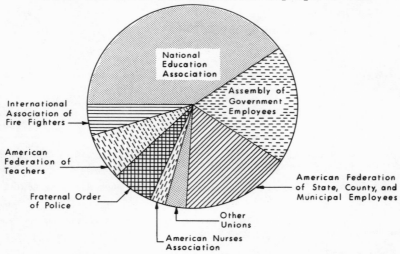

Source: Labor-Management Policies for State and Local Government Advisory Commission on Intergovernmental Relations (Washington, D.C., 1969), p. 6.

In the same year as the Condon-Wadlin Act
Congress tread a similar line, detouring from the
Taft-Hartley Act's principal concern with the private sector to provide for the unlawfulness of
strikes by federal employees, with strike sanctions
of immediate discharge, forfeiture of civil service
status, and ineligibility for reemployment for
three years.[9] The federal Hatch Act made it a
felony for a federal employee to belong to an organization that asserted the right to strike or to
engage in a strike against the government.[10]

The negative approach of state and federal
laws did not, however, stop strikes, such as the
New York transit strike in 1966. Theodore W. Kheel,
who played a major role in the resolution of that
dispute, made the following observations:

> The legal prohibition of strikes did
> not prevent workers from threatening
> disruptions of service and, on occa-
> sion, from carrying out the threat.
> The penalties assessed against indi-
> vidual workers did not deter them
> from concerted action. After a
> twelve-day transit strike in 1966
> that nearly brought New York City to
> a complete standstill, the need for
> change was apparent.
>
> Not only had the law failed to
> stop the strike, but it threatened to
> produce a second work stoppage be-
> cause of the penalty provisions. The
> enforcement of these provisions would
> have denied the transit worker the
> higher wages and other benefits nego-
> tiated under the Mayor's auspices.
> As a result, the governor and the
> legislature concluded that there was
> no alternative but to waive the penal-
> ties despite the clear violations of
> the statute. The law was in dis-
> repute.[11]

Eventually the severe restraints of New York's
Condon-Wadlin Act gave way to the new legislative

TABLE 4

Estimated Union Membership of Government Employees by State
and as Proportion of Total Government Employment,
United States, 1968[a]

State	Estimated Membership in Government[b] (thousands)	Government Employment		Ranking by Extent of Organization	
		Total (thousands)	Percent Organized	Government Unions	All Unions
Total	2,155	11,846	18.2		
Alabama	29	194	14.9	23	28
Alaska	5	32	15.6	19	10
Arizona	14	109	12.8	33	33
Arkansas	11	96	11.5	40	32
California	170	1,334	12.7	34	12
Colorado	21	166	12.7	35	24
Connecticut	36	140	25.7	5	23
Delaware	8	29	27.6	4	20
Florida	56	372	15.1	22	44
Georgia	42	269	15.6	20	43
Hawaii	6	69	8.8	48	19
Idaho	4	45	8.9	47	30
Illinois	128	599	21.4	8	8
Indiana	53	285	18.9	13	6
Iowa	19	163	11.7	39	25
Kansas	18	158	11.4	41	26
Kentucky	18	160	11.3	42	18
Louisiana	27	207	13.0	30	37
Maine	9	62	14.5	25	38
Maryland-D.C.[c]	91	589	15.4	21	26
Massachusetts	90	290	31.0	2	21
Michigan	117	484	24.2	7	5
Minnesota	54	216	25.0	6	15
Mississippi	12	127	9.4	46	47
Missouri	52	270	19.3	12	7
Montana	7	54	13.0	31	14

[a]Employees in government are represented by 59 unions, those in federal government by 57 unions, and those in state and local government by 18 unions.

[b]Total government membership of 2,155,000 includes 1,351,000 members in federal government, 804,000 in state and local government, and 65,000 outside United States or not classifiable by state.

[c]Federal employment in Maryland and Virginia sectors of Washington Standard Metropolitan Statistical Area is included in data for District of Columbia.

State	Estimated Membership in Government[b] (thousands)	Government Employment		Ranking by Extent of Organization	
		Total (thousands)	Percent Organized	Government Unions	All Unions
Nebraska	13	97	13.4	27	40
Nevada	5	34	14.7	14	17
New Hampshire	6	31	19.4	11	39
New Jersey	61	343	17.8	14	16
New Mexico	6	85	7.1	50	48
New York	309	1,116	27.7	3	4
North Carolina	24	227	10.6	43	50
North Dakota	6	46	13.0	32	34
Ohio	91	531	17.1	17	9
Oklahoma	30	180	16.7	18	41
Oregon	16	136	11.8	38	13
Pennsylvania	119	586	20.3	10	3
Rhode Island	17	52	32.9	1	22
South Carolina	13	134	9.7	44	49
South Dakota	6	50	12.0	37	45
Tennessee	27	217	12.4	36	29
Texas	85	636	13.4	28	26
Utah	14	99	14.1	26	35
Vermont	4	23	17.4	16	27
Virginia	38	283	13.4	29	42
Washington	41	230	17.8	15	2
West Virginia	9	95	9.5	45	1
Wisconsin	51	243	21.0	9	11
Wyoming	2	29	7.2	49	31
Membership not classifiable	65				

Source: Harry P. Cohany and Lucretia M. Dewey, "Union Membership Among Government Employees," Monthly Labor Review, July 1970, p. 19. Total government employment figures originally from Employment and Earnings, States and Areas, 1939-1968, U.S. Department of Labor, Bureau of Labor Statistics, BLS Bulletin 1370-6 (Washington, D.C., 1969).

provisions of the Taylor Law, which shifted the
primary effect of penalty from employee to union,
recognized rights and obligations to meet and confer, and established machinery for third-party recommendations to aid the resolution of impasse.[12]

The third historical period, beginning in 1959,
ushered in a decade of emerging law of public bargaining, commencing with the enactment by Wisconsin
of collective bargaining as a right rather than as
a tolerance in 1959, extended into a federal area
in 1962 by President Kennedy's Executive Order
10988, and further extended by Pennsylvania in 1970
with conditional strike rights.

The ten-year tempo of 1958-68 was marked by a
growth in the number of strikes, as well as a surge
in membership, as indicated in Figure 2. The 15
work stoppages of 1958 involved 1,720 public employees and a loss of 7,520 man-days. In contrast,
1966 witnessed 142 strikes involving 105,000 workers
and the loss of 455,000 man-days. This ninefold
increase of 1966 was nearly doubled in 1968, with
254 strikes involving nearly 202,000 workers and
causing a loss of over 2.5 million man-days.
Teachers played the lead in the cast of strikes,
with sanitation workers in the nearest supporting
role.[13]

Federal Scene and Executive Orders

The "establishment" of public labor relations
came about with the procedures that were developed
under federal Executive Orders and under the various
state acts for resolving disputes over (a) recognition, (b) grievances over working conditions, and
(c) impasses over new agreements. The most significant early development at the national level was
Executive Order 10988, issued by President Kennedy
on January 17, 1962, and supplemented on May 21,
1963, by the Presidential Memorandum "Standards of
Conduct for Employee Organization and Code of Fair
Labor Practices."[14]

FIGURE 2

Strikes and Other Work Stoppages
in Government, United States, 1958-68

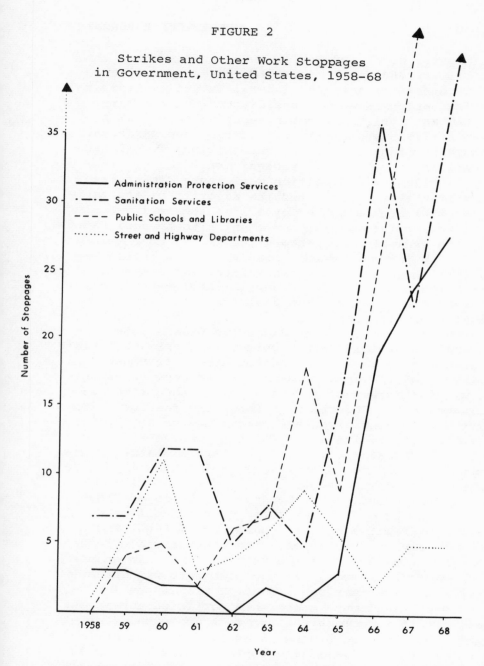

Source: Labor-Management Policies for State and Local Government, Advisory Commission on Intergovernmental Relations (1969), p. 25.

Executive Order 10988

Under the terms of federal Executive Order
10988 employees were granted the right to form,
join, and assist any employee organization or to
refrain from such activity. Employee organizations
could be granted informal recognition, formal recognition, or exclusive recognition.

Exclusive recognition was granted to an organization that represented the majority of the employees and thus spoke for all of the employees in
the appropriate unit. For a union to be designated
as the exclusive representative it had to obtain at
least 60 percent of the vote from the eligible
voters in an election. In further implementation,
as of January 1, 1964, federal agencies were authorized to check off union dues, pursuant to voluntary authorization.

Under the terms of Executive Order 10988 management officials were required to grant appropriate
recognition; to meet and negotiate at reasonable
times; and, if an agreement was reached, to execute
a written agreement. Section 11 of the order assigned to the Secretary of Labor the responsibility
for determining disputes concerning the appropriateness of bargaining units for the purpose of exclusive representation. The Secretary of Labor developed a procedure for advisory arbitration to determine such questions.

The "Standards of Conduct for Employee Organization and Code of Fair Labor Practices" were
jointly prepared by the Department of Labor and the
Civil Service Commission. The Standards of Conduct
for Employee Organization required the maintenance
of democratic procedures and practices within each
employee organization, including provisions for
periodic elections, membership participation in the
affairs of the organization, fair and equal treatment under the governing rules of the organization,
due process in disciplinary proceedings; the exclusion from office of persons affiliated with totali-
tarian movements and persons identified with corrupt
influences, the prohibition of business or financial
conflicts of interest on the part of officers, the

maintenance of fiscal integrity, and the furnishing
of financial reports to its members. These provisions were very similar to the "bill of rights"
provisions of the 1959 Landrum-Griffin amendments
to the Taft-Hartley Act.

The Code of Fair Labor Practices was similar
to the unfair labor practices provisions of state
and federal labor acts, and it prohibited the federal government and employee organizations from interfering with, restraining, or coercing employees
in the exercise of their rights under Executive
Order 10988 and from encouraging or discouraging
membership by discrimination in regard to hiring,
tenure, promotion, or other conditions of employment.

In addition, the federal government and its
agencies were prohibited from sponsoring, controlling, or assisting any employee organization or dis-
ciplining any employee because he had filed a complaint or given testimony under the program. The
federal government and its agencies were also
barred from refusing to grant appropriate recognition to an organization as required by the order or
refusing to hear, consult, confer, or negotiate
with such an organization.

Similarly, labor organizations were barred
from attempting to coerce an employee or member of
an organization as punishment or from imposing reprisals for the purpose of hindering or impeding
his duties as a federal employee. Public employee
organizations were also barred from calling a
strike, work stoppage, or slowdown; engaging in related picketing against the government; and dis-
criminating against any employee with regard to the
terms and conditions of membership because of race,
creed, color, or national origin.

The following statistics give an indication of
the impact of Executive Order 10988 during the
brief four-year period following its promulgation:

1. Among federal agencies 870 exclusive units
were established, in addition to some 24,000 local post office units.

2.   These exclusive units covered 870,000 employees, 515,000 of whom were employed by the
Post Office Department.

3.   There were 499 agreements negotiated, covering approximately 775,000 employees in 26 federal departments and agencies.

4.   There were 45 advisory decisions issued,
for the purpose of determining representation
questions and grievances.

5.   The status of exclusive recognition was
given to 30 bona fide employee organizations.[15]

The scope of the order embraced negotiations
on such topics as working conditions, promotion
standards, grievance procedures, safety, transfers,
demotions, reduction in force, and other matters
consistent with merit-system principles. Negotiations were excluded on matters concerning an agency's mission, budget, organization and assignment
of personnel, or the technology of performing its
work.[16]

Included within the basic subjects for bargaining were more finite provisions, and a 1964
survey by the Bureau of Labor Statistics of some
209 agreements lists 44 types of provisions negotiated by federal agencies and employee organizations. The more detailed subject matters covered
in the agreements included hours of work and overtime, holiday pay, rest periods, wash-up and clean-
up provisions, special clothing, work by supervisors, subcontracting, safety, leave policies, jury
duty, craft jurisdictions, wage surveys, promotions,
demotions, reductions in force, job descriptions
and ratings, apprenticeship and training, stewards
and representatives, visitation rights, dues withholding, mediation, and advisory arbitration of
grievances.[17]

Executive Order 10988 provided that collective
bargaining units could be established on a plant,
installation, craft, functional, or other basis
that would ensure a clear and identifiable community of interest among the employees concerned, but
no unit was to be established solely on the extent
to which the employees in the proposed unit had
organized.

Excluded from appropriate collective bargaining units were managerial executives, employees engaged in personnel work other than in a purely clerical capacity, and supervisors who officially evaluate the performance of employees whom they supervise. Professional and nonprofessional employees are also barred from being in the same bargaining unit unless a majority of the professional employees vote to be included in such a bargaining unit.

Disputes over appropriate bargaining units were resolved by advisory arbitration, and such early determinations received little criticism, except for the so-called 60 percent rule. This rule provides that 60 percent of the eligible voters must vote in an election before it will be considered valid. The rules also provided that, in the event of a runoff election, the 60 percent rule would also apply.

This same criterion for runoffs was later modified on the ground that the use of the 60 percent rule in a subsequent runoff election was inequitable because the desire of the employees for representation by a significant majority had already been determined in the first election. Labor organizations continued to criticize the 60 percent rule, however, for determining bargaining representatives by a greater standard than that which applied in private employment. The proponents of the 60 percent rule argued that it was necessary in order to ensure the choice of a true majority bargaining representative.

Criticism of Executive Order 10988 was voiced in four other problem areas. The first was the bargaining impasse.[18] Critics suggested that there was a greater need to develop mediation and fact-finding procedures and also to expedite referrals to higher authority within a governmental agency to bring the parties to an agreement. As of 1967 only about 10 percent of collective bargaining in the federal service provided for mediation.

The second problem area was the scope of negotiation. Some federal agencies had been averse to the use of mediation and advisory arbitration provisions to determine grievances and to deal with adverse actions by federal agencies, an adverse

action being an action in violation of the Code of
Fair Labor Practices.

The third problem area was regency review and
delegation of authority. The Executive Order required that all negotiated agreements be approved
by the head of the agency or an official designated
by him. The unions complained that agency heads
were second-guessing local officials and were also
overly restrictive in delegating sufficient local
authority to permit meaningful negotiations. In
response, the Civil Service Commission issued a
letter strongly encouraging agency heads to delegate more authority to ensure meaningful negotiations at the local level.

This problem was illustrated by a statement of
U.S. Secretary of Labor W. Willard Wirtz that what was
needed to make collective bargaining effective in
public employment was the establishment of bargaining authority on the part of public employer negotiators to enable them to say "I will" or "I won't"
rather than "I can't" at the collective bargaining
table.[19] This negative role of limited authority
is a problem by no means unique to the federal
service.

The fourth problem area was lack of advisory
arbitration of adverse actions. The unions complained that the use of federal agency hearing officers to determine allegations of the violation of
the Code of Fair Labor Practices was unfair. The
unions argued that agencies would not be objective
in evaluating their own compliance with the Executive Order and that the tendency would be to ap-
prove the actions of supervisors rather than to review them critically and objectively.

Federal officials recognized that the procedure in itself might appear to be unfair even if
its previous administration had not been unfair.
The use of outside arbitrators was recommended as a
means to remedy this situation.[20] There were also
suggestions for the creation of a federal employment relations board to act as an impartial agency
to administer the statute.

Criticism was also voiced with regard to
philosophical differences between the policies of
the Civil Service Commission and the Department of

Labor. Wilson R. Hart, a labor attorney and former
labor relations director for the Federal Defense
Supply Agency, felt that there was a gap between
the Department of Labor approach and the Civil Service Commission regarding employee-management relations. As he viewed it, the Civil Service Commission accepted the following proposition:

> that the art of public personnel man-
> agement has been so refined and devel-
> oped that there is neither need nor
> justification for strong unions in any
> public agency where this art is skill-
> fully practiced by personnel managers.[21]

A sharp rebuttal, expressed by the chairman of the
Civil Service Commission, emphasized the numerous
orders and directives that had been issued by his
agency in support of the policies of Executive
Order 10988 to encourage collective bargaining.[22]

Possible conflict in policy and implementation
among diverse agencies shaped up as an additional
problem, and the report of the Committee on the Law
of Government Employee Relations of the American
Bar Association for 1966 recognized the need for
uniformity in legislative and administrative policies under the Executive Order. The report suggested that a revised Executive Order or the establishment of a federal employee relations board was
necessary to eliminate the duplication and conflict
of regulations under Executive Order 10988.[23]

The American Bar Association report also recommended that supervisory employees be given the
right to organize and the right to negotiate collective bargaining agreements in units that include
only supervisors, but further recommended that supervisors should not actively participate in employee organization affairs except where the organization is limited to supervisors and excludes all
other federal employees.[24]

Executive Order 11491

These foregoing critical appraisals and new
Presidential evaluation led to Executive Order 11491

of President Richard Nixon, in 1970, which, in re-
placing the Kennedy order, established governing
procedures for federal labor-management relations.

Under the new order the term "labor organization" replaces employee organization. Employees
continue to have a free and protected right to join
or not join labor organizations. Organizations of
supervisors and managers are excluded from the term
"labor organization." Exclusive recognition is now
the sole form of recognition, to be accorded to an
organization receiving the majority of votes cast
in a secret-ballot election conducted in an appropriate unit.

Agencies and labor organizations are required
to meet and confer in good faith on personnel policies and practices and working conditions, subject
to applicable law and regulations and executive
written agreements or memoranda of understanding.
Excluded from the requirement to meet and confer
are the mission of the agency; its budget (including wages and fringe benefits), organizational
setup, number of employees, and grades and numbers
of employees assigned; the technology of its work;
and its internal security practices. The parties
may, however, negotiate agreements on arrangements
for employees adversely affected by the realignment
of work forces or technological change.

Management rights, in accordance with applicable laws and regulations, are specified and reserved. Although no agreement may require an employee to join or remain a member of a labor organization, dues check-off is authorized on the basis
of voluntary, written authorization. Grievance
procedures may be negotiated that meet the requirements set by the Civil Service Commission and may
include arbitration of employee grievances and disputes over the interpretation of existing agreements. Agreements must be approved by the agency
head if they conform to applicable laws and regulations.

Consultation rights may be accorded by an
agency on a national basis only to a labor organization that qualifies under criteria established by
the Federal Labor Relations Council. The labor

organization must be provided an opportunity to comment on proposed personnel changes, and its views will be carefully considered.

Supervisors or associations of supervisors will be provided a system for intramanagement communication and consultation within an agency. However, provision is made for continued or initial recognition of units for management officials or supervisors represented by labor organizations that traditionally or historically have represented such groups in private industry and that already hold exclusive representation for such units in any governmental agency.

Standards of conduct for labor organizations and management are extended, making them comparable to those for private-sector unions. Recognition may only be accorded to labor organizations that are free of corrupt influences and of influences opposed to basic democratic principles. They must file financial and other reports, provide for bonding of their officials and employees, and meet trusteeship and election standards. Certain practices by employers and by labor organizations are prohibited as unfair labor practices. Strikes continue to be banned by federal statute.

Major innovations in the new Executive Order include the centralization of basic aspects of the administration of the federal labor-management relations policy. A Federal Labor Relations Council consisting of the chairman of the Civil Service Commission, the Secretary of Labor, and other officials of the executive branch is to decide major policy questions, develop regulations, and handle appeals from actions of the Assistant Secretary of Labor for Labor-Management Relations. The latter will decide appropriate unit questions, supervise representation elections, prescribe regulations to effectuate the provisions on the conduct of labor organizations and management, and decide complaints of violation of these.

In negotiation disputes the Federal Mediation and Conciliation Service will provide assistance. In negotiation impasses a federal service impasse panel is established as an agency within the

Federal Labor Relations Council with discretion to
consider impasses on the request of either party
following failure of voluntary arrangements. The
parties may only use arbitration or third-party
fact-finding with recommendations to resolve an impasse on the authorization or direction of the panel.
   The following statistics give a partial indication of the impact of Executive Order 11491:

   1. Unions holding exclusive recognition
rights in federal agencies represented 1,542,111
executive-branch employees, or 58 percent, as of
November 1970--a significant increase over the
1,477,302 employees, or 54 percent, who were
represented as of November 1969.
   2. Excluding the Post Office, the percentage
increase in the number of employees covered by
exclusive recognition was even greater--48 percent, or 916,381, in 1970, compared with 42 percent, or 842,823, in 1969.
   3. There were 3,010 exclusive units of recognition in November 1970, up from 2,647 in November 1969.
   4. There were 1,509 negotiated agreements in
November 1970, up from 1,340, with 1,227,235 employees covered by agreements, up from 1,193,894
as of November 1969.
   5. Exclusive recognition covered 87 percent
of postal employees, 81 percent of wage system
(blue-collar) employees, and 35 percent of general schedule or equivalent (white-collar) employees in November 1970, compared with November
1969 figures of 87 percent postal, 72 percent
wage system, and 29 percent general schedule.[25]

   Executive Order 11491 was further amended by
President Nixon on August 26, 1971. The amended
order does away with informal and formal recognition with respect to bargaining rights. The amended
order does permit an employee to have certain consultation rights in connection with his membership
in social, fraternal, religious, or professional
associations that are not qualified as labor organizations with respect to matters of policies applicable to association members.

The amended order permits the use of official time, on a limited basis, for the purpose of negotiating an agreement. The amended order also makes certain changes in the grievance and arbitration procedures. It particularly provides that arbitration may be invoked only by the exclusive representative. Provision is also made for the resolution of a dispute about whether a matter is subject to arbitration by the Assistant Secretary of Labor.

Employee organizations generally welcomed the amendments but criticized them for not going far enough with respect to the scope of bargaining and for failing to establish an independent agency to adjudicate and administer the order.[26]

Direct Postal Bargaining

The procedures of the now extinct Executive Order 10988 were inadequate to meet the demands for full-scale collective bargaining by postal employees, and the unthinkable happened: a strike occurred among some 200,000 postal employees throughout the nation. As a result of that strike, the executive branch of the federal government engaged in direct collective bargaining with heads of the major postal organization, aided by the president of the American Federation of Labor-Congress of Industrial Organizations (AFL-CIO), and ultimately reached agreement on wage increases, wage progression schedules, fringe benefits, and endorsement of the Postal Corporation Act to apply new bargaining procedures for 750,000 postal employees.[27]

Congress largely confirmed the bargaining decisions reached at the table, which included binding arbitration of contract terms as a substitute for the prohibited right to strike. The president of the AFL-CIO endorsed the binding arbitration proposal, which, in providing for arbitration of interest disputes, as well as grievances, promises future significance for private and public dispute settlement.

The new postal law is based on private-sector principles set forth in the Taft-Hartley Act, excluding bargaining for managerial and supervisory employees and containing a detailed management prerogative provision. "Amtrak," the new national railroad corporation, further bridges the labor relations gap between the public and private sectors, with both the postal and rail commuter corporations suggesting similar state innovations.[28]

State Statutes and Experience

The changing of the establishment has been given impetus by state legislation. Justice Oliver Wendell Holmes, in one of his memorable dissents, stressed the wisdom of allowing states to make "social experiments that an important part of the community desires, in the insulated chambers afforded by the several states."[29]

Currently, 40 states, as well as the federal government, are engaged in a social experiemnt to determine whether the principles and practices of collective bargaining can be transferred from the private to the public sector. These principles and practices have been developed in private collective bargaining since the 1940s and have, as a premise, the right of employees to strike. The right to strike is prohibited, or at least not protected, in the public sector, except for the conditional strike rights enacted by Pennsylvania and Hawaii.

The various state statutes, their administrative machinery, and federal Executive Orders are serving as laboratories and guides for the establishment of orderly procedures for the resolution of public employer-employee disputes. Most of the above-mentioned statues establish the following:

1. The right of public employees to organize and to be represented in collective bargaining by representatives of their own choosing
2. Administrative machinery for the determination of questions of representation
3. The duty to bargain on the part of public employers and employee organizations
4. Certain unfair labor practices for public employers and public employee organizations
5. Dispute settlement procedures, including mediation services and, in the event of impasses,

fact-finding or advisory arbitration with non-
binding recommendations as alternatives to the
right to strike.

Until Wisconsin, in 1959, mandated bargaining
for the public sector, there was no state statutory
obligation for the employer to deal collectively
with its employees. By the end of 1970, 25 states
had enacted mandated statutes providing for either
"meet and confer" or stronger collective bargaining.
The remaining 15 of the 40 experimental states had
either permissive "meet and confer" provisions or
employer options to implement bargaining relationships.
The key provisions of selected state public
employee laws, including enactments as of spring
1970, are compared in Table 5, which illustrates
variations as to coverage, administrative machinery,
scope of bargaining, representation, dispute procedures, and strike limitations.
Although less than 20 of the state laws are
comprehensive in their coverage, the legislative
trend to full-scale bargaining laws is clear, as
state legislatures cope with conflicts arising in
all areas of public service. Among the most significant laws are statutes providing for binding
arbitration of new contract terms for policemen and
firemen in Michigan, Pennsylvania, and Rhode Island
and for firemen alone in Wyoming and Maine and those
providing for conditional strike rights in Pennsylvania and Hawaii.
In these latter two states public employee laws
set major precedents in expressly authorizing public employee strikes under certain conditions for
all public employees in Hawaii and for all except
police, fire fighters, mental hospital employees,
prison guards, and court personnel in Pennsylvania.
Montana grants a limited right to strike to nurses,
and Vermont permits strikes by municipal employees
and teachers.[30]
Both the Pennsylvania and the Hawaii laws mandate mediation and fact-finding, require avoidance
of public jeopardy, which is a test of "imminent or
present danger" in Hawaii and a "clear and present
danger or threat" in Pennsylvania. Additionally,

TABLE 5

Key Provisions of Selected U.S. State Public Employee Laws, Spring 1970

State	Employees Covered	Administrative Machinery	Bargaining	Representation	Dispute Provisions	Strike Provisions
Cal.	State and local employees (1968 amendments do not apply to state employees)	Governmental subdivisions	Required to "meet and confer in good faith" (1968 amendments authorized nonbinding memoranda of agreement with "determination" by governing body)	Subdivisions may adopt procedures after consultation with employee organizations; guides suggested for recognizing employee organizations	Authorized agreement on third party in local negotiations	
	Teachers	School district, county board of education, etc.	Required to "meet and confer"	Negotiating councils with proportional representation	None specified	
Conn.	Local	State Labor Relations Board (SLRB); Board of Mediation and Arbitration (BMA)	Duty to negotiate, including written agreement	SLRB determines representative; exclusive representation	BMA mediates, and fact-finding	Prohibited
	Teachers	Local boards of education; State Board of Education (SBE)	Duty to negotiate, including written agreement	Procedures set forth; exclusive representation	SBE mediates	Prohibited
Del.	State and local	State Department of Labor and Industrial Relations (SDLIR); State Mediation Service (SMS)	State and county--duty to negotiate; Municipalities--independent decision, including written agreement	SDLIR determines; exclusive representation	SMS mediates	Prohibited

	Teachers	Local boards of education; State Board of Education (SBE)	Duty to negotiate; authorizes agreement	Procedural guides for exclusive representation but administered by local boards; appeal to SBE	Authorizes local mediation and fact-finding but bans arbitration	Prohibited; exclusive representative loss of representation rights for 2 years, loss of dues check-off for 1 year
Me.	Local, including teachers	Commissioner, Department of Labor and Industry (CDLI); Public Employees Labor Relations Appeals Board (PELRAB); Board of Arbitration and Conciliation (BAC)	Duty to negotiate, including written agreement	Exclusive recognition; subdivisions may accord representation; elections, if required, conducted by CDLI; appeal to PELRAB	May call on BAC for fact-finding; permits binding arbitration, but advisory only on wages	Prohibited and may be enjoined; strikes are unfair labor practice
Md.	Teachers	Local boards of education; State Board of Education (SBE)	Required to meet and negotiate; negotiation includes duty to "confer in good faith" and "reduce to writing" agreed-upon matters	Procedures established; local board may designate majority organization as exclusive representative; SBE establishes rules for elections and supervises	SBE assistance; report and recommendations	Prohibited; penalties: revocation of exclusive bargaining representation for 2 years, loss of dues check-off for 1 year
Mass.	All local, including teachers	State Labor Relations Commission (SLRC); State Board of Conciliation and Arbitration (SBCA)	Duty to negotiate, including written agreement	SLRC determines; exclusive representation	SBCA fact-finding	Prohibited
	State	State Director of Personnel (SDP)	Duty to negotiate, including written agreement	Rules for determination by SDP; exclusive representation		Prohibited; strikes are unfair labor practice

TABLE 5 (continued)

State	Employees Covered	Administrative Machinery	Bargaining	Representation	Dispute Provisions	Strike Provisions
Mich.	All local, including teachers	State Labor Mediation Board (SLMB) (separate administration of labor relations and mediation function)	Duty to negotiate, including written agreement	SLMB determines; exclusive representation	SLMB mediates grievance	Prohibited; sanctions against strikes subject to appeal and court review
Minn.	State and local	Division of Labor Conciliation (DLC)	Required to "meet and confer"	DLC determines; formal recognition to majority organizations, informal to others	DLC mediates; then adjustment panel for findings	Prohibited; continues earlier penalties against individuals, with right to review
	Teachers	School boards	Required to "meet and confer"	Recognition to single organization; where more than one, proportional representation on teachers' council	Adjustment panel for findings	
Mo.	State and local except teachers, police, state police	State Board of Mediation (SBM)	Required to "meet, confer, and discuss"; results "reduced to writing"	SBM resolves issues; exclusive representation		Prohibited
Neb.	State and Local local	State and Local jurisdictions; State Court of Industrial Relations (SCIR)	Authorizes recognition, negotiation, and written agreement by public employers	Jurisdictions may grant exclusive recognition or conduct elections; SCIR certifies	SCIR jurisdiction may be invoked to determine terms	Prohibited; continues earlier penalties against individual

30

Teachers	School boards; State Court of Industrial Relations (SCIR)	"To meet and confer" is authorized on vote of majority of school board	Authorizes exclusive representation	Authorized parties to establish procedures for fact-finding; decision-making authority of SCIR may be invoked	Prohibited
Nev. Local, including teachers	Local jurisdictions; State Local Government Employee Management Relations Board (SLGB)	Duty to negotiate	No strike pledge as condition for recognition; exclusive representation accorded by local jurisdiction; appeals available to SLGB	SLGB notified and may appoint mediator; fact-finding if impasse persists	Prohibited; public employers may seek enjoinment; penalties for violation of enjoinment set out, by court, against employee organization (maximum fine), individual officers (maximum time on imprisonment), individual employees (dismissal or suspension); by public employers against individual or dismissal, demotion, or suspension; withhold salaries, cancel contracts
N.H. State	State Commission established	Obligation to negotiate for purpose of reaching agreement	State Commission conducts election and certifies results; exclusive representation		Prohibited, every agreement to contain no strike clause; employees subject to disciplinary penalties provided by law and personnel regulations for serious misconduct

31

TABLE 5 (continued)

State	Employees Covered	Administrative Machinery	Bargaining	Representation	Dispute Provisions	Strike Provisions
N.J.	State and local, including teachers	Division of Public Employment Relations (PERD) autonomous tripartite unit in Department of Labor and Industry; Public Employment Relations Commission (PERC) in PERD for policy and rule-making	Required to bargain, including written agreement	Majority Organization is exclusive representative; determined by employee designation or by election; elections conducted by and rules determined by PERC	PERC to aid in mediation; may recommend or invoke fact-finding	States that Act of 1968 is not to be construed to "diminish in any way the right of private employees to strike"
N.Y.	All state and local	Public Employment Relations Board (PERB) (autonomous in State Department of Civil Service)	Required to bargain, including written agreement	Procedures for recognition by local authorities, subject to "affirmation by such organization that it does not assert the right to strike against any government"; to PERB for resolution, if no local procedures, and for state employees	a) Parties establish own procedures b) or recourse to mediation and fact-finding through PERB c) Recommendations not accepted, legislative body or committee conducts hearing and takes action	Prohibited; organizations may be fined and chief executive of government involved required to notify PERB; for violation, PERB to order forfeiture of representation rights and dues checkoff for such period as PERB determines; chief executive required to deduct 2 days' pay for each day employee on strike; on probation without tenure for a year; right to review
N.D.	Teachers	Education Fact Finding Commission (EFFC)	Required to negotiate, and written agreement	Local board accepts majority organization or conducts election; if disagreement, EFFC rules govern	Determined by parties or call on EFFC for fact-finding	Prohibited; individual teacher may be denied full salary during period of violation

State	Level	Administering Body	Bargaining Duty	Representation	Impasse Procedures	Strikes
Ore.	Local	State and Public Employee Relations Board (PERB); State Conciliation Service (SCS); (PERB may assign duties to SCS)	Required to negotiate and enter agreement	Exclusive representation; local jurisdictions may determine or call on PERB	Local jurisdictions may determine or call on PERB for mediation and fact-finding	Prohibited
	Teachers	School boards	Required to "confer, consult, and discuss in good faith"	Local election to determine whether employee organization or committee representing teachers is to be exclusive representative	Mediation	
R.I.	Local	State Labor Relations Board	Required to bargain	SLRB determines; exclusive representation	Mediation by SDL with arbitration on request of either party (but decisions involving expenditures are advisory)	Prohibited
	State	State agencies	Required to bargain	Represents members		Prohibited
	Teachers	School boards; State Labor Relations Board (SLRB); State Department of Education (SDE)	Required to bargain	SLRB determines; exclusive representation	SDE mediation; either party may request arbitration, but decisions involving expenditures are advisory	Prohibited

33

TABLE 5 (continued)

State	Employees Covered	Administrative Machinery	Bargaining	Representation	Dispute Provisions	Strike Provisions
S.D.	State, local, including teachers	Individual jurisdictions; State Labor Commission (SLC)	Required to meet and negotiate with majority representative; settlements to be implemented by ordinance, resolution, or memorandum of understanding as may be appropriate	Formal recognition to majority organization only for members; informal recognition to any organization	Parties may call on SLC in case of impasse	Prohibited; state and local governments required to apply to courts for immediate relief; penalties against organization by courts set at maximum of $50,000 and/or imprisonment of officials for 1 year; employees right to appeal and court review, subject to a fine of $1,000 and 1 year imprisonment
Vt.	Local employees, excludes "professional employees"	State Labor Relations Board (SLRB); Department of Industrial Relations (DIR)	Authorized to bargain	SLRB determines; exclusive representation	Mediation by DIR and governor; effort to have parties agree to arbitration, otherwise fact-finding by labor emergency board	Prohibited; right of public employer to petition for injunction
	State	State Employee Labor Relations Board (SELRB)	Required to bargain; written agreement	SELRB certifies; exclusive representation	SELRB may authorize fact-finding	Prohibited; strikes are unfair labor practice
	Teachers	Local boards of education	Required to negotiate, and written agreement	School board may waive elections for exclusive representation or follow procedures in statute	Parties may use mediation or fact-finding	Injunctions by court only after due hearing that action "poses clear and present danger to sound program of school education... is in best public interest to prevent"

34

Wash. Local	Department of Labor and Industries (DLI)	Required to bargain and written agreement	Exclusive representation; parties may decide or invite DLI to decide and conduct election if necessary	Mediation	Prohibited
Teachers	School districts; State Superintendent of Public Instruction (SSPI)	Required to meet and negotiate	Procedures adopted locally; exclusive representation	Assistance of committees of educators and school directors appointed by SSPI	
Wisc. Local	Wisconsin Employment Relations Board (WERB)	Required to bargain	WERB determines, exclusive representation	WERB fact-finding; unless local authorities have established comparable procedures	Prohibited
State	Wisconsin Employment Relations Board (WERB)	Required to bargain	WERB determines, exclusive representation	WERB fact-finding	Prohibited

Source: Joseph P. Goldberg, "Changing Policies in Public Employee Labor Relations," Monthly Labor Review, July 1970, pp. 8-10.

as a "safety valve" Hawaii provides for a 60-day
cooling-off period between dispute procedures and a
strike.

The pattern of full-scale bargaining, short of
the conditional strike rights of Pennsylvania and
Hawaii, had been initiated by the Wisconsin Municipal Statute in 1962, which fashioned the legislative look for several other states. The Wisconsin
legislature also enacted a comprehensive collective
bargaining law for state employees, Section 111.80,
effective January 1, 1967. The Wisconsin Employment Relations Commission was assigned the responsibility for determining bargaining units, conducting representation elections, enforcing unfair
labor practice provisions, mediating labor disputes,
appointing grievance arbitrators, and appointing
fact-finders to make public recommendations for the
resolution of impasses.

The Wisconsin legislation contains a management-
rights clause and defines the scope of collective
bargaining to include the following conditions of
employment over which a state appointing officer
has discretionary authority:

1. Grievance procedures
2. Application of seniority rights as affecting the matters contained in the legislation
3. Work schedules relating to assigned hours,
days of the week, and shift assignments
4. Scheduling of vacations and other time off
5. Use of sick leave
6. Application and interpretation of established work rules
7. Health and safety practices
8. Intradepartmental transfers
9. Such other matters consistent with this
section and the statutes, rules, and regulations
of the state and its various agencies.

The state is not required to bargain over
wages, promotions, layoffs, fringe benefits, examinations, discipline, merit salary determinations,
and other matters governed by the civil service
rules. As a practical matter, the state has

engaged in bargaining with a union representing
state employees on wage and fringe benefits, and
the legislature is currently considering formally
widening the scope of bargaining to include wages
and hours.

The statute also contains a prohibition against
strikes and specifies that striking employees are
subject to discipline--including discharge, suspension without pay, and cancellation of their civil
service status because of their participation in a
strike--and provision is made for the right of the
state employer to seek an injunction or the imposition of fines and to sue for damages. A strike
is broadly defined to include concerted slowdowns,
as well as work stoppages.

The Taylor Law in New York State authorized
bargaining for state employees, with the employee
organizations quickly taking advantage of their
rights. Since September 1, 1967, when the Taylor
Law went into effect, 1 million state and local employees have been brought under its protection.
Presently, some 1,100 public employers are bargaining with 900,000 employees in some 2,500 negotiating units.[31]

These state statutes have invoked litigation,
thus confronting courts with necessary rulings on
membership and organization rights; appropriateness
of bargaining units, with emphasis on supervisor
units; duty to bargain collectively; legality of
strikes; and enforcement of agreements. The question of state public employee relations, where
Justice Holmes' laboratory for social experiment
has become something of a launching pad for soaring
problems, will be looked into further in the discussion of strikes and typical operative problems
calling for possible legislative solution, below.

SOME PROBLEM AREAS

The development of public collective bargaining has given rise to the following problem areas,
which occur regardless of the level of bargaining:

1. Since the establishment of the bargaining unit will have a substantial impact on the collective bargaining relationship not only of the employees in the proposed unit but also of other proposed units and unrepresented employees, both the collective bargaining organizations and the municipal employers must concern themselves with the appropriateness of the unit. Municipal employers generally favor the largest possible collective bargaining unit, but with separate units for craft, professional, or occupational groups, whereas employee organizations inclined also to craft and professional groupings tend additionally to favor the establishment of bargaining units based on how the union is structured or according to the capacity to win membership. Special provisions may be required by law or occupational preference, for its classification of uniformed forces--that is, police and firemen.

2. The definition of employee organization creates a problem, particularly if the organization does not exclude supervisory personnel and confidential employees.[32] The term "confidential" is keyed to a related labor relations role within the meaning of the labor relations acts; it usually means persons who have the authority to hire, transfer, suspend, promote, discharge, assign, reward, or discipline employees, adjust their grievances, or recommend such action effectively. The conflict-of-interest problem invoked by supervisory participation in employee organizations can be a particularly difficult one in both the negotiation and the implementation of agreements.

If teacher organizations include administrators within their membership and if such supervisors participate in the collective negotiating activities, then the system of lay control of education in this country may change. It has been observed that, to the extent that administrators are separated from the management side of the bargaining table and seek to represent their own interests, school boards are divested of some of their most effective spokesmen at the bargaining table. It has also been noted that school

boards that have thoughtfully considered the conflict have shown a preference for collective bargaining modeled on the traditional pattern of
leaving the policy-implementing administrative
staff wholly intact and out of the "rank and
file" organization.[33] The same problem exists in
varying degrees with respect to the effect of the
participation of supervisory employees in the
bargaining units and negotiating processes of the
police and fire departments and of other governmental units.

3. The enforcement of the mutual duty to bargain in good faith on the part of both municipal
employer and employee organizations is as complex a problem here as it is in the private sector. Even where the statute specifically contains such a provision, enforcement of this duty
is not easy. Since good-faith bargaining is a
two-way street, however, the whole spirit and intent of collective bargaining statutes depend for
fruition upon the good faith of the parties in
trying to make the collective bargaining process
work.

The dual role of collective bargaining and
legislation in protecting employment conditions
requires that public employee organizations
should not change stance or attempt to improve
upon the terms of the bargain before the ratifying legislative body if it has agreed to forego
such improvement during negotiations in consideration of other benefits granted.

For example, if a city council agrees to grant
a wage increase of 7 percent to its employees on
the agreed-upon condition that the public employee
organization drop its request for a work-week reduction from 44 to 40 hours without loss of take-
home pay, then the union should be obligated to
forego, at least for the term of the agreement,
any request to the state legislature or the local
legislative body to reduce the work week. Similarly public bargaining representatives who have
agreed with local union representatives on the
terms of a new labor agreement should not renege
on their promise to recommend acceptance of the

proposal to the full legislative body--city council or county board--nor should they ask their
fellow legislators to take them off the hook.

It is unrealistic to expect or even to encourage public employee organizations to abandon traditional methods of lobbying and other means of
public persuasion to secure protective legislation affecting the terms and conditions of employment. What is suggested is that, where collective bargaining is practiced or protected by
statute, the public employee representatives
should not work at cross-purposes, before legislative bodies, to the efforts made by their collective bargaining representatives.

A serious and related problem is the refusal
or the failure of the legislative body to implement the agreement when such action is necessary.
The problem becomes particularly acute when the
legislative body refuses to act at all on the implementing legislation, which was the case in the
1971 major strike in New York City by bridge-
tenders, sewer workers, and other public works
employees who struck when the legislature refused
to vote on pension improvements negotiated between the city and District Council 37 of the
American Federation of State, County, and Municipal Employees (AFSCME).[34]

4. The authority to bargain is a serious
problem in public employment. The division of
powers between the executive and legislative
branches in government, so essential to democracy,
often results in a lack of focused bargaining.
This problem does not exist in private employment.
As previously mentioned, what is needed to make
collective bargaining work in government is development of government bargaining teams with
authority to say "I won't," rather than "I can't."

The choice of representative--whether such
bargaining teams are made up solely of members
of the legislative department, the executive department, or a combination thereof--is secondary
to the establishment of spokesmen with authority
to make effective recommendations. Without such
authority, the bargaining process will break down,

because employee representatives will bypass the
formal bargaining table, seeking legislative or
executive decision.

5. The problem of good faith also involves
the question of bargaining in executive session
versus the public's right to know the public
business. Experienced practitioners of collective bargaining, in both public and private employment, know that it is virtually impossible to
conduct constructive negotiations in a goldfish
bowl. This is not because the representatives
have any business to hide that cannot ultimately
be made public but only because it makes bargaining so difficult.

Aside from the tactics and techniques of
bargaining, the almost irresistible temptation of
the public official, as well as the public employee representative, when faced with a television camera, a microphone, or a reporter's note-
book, is to make statements for the benefit of
his constituents, rather than to concentrate on
how the positions at the bargaining table might
be modified in order that an agreement may be
reached. There is a difference between making
the news and reporting the news. The public has
a right to know about the recommendations made by
its public officials to the legislative body,
which require hearings and debate on tentative
recommendations as a prerequisite to final, formal action.

Furthermore, there should be a reasonable period of time for the study of such recommendations prior to ratification. Last-minute settlements that permit no public study bring charges
of secrecy in government. Experience in private
employment, however, evidences that, too frequently, agreements are upset due to premature
press releases, circumscribing the "due process"
of boards of directors.

An attorney general's opinion in Wisconsin,
holding that the Anti-Secrecy Law does not prevent the conduct of mediation meetings in public
employment in executive session, has recognized
this problem: "Where a bargaining system is

adopted akin to that operating in private industry, it is not likely that the legislature intended a municipal employer to be more seriously
handicapped than private employers."[35]

6. A continuing problem in the public sector
concerns the scope of bargaining. Several of the
statutes that have been enacted do not provide
for negotiation of the traditional subjects of
wages, hours, and conditions of employment. Determining the applicability of wages, hours, and
conditions of employment to specific demands or
proposals is no easier interpretation than in
private employment. The U.S. Supreme Court has
been called upon to resolve questions of pensions,
subcontracting, or the closing of a business as
mandatory subjects of bargaining.

Questions exist in some jurisdictions about
the legality of including grievance arbitration
procedures and union security agreements in public employee labor agreements. The issue of
grievance arbitration concerns not only the argument of the delegation to a third party--namely,
the arbitrator--of the authority to determine
disputes under a contract, but also the accommodation of grievance arbitration procedures to
existing civil service procedures for reviewing
employee grievances or other unilateral grievance
procedures.

Further, the question of the legality of union
security agreements in public employment requires
consideration of the legal authority to enter into
such agreements, the question of whether such
agreements are good public policy, the conflict
concerning civil service tests of "merit and fit-
ness," and appropriate limitations regarding the
use of dues money for direct political purposes.
The check-off of dues is in practice in a number
of jurisdictions, but union security practices
are rare. It is expected that there will be increasing demands for the inclusion of such agreements in collective bargaining contracts, but
legislative authority or judicial approval may be
required before such agreements are widely accepted.

Further difficulty exists in defining the scope of public employee organizations, which goes beyond the subjects of wages, hours, and conditions of employment. For example, the National Education Association states that its goals of negotiation include "all matters which affect the quality of the educational program," whereas the American Federation of Teachers speaks of its intent to negotiate "anything that affects the working life of the teacher." Thus, disputes arise over classroom size, the curriculum, the school calendar, and other subjects that involve educational policy, as well as working conditions.

7. The budget-making process affects the scope of negotiation, the timetable for bargaining, and the length of the collective bargaining agreement. Bargaining is also affected when the employer is wholly or partially fiscally dependent on another governmental unit. School boards, for example, are frequently totally or partially dependent for funds upon another local or state taxing unit. The stretching-out of the budget process and bargaining has, however, made budget deadlines unrealistic in some jurisdictions, including New York City.

8. Bargainers in the public sector must consider the existence and coverage of other statutes and civil service rules regulating discipline procedures that control promotional or other personnel policies. Experience in Wisconsin and New York City and observation of the administration of Executive Order 10988 point out that, although certain conflicts do exist with respect to the scope of bargaining in civil service, the essential merit principles of the civil service system to recruit and appoint qualified candidates and to appoint qualified persons to the public service have not been impaired by the collective bargaining process.

The existence of laws regulating the employment of teachers and the authority of police and fire chiefs and police and fire commissioners may conflict with the bargaining process. Imaginative

collective bargaining and, in some cases, amendments to existing statutes may be necessary to
accommodate the collective bargaining process to
other existing statutes. A conflict-of-laws provision in a collective bargaining statute might
set forth the priorities of the respective statutes regulating public employee relations.

9. The question of exclusive representation
and minority rights causes some special problems
in public employment for the reason that in public employment citizens have constitutional
rights to petition their government and to be
heard over and beyond the rights established by
collective bargaining statutes. The duty of fair
representation for minority groups and individual
employees resulted in the enactment of the "Bill
of Rights" provisions in the Landrum-Griffin Act
in private employment. Similar protections, as
included in the Standards of Conduct for Employee
Organization under Executive Order 10988, are
likely to be enacted into local bargaining statutes and will be administratively implemented.

10. The question of whether a collective bargaining agreement in public employment can be reduced to writing has been the subject of legal
argument, but this objection has been overcome in
a number of jurisdictions by statute and practice.
Legality aside, one should not lose sight of the
fact that the collective bargaining contract is
regarded by labor organizations as a symbol of
recognition and the culmination of the collective
bargaining process.

11. Related to the question of written contracts is the question of contract bar and subject of the time for representation elections.
Several statutes have adopted the principle of a
contract bar providing that no representation
election can be conducted until near the expiration of an existing bargaining agreement and that
representation elections may be permitted only
every two years.

12. There is a great need to establish criteria for determining bargaining units, as is
evidenced in a number of statutes or legislated

bargaining units. Failure to establish reasonable guidelines permits units to be established
on the basis of extent of organization, which results in a fragmented, disordered bargaining
structure.

Multiple units of employees in the same basic
occupational group lead to leapfrog bargaining
or me-tooism and one-upmanship. New York City is
the best, or worst, example of this problem.
Units should be established, insofar as possible,
along broad occupational lines--blue-collar,
white-collar, administrative, skilled, technical,
professional, uniformed services, and similar
groupings.

RIGHT TO STRIKE

New York City--a Case Example

Nineteen sixty-eight was New York's year of
the strike in public employment. The New York City
sanitation strike, the tragic strike of sanitation
workers in Memphis, and the New York City teachers'
strikes were the most dramatic public employee disputes of 1968, but there were many less publicized
strikes with significant local impact in all parts
of the country.

The number and effect of these disputes, par-
ticuarly in New York City, crystallized the political positions of many candidates in municipal,
state, and national elections. (See Table 6.)
Candidates, newspaper editors, and government administrators generally expressed dismay at the
work stoppages and their frequently accompanying
acts of civil disobedience.[36]

The increase in the incidence of public-sector
strikes may be explained in part by the extraordi-
narily rapid growth of unionization among government employees. In New York State, for example,
almost 900,000 workers, nearly 75 percent of all
its state public employees, are now organized. In
New York City alone, more than 95 percent of those
city workers employed by municipal agencies that

are not headed by mayoral appointees are represented by some labor organization.   Representation
exceeds the percentage of actual union membership,
however.[37]

TABLE 6

New York City and State Strikes, 1965-68

Year	Strikes	Workers	Man-Days Idle
New York City			
1968	8[a]	69,800	1,930,000[b]
1967	10	63,900	785,000
1966	9	40,000	291,500
1965	3	6,750	118,000
New York State			
1968	8	800	7,360
1967	5	64	9,000
1966	6	70	2,500
1965	1	[c]	[d]

[a]Tentative 1968 figures; do not include consideration of New York State Department of Mental
Hygiene strike.

[b]Teachers accounted for 1,860,000 man-days idle;
sanitation workers, 60,000 man-days idle.

[c]Welfare workers, 6,500 involved.

[d]Fewer than 1,000.

Sources: 1965-66 figures from "Work Stoppages
in New York State," New York State Department of
Labor Division of Research and Statistics.   Figures for 1967-68 and January-December 1, 1968, supplied by Jack Herbst, New York State Department of
Labor, Division of Research and Statistics.

Legislatures in a growing number of states have contributed to the increase in public-sector unionization by passing comprehensive statutes that recognize the right of public employees to organize and bargain collectively. Other states have enacted enabling legislation that establishes collective bargaining rights for selected public employee groups.[38] Only two of these statutes, those of Hawaii and Pennsylvania, recognize the right of some public employees to strike under certain limited conditions.[39]

It should never have been supposed, however, that mere strike prohibition means the demise of public employee work stoppages. Indeed, the experience in Michigan following the passage of its Public Employment Relations Act suggests that the introduction of collective bargaining rights to public employment in an already highly unionized state might cause an increase in work stoppages.[40] In the first year under the Michigan act, there were 12 strikes by municipal employees, contrasted with 13 in the previous 17 years.[41]

New York's Taylor Committee, drawing upon the earlier Michigan experience, anticipated that the immediate impact of its proposed statewide mandate to grant exclusive recognition and bargaining rights to public employee unions in New York might be to increase the number of illegal strikes.[42] Still, the public, which had hoped that the new Taylor Law would bring labor peace to the public sector, was not prepared for the rash of ensuing strikes.[43] Governor Nelson Rockefeller, in his annual message to the New York legislature, declared that the Taylor Law "is not a perfect instrument. Judged solely on its ability to prevent such stoppage, it is indeed imperfect."[44]

Yet it would be misleading to conclude from the experience in Michigan and New York that the way to prevent public-sector strikes is to abolish laws that confer bargaining rights on public employees. Major public employee strikes have also occurred in many states without such laws. Teachers struck in Florida, policemen in Ohio, firemen in Georgia, and hospital workers in Illinois.

In a number of states there seems to be tacit recognition that public-sector collective bargaining is here to stay, leaving unsolved the question of what to do about the strike issue. Is collective bargaining in public employment possible without the right to strike? Given strong political pressures favoring labor peace, is it realistic to suppose that private-sector collective bargaining techniques can be adopted to normalize labor relations in government?

Closely related to the debate over the right to strike is the controversy over appropriate sanctions. What can be done to avoid strikes or terminate those that do occur? In New York State the argument seems to center on whether the penalties for violation of no-strike laws should be increased. The Taylor Committee reiterated its original position in favor of unlimited fines against striking unions.[45] In response to this proposal and other community pressures the New York legislature amended the Taylor Law on March 4, 1969, to provide for stiffer penalties against striking public employees and their unions.[46]

The short history of unionism in the public sector demonstrates graphically that merely declaring public employee strikes illegal will prevent neither collective bargaining from developing nor strikes from occurring. At all levels of government, legislatures, executives, and the courts have been forced to deal with the problem. But they can no longer afford the luxury of debate about strike policy. Stark realities require confrontation and search for solution.

The existence of collective bargaining in the public sector, however, does not depend upon a resolution of public policy on strikes. For amid all of the outcry the fact remains that a great many collective bargaining contracts are concluded without strikes. New York City, for instance, is obligated to deal with more than 80 unions in approximately 170 different collective bargaining relationships. The vast majority of these negotiations are resolved without a strike or the threat of a strike.[47]

In those instances in which impasse panels
have been appointed under the city's collective
bargaining statute, the city and public employee
organizations involved have accepted the recommendations.[48] At the state level, of the 370 impasses
that were referred to the New York Public Employee
Relations Board (PERB) in its first year of operation, only five cases (which involved a total of
fewer than 1,700 employees) resulted in work stoppages.

Nevertheless, there were other work stoppages
in which the impasse procedures of the Taylor Law
were not utilized.[49] The experience in other states
that have adopted public-sector collective bargaining laws is similar; countless contracts have been
negotiated without strikes. But strikes, when they
do occur, make the headlines because of their great
political, if not economic, impact on the public.

Experience indicates that in most instances
the right to strike is not an essential part of the
public employment collective bargaining process.[50]
Thus, crucial attention focuses on making the collective bargaining process so effective as to ob-
viate work stoppages. Certain proven impasse resolution procedures like mediation, fact-finding, and,
in some cases, even arbitration, can be substituted
for the strike weapon in public bargaining so as to
preserve its making the process functionally comparable with the private sector.

Thus, it may be unnecessary for state legislatures to resolve the difficult policy dispute over
whether public employees should be given the right
to strike. Still, it is useful to examine the arguments for and against the right to strike in public employment in order to evaluate the various
proposals for making public-sector collective bargaining orderly and effective.

Theory and Practice

The debate over the right to strike in public
employment has tended to center around two polar
extremes. Some argue that public employees should
have an unequivocal right to strike.[51] Others

contend that strikes in the public sector must be
prohibited in all circumstances. To present the
issue in such stark terms, however, is to miss the
point that there is a viable middle position.
Those who favor the right to strike seem to take
the position that true collective bargaining depends upon a balanced power relationship between
the negotiation parties.

They assume that without the strike weapon
public employees would not have sufficient power to
achieve real bargaining leverage. In support of
this assumption they state that the right to strike
has been the equalizer in employer-employee relations for one-third of a century in private employment collective bargaining and that the transfer of
private-sector collective bargaining procedures
into the public sector must necessarily be accompanied by the strike weapon.[52]

But this position tends to overlook the fact
that there is no such thing as an unlimited right
to strike in private employment. Congress, state
legislatures, and the courts have for many years
prescribed limitations on the right to strike; occasionally legislatures have enacted emergency provisions to delay strikes or prevent them altogether
when necessary to protect the public's health,
safety, and welfare.[53]

The right to strike has not been equated with
any constitutional guarantee. Moreover, restrictions on concerted work stoppages do not raise an
issue of involuntary servitude. The courts have
always interpreted the constitution's provisions
on involuntary servitude as running to the individual; they have never found that these provisions
intend so far as to create a collective right to
terminate employment. There are a number of
grounds upon which to distinguish public-sector
employment rationally from that of the private sector.

The strike is an instrument for applying economic pressure. In the private sector it has been
an effective weapon in the hands of employees because employers have been constrained by the need
to compete in a product market or else go out of

business. But political, rather than economic, forces are the dominant constraints in the public sector. It is this distinguishing factor that most judges and commentators rely upon to justify the prohibition on public employee strikes.

In City of New York v. DeLury,[54] a case that upheld the ban on strikes in the Taylor Law, Chief Judge Stanley Fuld wrote the following for a unanimous New York Court of Appeals:

> the necessity for preventing goods or services being priced out of the market may have a deterrent effect upon collective bargaining negotiations in the private sector, whereas, in the public sector, the market place has no such restraining effect upon the negotiations and the sole constraint in terms of the negotiations is to be found in the budget allocation made by responsible legislators.[55]

From this Judge Fuld reasoned that "the orderly functioning of our democratic form of representative government and the preservation of the right of our representatives to make budgetary allocations free . . . from the compulsion of crippling strikes" requires the prohibition of public employee work stoppages.[56] Dr. George Taylor stated the following:

> In a democratic society, consumer choice with respect to governmental services is ultimately exercised, not in the market place, but in the legislative authorization of laws to be passed, taxes to be levied, and budget expenditures to be made, and of loans to be floated. This is the final arbitrament of conflicts of public interest.[57]

Thus, although the existence of a product market is a relevant consideration in private-sector

or public-utility bargaining, political factors
often overshadow economic considerations in public-
sector bargaining. This predominance of political
over economic constraints will frequently lead to
inefficiency or inequity in the management of
public-sector services. Although the complete
avoidance of these inequities and inefficiencies is
impossible, it would seem that the inequities created by strike pressures in the public sector are
greater than those that would result from the recommendations or decisions of fact-finders or arbitrators.

The Illinois Supreme Court advanced another
possible distinction between private-sector and
public-sector unionism in that private parties have
no right to interfere with a governmental function:

> The underlying basis for the policy
> against strikes by public employees
> is the sound and demanding notion
> that governmental functions may not
> be impeded or obstructed, as well as
> the concept that the profit motive,
> inherent in the principle of free
> enterprise, is absent in the govern-
> mental function.[58]

Related to the notion that there is no right to
interfere with a governmental function is the concept of loyalty; with both concepts grounded in the
well-worn idea that public employee strikes constitute an intolerable interference with the sovereignty of the state.

Advocates of the right to strike in public employment usually make it clear that they are not
actually calling for an unqualified or an unlimited
right. Instead, they argue that lifting the strike
ban in public employment labor disputes and granting a qualified right to strike in nonessential
public services would move the parties toward more
equal collective bargaining power and greater labor
peace.

Various legal mechanisms to distinguish between essential and nonessential government services

have been suggested. Some of these provide for
prior settlement of the issue of essentiality.[59]
Other mechanisms contemplate modes of emergency
resolution after the occurrence of a strike, to
determine the essentiality of a service to the community's health, safety, and welfare.[60]

The Pennsylvania statute confers the right to
strike only after the exhaustion of mediation and
fact-finding procedures, and then only if a strike
would not endanger the public's health, safety, and
welfare.[61] The right to strike, under Pennsylvania
statutes, does not apply to policemen and firemen,
who are prohibited from striking but are provided
with the alternative of a compulsory arbitration
procedure.[62] Similarly, prison guards, mental hospital employees, and certain court employees are
barred from striking but are afforded the arbitration alternative.

Proposals for a qualified right to strike present some difficult practical problems. The ultimate resolution of public policy toward the strike
issue is likely to affect the private as well as
the public sector because it is difficult to distinguish between essential public and private services. Resolution of this problem is, in turn,
further complicated because federal law protects
the right to strike in private employment, whereas
public employment disputes are a matter for state
regulation.

But any test that purports to relate the right
to the essentiality of the service involved cannot
operate to prohibit strikes in the public sector
alone; the private sector also provides countless
vital services affecting the health and safety of
the public. A determination of essentiality might
easily be made in advance with respect to police
and fire services, but it would be difficult to
categorize many other situations. That making such
determinations would be difficult for administrators and judges should not by itself cause the idea
to be discarded. Such determinations have been
frequently made under the Taft-Hartley Act in the
private sector.[63]

In Rankin v. Shanker, the majority of the New
York Court of Appeals distinguished public from
private employment in order to deny a right to jury
trial to public employees in a criminal contempt
case.[64] Judge Kenneth Keating, in a strenuous dis-
sent, emphasized the point that public-sector
strikes cannot be distinguished from private-sector
strikes solely on the basis of the essentiality of
the services involved:

> When it is remembered that employees
> of private utilities have the power
> to plunge one of the great cities of
> the world into total darkness or com-
> plete silence, that employees of pri-
> vately owned railroads and shipping
> lines have the power to deprive the
> residents of that city of vital food
> and fuel, that private sanitation
> workers, who carry away a substantial
> portion of the refuse in New York
> City, have the power to endanger the
> health of millions of its inhabitants
> and that thousands of other workers,
> carrying out activities vital to the
> life and safety of the city, may de-
> mand a trial by jury if they are
> charged with violation of a court
> order restraining a strike, the fal-
> lacy in the reasoning which would
> deny a jury trial to these defendants
> is really exposed. References to the
> dangers to the children from the
> teacher's strike, real as those dan-
> gers may be, are not a substitute for
> a penetrating analysis of the labels
> "public" and "private" employees.[65]

Still, the question remains whether the essential services distinction is an equitable method
for determining wage and employment policies in the
public sector. This distinction puts a premium
upon an employee group's capacity to injure the
public. Those employees with the greatest capacity

to cause a disruption of public services will be
able to exert considerable pressure by way of a
strike, provided the disruption is difficult to
predict. Those employees whose services can occasionally be interrupted without serious consequences
will be given the right to strike precisely because
it will give them little leverage.

If the distinction between public and private
employment on the basis of essential services is
not legitimate, denial of the right to strike to
public employees alone could be challenged under
the equal protection clauses of the federal and
state constitutions. It should be remembered, however, that state legislatures have been accorded
wide discretion to draft laws that affect one group
of citizens differently than another, so long as
the distinction is rationally related to some lawful objective.

Whether the individual states will be willing
to enact the sophisticated labor relations legislation necessary to provide for the professional administration of emergency procedures remains to be
seen. The new Hawaii and Pennsylvania statutes
will provide the experience to determine whether
such a qualified strike right is effective in encouraging collective bargaining and dispute settlement.

The advocates of a qualified right to strike
in public employment generally recognize that state
legislatures must provide the judiciary or some administrative official with the authority to fashion
appropriate remedies for the violation of a limited
strike prohibition. But fashioning realistic penalties for violations of strike prohibitions has
proved to be an inordinately difficult task. In
1967 the New York State legislature repealed the
rigid penalties of the Condon-Wadlin Law as unworkable.[66]

The governor of Pennsylvania signed a teacher
amnesty bill that enabled local school boards to
grant pay increases to teachers who had participated
in illegal strikes.[67] A governor's study commission in that state pointed out that, because of the
difficulties of teacher recruitment, the prohibitions

against reemployment of striking teachers had
worked to the disadvantage of several school districts that were forced to impose penalties; other
communities were more anxious to hire teachers who
had been disciplined by denial of pay raises.[68]

The imposition of jail sentences against union
leaders has done little more than to provide them
with an aura of martyrdom that has enhanced their
prestige and job security. The practical necessity
of bringing union leaders to the negotiating table
in order to settle a strike led to delays in the
sentencing process and persuasive requests for
their early release from jail by the very authorities who prosecuted them.

Furthermore, limited fines on some union trea-
suries have been too small to deter strike action.
Even a large fine is not excessively burdensome if
it can be spread among the membership of a large
union. And, as has been seen in New York City,
individual and union fines may even be paid by
other segments of the labor movement. Summarizing
these difficulties, one writer has suggested that
prohibitions of strikes will not survive in the
American political climate if their maintenance depends primarily on the severity of the penalties
for violation.[69]

Opposition to public strikes swells from the
argument that statutory strike prohibitions are
based on the conviction that the political process
can be substituted for the strike weapon as an
orderly method of dispute resolution. The rationale
is that decisions affecting the wages, hours, and
working conditions of public employees are primarily
political rather than economic. In short, public-
sector collective bargaining concerns the allocation of public resources posing which government
employees receive how much of the tax revenues of
various governmental jurisdictions.[70] Since this
is a political matter, a system of political settlement is preferable to an impasse resolution
mechanism that depends upon economic coercion.

Thus, some state legislatures have provided
for fact-finding, with recommendations as a substitute for the strike weapon.[71] Other legislatures

have provided for advisory arbitration and, in some
instances, even compulsory arbitration as a method
of dispute settlement.[72] The theory behind these
laws is that fact-finders or arbitrators, empowered
to make recommendations that are advisory awards or
final and binding determinations, will be able to
provide an effective political substitute for the
strike. The laws are also premised upon the assumption that the recommendations or decisions of neutral parties will be binding, or at least persuasive
to the body politic, as well as to the participating
unions, employees, and employing agencies.

Opponents of the right to strike point out
that strike rights for many categories of nonessential public employees would be virtually meaningless
unless work stoppages could be carried out in association with other groups of public employees engaged in more critical services. Preserving the
right to strike for librarians, custodians of cultural institutions, or tax collectors, for instance,
is not likely to confer on such employees or their
representatives a powerful bargaining weapon.

This observation is in no way intended to de-
mean the importance of these public services; their
interruption would obviously be felt in due course.
Striking payroll clerks and some computer operators
would be missed the very first pay day; but a strike
of tax collectors could last somewhat longer before
the day of reckoning occurred. Thus, the power of
political persuasion through the utilization of
fact-finding or arbitration, accompanied by public
recommendations, is likely to be a much more effective balancing force for such employees than is
the strike.

This argument is supported by bargaining experience with some white-collar employees in the
private sector. This experience demonstrates that
collective bargaining based upon the right to strike
and upon militant union activity has not been as
effective a balancing force for white-collar groups
as it has been for blue-collar employees.[73]

The political nature of public employee bargaining poses the question of whether legalized
strikes would have bred different collective

bargaining results. In some emergency situations
involving essential services a strike would have
been enjoined in any event. For instance, even if
the 1968 strike of sanitation workers in New York
City had been lawful initially, it is likely that
an injunction would have been sought against the
work stoppage on the ground that its prolongation
constituted a health emergency.

Also, legalizing strikes might force some labor organizations to engage in a strike when they
might not otherwise have done so in order to demon-
strate to their membership that they have exhausted
every possible avenue of dispute resolution. Finally, if public employee strikes were permitted,
the attitude of government employers toward collective negotiations might change drastically.

The public employer would be forced to assume
the role of a private employer in many situations,
using the tactics of brinkmanship and power, including use of a lockout, consistent with the maintenance of essential services. The public employer
might also attempt to break strikes by hiring replacements and resorting to other lawful reprisals
against striking employees.

But it would be difficult, as a practical matter, for a public employer, who has political responsibilities not shared by his counterparts in
private employment, to play this role. In the
first place, supervisory employees are themselves
highly organized in many jurisdictions; moreover,
automation is less prevalent in public employment
than in private industry. Both factors would make
it more difficult for an employing agency to bring
in replacements, even in nonessential services.

Legalizing strikes in the public sector would
tend to increase the occasions for confrontation
between the public employer and employee organizations. Public employee strikes increasingly involve disputes over social policy, as well as over
conditions of employment.[74] A teachers' strike in
New York City, for instance, involved questions of
decentralization and community control of schools,
going beyond economic benefits for teachers. Earlier strikes of welfare employees in New York City

involved questions of the level of benefits to be
made available to relief recipients.

Resolution of such public policy questions has
traditionally been the responsibility of the legislative and executive branches of government. The
scope of bargaining can be limited by statute to
reserve to the governments the authority to make
these decisions. Legislation of strikes, however,
might tempt exploration and adventure into insulated
statutory boundaries.

For these and other reasons it is not clear
that legalizing strikes by public employees would
contribute significantly to equality of bargaining
power in the public sector. Purely from the point
of view of policy, therefore, it would seem that
substitution of a political process of impasse resolution for the strike weapon would move things
closer to an orderly pattern of public-sector collective bargaining. It remains to be seen whether
the political and economic differences between public and private employment are sufficient to support a differential treatment of the right to
strike in the two sectors.

SETTLEMENT OF DISPUTES

Office of Collective Bargaining

In New York City the Office of Collective Bargaining coordinates the labor relations activities
of municipal agencies and such other public employers who, with the mayor's approval, elect to use
its procedures.[75] The office is charged with the
responsibility of implementing a three-part procedure of impasse resolution consisting of mediation,
fact-finding, and, ultimately, public recommendations for settlement.

The majority of contract disputes are settled
by the direct bargaining of the parties. Moreover,
inherent in the concept of advisory recommendations
--at least in New York City--is the possibility
that a given dispute might be referred to mediation
or binding arbitration. Indeed, the disputing

parties may call upon the same panel that conducts
mediation to arbitrate a particular issue; on other
occasions, a public board may ask the mediation
panel to make advisory recommendations on issues
that the parties will not refer to arbitration.
The panel may actually engage in all three processes under the general heading of fact-finding.

During the first three years of operation of
the New York City Office of Collective Bargaining,
61 impasse cases were settled by report and recommendations of a panel that was accepted by the
parties; three cases were settled when the parties
reached agreement before the panel operated; one
case was diverted to arbitration as a grievance
under contract; five cases were diverted to, and
settled by, mediation; two cases were diverted to
the Board of Collective Bargaining for binding determinations; and one case was not within the jurisdiction of the office.[76] In only two cases did
one party initially reject a fact-finder's report
and recommendations. In both cases the unions
initially rejected the findings, but in neither
case did a strike result; moreover, the unions involved subsequently reconsidered their position and
accepted the recommendations.[77]

Fact-Finding

The nature of the fact-finding process itself
perhaps explains the variety and flexibility of
impasse resolution procedures that have been observed in jurisdictions such as New York City. The
fact-finder typically collects evidence in a quasi-
judicial hearing in order to examine critically the
merits of a given dispute. With this information
in hand, he may make a report to a political authority, recommend a settlement to the parties, or
make a public recommendation designed to bring
pressure of public opinion to bear on an intransi-
gent party.

Fact-finding has been described as a "logical
extension of collective bargaining because it con-
tinuously keeps open the possibility of voluntary
settlement."[78] It is this possibility of voluntary

settlement throughout the process that distin-
guishes fact-finding from compulsory arbitration.
Theodore Kheel noted another important distinction
between arbitration and fact-finding in his report
to the speaker of the New York State Assembly:
fact-finding success is measured by the "acceptability of recommendations," whereas arbitration
measures the "equity of the claims."79

Arbitration and fact-finding may, however,
converge at a number of points. The nature of the
investigation, the scope of the parties' submission
or stipulations, the language of written decisions,
and even the unstated criteria are often the same
or similar. This may be the result of what Kheel
terms "practitioners' confusion."

It may also reflect the fact that practitioners
tend to shape a new process like fact-finding, as
professional arbitrators who may find it difficult
to abandon their firm commitment to equitable notions. Indeed, it may not be desirable for them to
do so as long as they firmly believe that the fact-
finding process works because the parties respond
to equitable recommendations. An arbitrator is in
one respect a fact-finder:

> Arbitration is in itself unique be-
> cause it normally concentrates in the
> arbitrator the primary function of
> fact-finding, which is performed by
> the trial court, and the secondary
> function of review, which is confided
> in the intermediary and final appel-
> late court system.80

It is also common that fact-finders are constrained
by the parties' submission agreement from making an
independent investigation to uncover relevant facts
and must rely upon briefs and evidence submitted
during the hearing.

Fact-finding should be seen as an occasional
extension of bargaining or as an adjunct to bar-
gaining--a process that is valuable because it presents carefully framed terms of the agreement that
are closely related to the prior bargaining of the

parties. These terms of agreement are likely to be
"acceptable" because they are couched in the realm
of the reasonable--if not equitable--expectations
of the parties.

Recommendations will be all the more acceptable if the fact-finder identifies the issues in
full view of the public and the union's rank and
file. If one disputing party's miscalculation about
the reasonable expectations of the other party is a
common cause of strikes, as noted by one outstanding
economist, then a process within a particular bargaining history and in a particular labor market is
a process premised on persuasion and voluntary
agreement rather than adjudication.[81]

The substitution of fact-finding, with recommendations, for the strike weapon is not advanced
as a panacea for dispute resolution; there are no
such easy answers. But fact-finding is an alternative to legalizing public employee strikes because
of the flexibility and equity it affords in dispute
resolution. Recent experience, cited above, shows
that the majority of public employee disputes are
settled short of recommendations by mediators, that
the great majority of recommendations have been accepted, and that the problems posed by rejection of
recommendations are not peculiar to the process of
fact-finding.

Arbitration

The ultimate in fact-finding is, of course,
binding arbitration, frequently concealed behind
semantic disguises such as mediation to finality.
The basic argument against compulsory arbitration
is that it results in an unconstitutional delegation of the authority of elected officials and particularly legislators to fix wages and conditions
of employment.

It is also argued that, even if these legal
obstacles can be overcome, the delegation of authority to a private third party to fix the terms
and conditions of employment and, thus, in effect,
the budget and tax rates, means an abdication and
derogation of the representative form of government.

These arguments need to be considered seriously
from both the legal and the practical point of view.
The constitutionality of the recently enacted
Rhode Island, Pennsylvania, and Wyoming statutes
has been upheld by court decisions.[82] The Wyoming
Supreme Court specifically dealt with the question
of whether a compulsory arbitration statute for
firemen was unconstitutional on the ground that it
delegated to a board of arbitration powers expressly
reserved to the state legislature. The court, in a
sweeping decision, found the compulsory arbitration
statute constitutional and stated that the statute
conferred on arbitrators the power to execute the
law and the power to make the law. The court reasoned that the state had the authority to fix the
minimum salaries to be paid to firemen and thus had
equal authority to establish a "formula" through
the medium of arbitration for fixing a specific
amount above the minimum.[83]

The court cited with approval an earlier decision of the Pennsylvania Supreme Court that set
forth the distinction between delegable and nondel-
egable functions:

> If the delegation of power is to make
> the law, which involves the discretion
> of what the law shall be, then the
> power is nondelegable. If the con-
> ferred authority is the power of dis-
> cretion to execute the law already
> determined the delegation is unob-
> jectionable.[84]

Compulsory arbitration is old hat in some of
the Canadian provinces loke Ontario, where binding
arbitration of contract terms for policemen and
firemen has been applicable for 25 years.[85] The
Public Service Staff Relations Act of Canada now
provides for compulsory arbitration of disputes over
new contract terms for federal employees.[86]
The record in Canada, Pennsylvania, and Michigan suggests that compulsory arbitration is working
well in giving effective leeway to harmonious collective bargaining and, at the same time, standing
available to protect very necessary public services.

Compulsory arbitration is receiving intensive testing as an effective and equitable means of dispute settlement in the public service. What the long-range impact will be on the collective bargaining process remains to be seen. The early evidence is that compulsory arbitration is working to resolve disputes and that it has not harmed or destroyed the collective bargaining process.

It is possible that the parties to public employee disputes will concern themselves primarily with the selection of the arbitrator or persons who are to appoint the arbitrators and thus make no serious effort to bargain. The result would be the accumulation of a whole host of issues to be submitted to the arbitrator. The resulting confusion, loss of time, and possibly ill-considered decisions are pictured as real horrors.

The concern is valid. The problem has occurred occasionally in fact-finding proceedings and, for that matter, in private-sector bargaining, where parties pile up issues for last-minute negotiation. Despite a few horrible examples, however, the fact-finding process demonstrates that the parties tend to resolve and narrow the issues significantly before submitting the remaining difficult issues to an impasse panel.

Sound administration of arbitration statutes can be helpful here by declining or deferring the submission of disputes to arbitration or impasse panels until serious efforts at negotiation or mediation have been tried. In this atmosphere there is still the danger that the parties will disregard a number of tentative settlements when arbitration is commenced. The same problem exists in the private sector when some issues are brought back to the bargaining table if there is a strike or rejection of a settlement offer.

As has been observed, if compulsory arbitration enervates the bargaining process, it will be because the public and the parties to the negotiations want it that way, preferring settlement to the free collective bargaining process.[87] The availability or use of compulsory arbitration should not put voluntary arbitration and mediation

to pasture.   Certainly a voluntary use of arbitration affords the parties involved greater flexibility in defining the scope of arbitration and in
adopting their own procedures.

The voluntary nature of arbitration normally
gives the parties the freedom of choice to agree
upon the person or persons to serve as arbitrators,
or at least a choice of how the third-party arbitrator is to be selected.   The voluntary method
assumes a greater responsiveness of the arbitrators
to the parties than to the appointing agency.   Voluntarily selected arbitrators may be more amenable
to seeking means of accommodation and more concerned
with the acceptability of their awards than are arbitrators appointed unilaterally under a compulsory
statute.

Voluntary arbitration, however, possesses some
of the same shortcomings as binding arbitration.
If arbitration is voluntary, there is no assurance
that it will be used, that strikes will not occur,
that the employees will accept the awards, or that
the employer will implement the terms of the award.
Legislation may be necessary to authorize voluntary
and binding arbitration of contract terms and to
establish standards and criteria for the arbitration to overcome the arguments over unconstitutional
delegation of legislative authority and the absence
of standards for arbitrators.

Mediation

The role of mediation should also not be den-
igrated or derided, because this settlement aid is
by far the most effective and the most important
means of third-party aid in settling public employee
disputes.   Just as in private employment, mediation
has been and will be an effective means, regardless
of what happens to the strike or arbitration questions.   At times, mediators are requested by both
parties to make recommendations for settlement in
a role difficult to distinguish from fact-finding
or advisory arbitration.   But, when mediation fails,
other means of settlement must be considered.[88]

SUMMARY

Collective bargaining in the public service is
changing the "establishment" of government at all
levels. The impact of collective bargaining on the
structure of government will likely be as profound
as the one-man, one-vote, and civil rights decisions of the U.S. Supreme Court.
One effect should be the consolidation of local governmental units. Another effect has been
the codetermination of conditions of employment.
In time, collective bargaining will have as significant an effect on governmental institutions as it
has had on political and economic institutions in
the private sector.
The revolution in government employer-employee
relations wrought by collective bargaining has been
for the most part brought about by nonviolent means.
The tragic loss of Dr. Martin Luther King in a
struggle to establish bargaining rights for public
employees was an exception to the largely peaceful
and orderly, by today's standards, growth of public
employee bargaining.
Although collective bargaining has not been
fully extended to all municipal and state employees
or fully extended in terms of the scope of bargaining to all federal employees, the practice of public bargaining is now so clearly established in law
and in fact as to be a permanent way of life.
The task of the next decade is to fashion orderly procedures at the local, state, and federal
level; to make the system of bargaining work in an
equitable and effective manner; to meet the needs
of public employers for an efficient and responsible
public service; and to fulfill the desires of public
employees for an increased share of public resources
and for a right to participate in the decisions affecting their wages, hours, and conditions of employment.

BELGIUM
Marc Somerhausen

HISTORY AND EVOLUTION OF
PUBLIC BARGAINING

One of the first steps of the provisional
government of Belgium, which took power on September 26, 1831, was to proclaim the freedom of association. The eleventh issue of the Official
Journal of the new independent state published an
ordinance of the provisional government, issued on
October 16, that read as follows:

> Considering that all fetters set
> to the freedom of association are
> infringements upon the sacred rights
> of individual and political freedom,
>   The provisional government
> decides:
> Article 1. Citizens are free to asso-
>   ciate as they please for political,
>   religious, philosophical, literary,
>   industrial or commercial aims.
> Article 2. The law will interfere
>   only with unlawful acts of the as-
>   sociation or of the associates, but
>   not with the right to associate
>   itself.
> Article 3. No preventive measure can
>   be enacted against the right to
>   associate.

This right had been written into the Bill of Rights, which heads the constitution of Belgium enacted by the National Congress on February 7, 1831; it is still unchanged: Article 20 reads "The Belgians have the right to associate; this right can not be submitted to any preventive measure."

To the founding fathers of the Kingdom of Belgium this did not, however, mean that trade unions could be organized. According to the laws of the French Revolution, which were still valid, stoppage of work to enforce higher wages was a criminal offense and remained so up to 1866, when the pertinent articles of the penal code were abrogated under the influence of liberal ideas prevailing in Western Europe.

Trade unions could henceforth be organized legally. A statute of March 31, 1898, even provided a framework for "professional unions" endowed with legal status. Their rules had to be published in the Official Journal; their committees had to be approved by a governmental agency; their accounts had to be submitted to this agency; the list of members could be consulted by anybody; and the professional union could sue and be sued on behalf of its members.

Thousands of such professional unions were created by businessmen, craftsmen, peasants, physicians, and pharmacists; but wage earners never made use of this legal framework. Trade unions remained voluntary associations without any legal status, as they were in Great Britain. They still, to a great extent, have this de facto existence today.

Thus, the right to organize has existed since 1866, but special provisions were written into the penal code against outrages, violence, and insults occurring during a strike (art. 310). Peaceful picketing was not punished, but calling somebody a scab, spitting on his footsteps, or even making a grimace could send the culprit to jail. The courts had little sympathy for industrial disputes and applied Article 310 of the penal code with severity.

This repression did not, however, check the growth of the trade union movement--or, rather, the trade union movements--because two parallel

organizations developed: the socialist and the
catholic unions, the latter set up with the help of
the clergy. Later, liberal trade unions were also
founded with the help of the liberal party, liberal
in the British sense, not the American.

World War I brought about a great change:
Belgium was almost completely invaded; the Belgian
Government ordered the railwaymen to discontinue
work and advised the employers to close their factories if their products could in any way be useful
to the enemy. The government, one might say, organized a general strike and a general lockout in resistance to the invader.

The mass of the population was "on the dole"
and was fed with the help of the American Relief
Fund, headed by Herbert Hoover. To organize the
relief work in the cities and the villages throughout the country all public-minded citizens were
called upon, and, naturally, in the industrial regions employers and trade unionists joined in this
patriotic venture. Where class struggle, often in
an acute form, had prevailed, a spirit of cooperation was born.

When Belgium was liberated after Armistice Day,
the poverty was appalling. The membership of the
trade unions grew enormously, and a number of demands were made by the labor movement--among others,
the deletion of Article 310 from the penal code.
The national government set up by King Albert after
his return as liberator accepted the demands of the
labor movement. Article 310 was removed, and a law
was enacted to guarantee the right of association.

This new law provided that proceedings could
be instituted only against those who had made the
conclusion or the continuation of a wage contract
dependent upon the affiliation or the nonaffilia-
tion of one or more persons to a given association
--and that only if it was done maliciously, with
the will to infringe upon the freedom of association.
In other words, prosecutions against strikers could
only succeed if a special malicious purpose was
proved to exist.

Shortening hours or increasing wages were
termed lawful reasons for striking. The Supreme

Court (Cour de cassation) interpreted the new law
in a very liberal way; and, since 1923, few legal
procedures have been instituted against strikers by
the public prosecutors, except when they had committed offenses falling under the general provisions of the penal code.

The right to organize was denied even after
1866, however, as far as government employees were
concerned, not because of any legal prohibition but
because the government thought that it was contrary
to the duties of anybody in public service to "oppose the chiefs" or to "discuss the acts and ordi-
nances of the administration" and that it could
even be considered as encroaching upon the privileges of the public officials who had set up the
rules.

In 1881 a federation of the employees of the
Ministry of Public Works, which at that time was
responsible for the Belgian railways, was created,
but the minister published a circular forbidding
his personnel to join that federation. The matter
came up before Parliament, and the majority upheld
the government. In 1891 a federation of letter
carriers came into being, but the Minister of Railways, Post, and Telegraph again issued a circular
prohibiting government employees from joining this
new organization, noting "those who will disobey
will be discharged."

A member of the liberal opposition declared
this measure to be unconstitutional. The minister
argued successfully that this organization was political, since a motion had been passed by them
asking for a universal manhood franchise. In 1905
a federation of retired employees of the Ministry
of Railways, Post, and Telegraph announced a public
meeting in a provincial town, where a Labor Party
Member of Parliament (M.P.) would speak on "the
right to organize, the claims and the overwork of
the personnel." The minister immediately had post-
ers set up in the railroad yards threatening the
railway workers who would attend this meeting with
severe punishment. The Labor M.P. claimed that the
government had violated the constitution; the debate lasted for three days, but the motion of the

opposition was defeated 64 to 57, with 13 abstentions. This close vote shows that things were on
the move.

In 1910 a bill was brought in by the government to allow unions of the agents of the Ministry
of Railways, Post, and Telegraph, but only between
"such agents who had the same professional activity." In other words, craft unions were allowed.
Any union that disregarded the law would be dissolved by the King. This bill was never adopted,
but in the meantime the minister ruled that craft
unions were permitted in his department if they abstained from criticizing the administration, from
any political activity, and from any interference
by outsiders.

After World War II the Declaration of Human
Rights recognized the right to organize (art. 23,
sec. 4) and the International Labour Office (ILO)
conference at San Francisco drafted a convention on
the subject that was approved by the Belgian law of
July 9, 1951. During the discussion of the bill
approving the ILO convention members in both houses
of the government, whether of the majority or of
the opposition, declared that no change in the national legislation was required to comply with the
rules laid down by the ILO. The European convention
for the safeguard of human rights, approved by the
Belgian law of May 13, 1955, again reaffirms the
right to organize and to found trade unions (art.
11).

Both the ILO convention and the European convention have limitations concerning certain public
employees--the first concerning armed forces and
police; the second concerning armed forces, police,
and government employees (art. 11, sec. 2). The
European Social Charter also guarantees the right
to organize and makes no exception for public employees. This charter has been signed by the Belgian Government but has not been submitted to Parliament for approval.

There is no valid argument to exclude the civil
servants from the benefit of Article 6 of the European Social Charter. On the contrary, writes Louis
Paul Suetens, "during the discussions of the Charter

it was always admitted that it applies to civil
servants."[1] Another Senator recently said that
"the hesitations of the various governments concerning the clause of the European Social Charter
could well be understood, because it would imply
the right of public officials to strike."[2]

Although the right to organize has been recognized in Belgium since 1866, collective bargaining
was not practiced systematically before World War I,
at least not between employers and wage earners. A
sort of collective bargaining took place--curiously,
as a consequence of political strikes that occurred
before 1914. The franchise was limited to a small
number of citizens by the Belgian constitution of
1831. Labor demanded a general franchise to enforce it.

The Socialist Party initiated several general
strikes. The first one in 1882 led to violence and
arson and was suppressed by the militia and the
army; the second one in 1892 was called off after
secret negotiations between the leader of the Belgian Labor Party, Emile Vandervelde, and the prime
minister, which were followed by the revision of
the constitution.

As a result of this revision universal suffrage was established, but with plural votes for
citizens paying a certain amount of taxes or having
certain degrees. The number of voters rose from
134,000 to over 1 million. A third general strike
was called in 1902 and was forcibly repressed, and
a fourth one was called in 1913, which was the occasion of negotiations between Vandervelde and the
prime minister, De Broqueville. Universal suffrage
(one man-one vote) was enacted only after the end
of World War I.

Collective bargaining in the industrial field
began only after World War I. Inspired by the example of the Whitley committees and councils in
Great Britain, joint committees were instituted in
several industries by the Minister of Labor, Joseph
Wauters.* There was no law empowering the government

---

*For a discussion of the Whitley committees and
councils, see the section on the influence of Whitleyism in Chapter 3, below.

to do so. The first one was created in the mining
industry by royal decree. Others were established
by ministerial decisions for ore smelters, engineering, gas and electricity, the building trades,
glass, wood and furniture, bakeries, hotels, res-
taurants, and inns. Regional joint committees were
established for the textile industry, the harbor
of Antwerp, flax-processing, and wooden-shoe manufacture.

These joint committees consisted of delegates
of workers' and employers' organizations sitting in
equal numbers, under the presidency of an impartial
chairman. Their mission was to discuss wages and
conditions of work and to reach agreements on these
matters. Decisions had to be unanimous but even
then were not binding.

Although there have been cases where unanimous
decisions reached in some joint committees were
disregarded by the trade unions, generally the
agreements set up in the joint committees were applied by all parties concerned. The agreement
granting a certain quantity of coal free of charge
to the mine workers was even enforced by the labor
courts, which decided that the agreement had to be
considered as a custom of the industry and, as such,
binding.

The first joint committee to be set up by law
was established for railroad personnel. In 1926 a
tremendous monetary crisis occurred. To stabilize
the Belgian franc, the state railroads were handed
over to a corporation whose shares were exchanged
more or less compulsorily for the bonds of the
floating debt of the government. The state, in
fact, kept complete control over the railroads, but
outwardly public ownership had ceased. In order to
appease the railwaymen it was decided that their
status would be fixed by a joint committee and
could not be altered later on without the agreement
of this joint committee. In other words, this
joint committee, whose decisions were reached by a
two-thirds majority, received a quasi-legislative
power that it has kept up to this day.

The same system was enacted in the National
Corporation of Belgian Railroads. The same year a
joint committee was established in the Ministry of

Railroads and Ministry of Post, Telegraph, and
Telephones but did not receive the extensive power
of the joint committee of the National Corporation
of Belgian Railroads, for the former had only a
consultative role.

A new step occurred in 1937, when the government established common rules for the personnel of
all ministerial departments concerning selection,
promotion, discipline, and so on. It provided for
the establishment of personnel committees in each
department in order to foster close collaboration
between the trade unions and the administration.
Formally, there was no mention of trade unions
(syndicates); a milder term, "organisations professionnelles," was used instead. In 1937 a difference was still thought necessary between the
syndicates of the private sector and the organisations professionnelles of the public sector.

The details of the new scheme of collaboration
between government and its personnel were laid down
in the royal decree of December 14, 1937. A personnel committee was created in each ministry, and
an interdepartmental committee was created for the
government at large. Questions concerning one department were discussed in the personnel committee
of that department. As soon as a problem concerned
more than one ministry, the interdepartmental committee was to be consulted. All problems relating
to the functioning of services and the improvement
of labor conditions were to be submitted to the
committees, which were asked to express their opinion. The government was not bound by the advice of
the committees.

The committees were organized after the model
of the Whitley councils: half of a committee's
members representing the government and the other
half representing the personnel. The chairman was
to be the secretary-general of the department; that
is, the permanent undersecretary, according to the
British terminology.

The delegates of the personnel were chosen by
the trade unions after an election that was held in
order to determine the influence of the various
unions. This election was quite peculiar: no

individual candidates ran for election; the personnel were asked to vote for the socialist, catholic, or liberal union or for a craft union of some sort. The votes were counted, and each union was asked to propose its delegates according to its strength as revealed at the polls.

The vote was compulsory--a usual trait of Belgian electoral law--and secret, of course. In order to allow diplomats or consular agents to participate, voting by mail was provided for--which was only introduced in Belgium for national elections by a Law of 1969. According to the freedom of association guaranteed by the constitution, anybody can set up a trade union: one just has to say "I am the president" and persuade his colleagues to join him. Not every union was admitted to the election, however; only those that, after having submitted their rules, were accepted by the minister.

The first elections were held in 1938, but, hardly had the committees been organized, then war broke out. The country was invaded, and during the occupation a few unions collaborated with the Germans. It was therefore not possible to maintain the committees resulting from the 1938 elections. The government set up new committees after the liberation, called "comités de consultation syndicale." The representatives of the personnel were chosen by the government without election, but the other features of the royal decree of 1937 remained unchanged. New elections were provided for by a decree of the Regent of July 11. About 115,000 civil servants took part. The socialist unions got 45 percent of the votes, the catholic unions 36 percent, the liberal unions 7 percent, and the craft unions 11 percent.

The system was again changed in 1955, in order to include, besides the personnel of the ministries, the personnel of a large number of public or quasi-public corporations, called in Belgium "organismes parastataux." The term "parastatal" was coined in Italy and is unknown in France. A precise definition of what is parastatal and what is not is a question of dispute among lawyers and is gradually being settled, although the Supreme Court and the Conseil

d'Etat (Council of State) have not always had the
same opinion on this matter. But for the moment it
suffices to know that because of the extended scope
of the royal decree of June 20, 1955, 200,000 people
took part in the trade union elections of the public
sector.

Elections were held under the new scheme in
1955; the socialist unions received five seats in
the Comité Général de Consultation Syndicale, the
catholic unions five, and the liberal unions two.
The last trade union elections were held in 1959.
No elections took place in 1963 and 1968, because
negotiations were going on between the government
and the main unions in order to set up another system. In the meanwhile, the comités de consultation
syndicale set up in 1959 went on advising the government.

The royal decree of June 20, 1955, also en-
larged the advisory competence of the committees,
which were to be consulted about (a) all bills,
royal decrees, or circulars concerning admission,
promotion, discharge, salaries, and pensions; (b)
the organization of work and of services; and (c)
safety, hygiene, and the improvement of offices and
workshops.

If a bill relating to salaries or pensions is
not submitted to the Comité Général de Consultation
Syndicale, there is no redress. The opposition may,
of course, criticize the government for not having
sought the advice of the committee, but for the individual official there is no legal remedy once the
bill has become law.

If a royal decree or a ministerial ruling of
any sort has not been submitted to the competent
committee, the unions or any official concerned can
seek its annulment by the Conseil D'Etat. This administrative court considers that the government or
the authorities of a parastatal have acted ultra
vires if they fail to consult the competent committee. Quite a few measures have thus been quashed
by the Conseil d'Etat.

To revert to the private sector, as stated
above, joint committees were set up after World War
I in various industries and economic activities,

but during World War II the Germans dissolved them.
As soon as Belgium was liberated, the government--
acting under its emergency powers--gave these joint
committees legal status (arrêté loi du 9 juin 1945
fixant le statu des commissions paritaires). The
King was empowered to establish joint committees in
each branch of industry, commerce, or agriculture.
A later law added the "liberal professions." Eventually 81 such committees were set up.

The jurisdiction of these committees is determined by the King. They may be competent for workers only or for white-collar employees, or for both;
they may have jurisdiction over the entire country
or over only one region. The King may alter the
jurisdiction of a committee. The King is thus empowered to settle jurisdictional disputes between
trade unions or between employers' unions.

How does the King know which trade unions or
employers' organizations are to be represented in
the joint committees and in what proportions? In
the private sector there are no elections as in the
public sector. The Minister of Employment and Labor announces in the Official Journal that a joint
committee will be set up for this or that particular activity and asks the organizations concerned
to present a double list of candidates. They are
also invited to state their membership or the importance of their personnel. The government decides then which associations are sufficiently representative to have delegates on the committees and
how many. If the government omits this preliminary
inquiry or grossly disregards the facts revealed by
the inquiry, the appointment of the members of the
joint committee can be quashed by the Conseil d'Etat.

The joint committees have the power to determine the rates of wages for the various classes of
skills. In other words, they may set up collective
agreements. They also must prevent or conciliate
any dispute that threatens to arise between employers and workers. The decisions must be unanimous.
A single delegate of either the employers or the
employees can thus kill any proposal of settlement,
but this rarely occurs. In general, bargaining
goes on up to the moment a unanimous decision--or

agreement--can be reached. The chairman of the
joint committee is an independent person, often an
official of the Ministry of Employment and Labor.
The chairman has no vote but has a great influence
as a middleman.

Once a unanimous decision has been reached,
the King may make it binding for the branch of activity concerned. Violation of a unanimous decision made binding by the King is an offense punished
by a fine from 2,000 francs to 2 million francs.
Workers and employers can be fined, but the employer
will be fined as many times as there are members of
his personnel concerned. Convictions on this basis
are extremely rare, but the sword of Damocles is
very effective.

Unorganized employers or employees have to
abide by the decisions of the joint committees as
soon as they have been made binding by the King.
The King's decision may, however, be quashed by the
Conseil d'Etat if the joint committee is not legally
set up, if the decision was not unanimous, or if an
unreasonable retroactive effect is given to the
royal decree.

The Napoleonic Code--many of whose essential
provisions are still in force in Belgium--states
that the law provides only for the future and has
no retroactive effect (art. 2). The decision of
the joint committee is not law, but, once it has
been made binding, it becomes law. In principle,
this sort of quasi-legislation should have no retroactive effect. But the decision is the result of
negotiations between employers and employees; these
negotiations often last for several months before
unanimous consent is reached within the joint committee.

The unions insist, therefore, that the new
wage rates should be effective from the time of
their original demands, and the employers agree to
this demand or to some intermediate date. The King
will eventually make the agreement binding, but he
does not do so immediately. The government often
thinks the matter over, and a few more months elapse
before the royal decree is published in the Official
Journal.

The retroactivity--which means the payment of considerable sums of back wages--is certainly not in accordance with the principle of Article 2 of the Civil Code of Napoleon. The Conseil d'Etat, which had been asked to annul a royal decree that made a retroactive collective agreement compulsory, refused to do so, however. The legal reasoning was that the arrêté loi of June 9, 1945, had implicitly amended Article 2 of the Civil Code.

The main aim of this legislation was to ensure peace in the economic world. If the negotiations between unions and employers' organizations could settle the dispute for the future only, without any back payments, it would be an enticement for the less socially minded employers' delegates to prolong the discussions, and the trade unions would be induced to strike rather than to bargain. The Conseil d'Etat adopted an Anglo-Saxon standard in this regard. The retroactivity must be reasonable. If the King waits for several years before he makes a collective agreement binding, he delays his decision unreasonably and then acts ultra vires.[3]

Public bargaining is presently regulated by the law of December 5, 1968 (loi sur les conventions collectives et les commissions partitaries), which defines the collective agreement as follows:

> The collective labor contract is an agreement between one or several organizations of employees and one or several organizations of employers which determines the individual and collective relations between employers and employees within plants or within a branch of activity and fixes the rights and duties of the contracting parties.

The recent law is more detailed than is the arrêté loi of 1945 but does not alter the system that has been described under it.

There are, however, new features: collective agreements can be made not only in the joint committees of a branch of activity but also in the

National Labor Board (Conseil National du Travail)
if an agreement applies to more than one branch of
activity, if no joint committee exists for a particular branch of activity, or if an existing committee does not function.

Furthermore, it is expressly stated that trade
unions, although not incorporated, may sue on behalf of their members to enforce the collective
agreements; trade unions may be sued for breach of
the collective agreement to which they were a party,
but only if they have accepted this responsibility
in the agreement. Collective agreements have to be
registered at the Ministry of Employment and Labor.
The royal decree making the collective agreement
binding may be retroactive, but the retroactivity
may not exceed one year before the publication of
the decree.

SCOPE OF PUBLIC SECTOR

The public sector includes the personnel of
the state, the provinces, the local authorities,
and public or quasi-public corporations. The state
has approximately 100,000 officials and employees
working for the various ministries: the ministries
of finance; interior; national defense; justice;
economic affairs; foreign affairs and foreign trade;
agriculture; middle class; communications; post,
telegraph and telephone; national education and
culture; employment and labor; social affairs; and
public works.

This personnel corresponds to the British
civil service but is somewhat more extensive; it
includes messengers, elevator operators, carpenters,
and so forth. The civil service is divided into
four classes: the first class (less than 10,000)
consists of officials with a university education;
the second class (20,000) comprises those employees
who have completed their secondary education; the
third class (22,000) takes in people with only a
limited secondary education; and the fourth class
(37,000) includes typists and manual workers.

According to the Belgian constitution appointments in government service are made by the King,
unless otherwise provided by law. Traditionally it
has been admitted that the right to appoint implies
the right to determine the rules of employment. A
uniform set of rules has thus been set up for the
personnel of the various ministries by a royal decree of October 22, 1937.

According to the Belgian constitution education
provided by the state is regulated by law. State
universities, state high schools, and state primary
schools have a staff of nearly 60,000. There are
also municipal schools, with 34,000 teachers.
Schools organized by the Catholic church are an important factor in Belgian education. These schools
are subsidized by the state, and the pensions of
their retired teachers are also paid out of public
funds. There are nearly 100,000 teachers and
100,000 personnel in the Catholic schools.

According to the Belgian constitution the
rights and duties of the members of the armed forces
are determined by law. Not counting 50,000 soldiers
drafted for military service, over 50,000 officers,
noncommissioned officers, and soldiers are serving
in the Belgian army. Besides these, the national
police corps (gendarmerie), subject to military
discipline, has 13,000 members.

Local authorities employ 85,000 people, including the personnel of the municipal hospitals.
In addition, 10,000 employees work for intercommunal
associations, mainly for water, gas, and electricity
distribution. The courts employ barely 5,000 people, ranging from the members of the Supreme Court
to the detectives (police judiciaire) and court
messengers. Their employment is ruled by law.

Finally, the public and quasi-public corporations have a staff of nearly 200,000. There are
about 100 of these corporations, including the Belgian railroads; the telegraph and telephone corporations; the state savings bank; Belgian radio and
television; various institutions of social security;
the port authorities of Brussels, Liège, and Bruges;
the airports' authority, and so on. Each of these

corporations has been set up by law, and their sta-
tuses vary considerably since they are concerned
with financial, economic, welfare, and other activities.

A law of March 16, 1954, empowered the King to
set up rules for their 200,000 members. One set of
rules has been laid down for the staff of the social security institutions (royal decree of February 14, 1961), for the other institutions their
former rules are still applicable, and for the airports' authority there are as yet no written rules.

All in all, nearly 650,000 men and women are
active in the public sector (exactly 648,216 according to a census taken on June 30, 1969), for a total population of nearly 10 million inhabitants and
for a total of over 3,800,000 people gainfully employed at the same date.[4]

In a wider sense, the medical and paramedical
professions might be included in the public sector,
although their members are generally not salaried.
The income of surgeons, physicians, dentists, opticians, nurses, and the like depends to a great
extent on fees that are regulated by government
within the system of compulsory insurance against
disease and invalidity. This system covers not
only white- and blue-collar employees but also the
middle class, civil servants, and students.

In other words, practically the entire population of Belgium is insured and pays contributions
to the social security system. These contributions,
however, do not suffice, and one-third of the cost
of the insurance against disease and invalidity is
paid out of the national budget. The fees of the
medical and paramedical professions are regulated
by the government. Joint committees have been set
up for each medical and paramedical profession (law
of August 9, 1963). Constant bargaining is therefore going on with the medical and paramedical pro-
fessions--in total, 46,000 men and women.

In the 1960s the medical unions gave the government more headaches than did any other. Statistics on the number of people in the medical and
paramedical professions and the average yearly income of physicians follow:[5]

Physicians (including surgeons)
general practitioners	8,557
specialists	5,773
Total physicians	14,330
Dentists	2,249
Pharmacists	4,854
Opticians	2,845
Nurses	13,606
Kinesists	4,249
Midwives	1,856
Orthopedists	576
Acousticians	427
Bandagists	1,179

Average Yearly Income of Physicians

	Francs	Dollar Equivalents
1963	328,000	6,400
1964	506,000	10,000
1965	699,000	14,000
1966	800,000	16,000

JOINT COMMITTEES IN PUBLIC SECTOR

A central joint committee has jurisdiction for the personnel of the various ministries and for the public and quasi-public corporations, with the exception of the financial institutions. This committee has 24 members; 12 are chosen by the government and 12 by the trade unions. The 12 seats of the trade union representation are allotted to the most representative national unions on the basis of a secret ballot taken in 1955. All members of the personnel not only have the right to vote but are obliged to do so, whether they are affiliated with a trade union or not. As a result of this ballot, five seats were allotted to the socialist union, five to the catholic union, and two to the liberal union.

In each ministry and each public or quasi-public corporation a joint committee is set up. According to the size of the personnel, the number of members of the committee varies from four to 20,

half of them chosen by the minister or the ruling
body of the corporation, the other half chosen by
the trade unions. The National Corporation of
Belgian Railroads has its own joint committee consisting of 20 members; 10 are chosen by the board
of the society, and 10 by the organizations encompassing the personnel (organizations groupant le
personnel) (law of July 23, 1926).

A year later, a similar system was established
for the rural railways (chemins de fer vicinaux),
which was run by a national society created in 1885.
The shares of this company were subscribed by the
state, the provinces, and the municipalities to
private persons. The dividends could not exceed
4.5 percent. The joint committee consisted of 14
members, of which half were appointed by the board
of the society and half by the trade union organizations encompassing the personnel (law of July 20,
1927).

Joint committees have been set up for the
Catholic schools (law of May 29, 1959), primary
schools, high schools, and technical schools. They
are composed of equal numbers of representatives of
the church and of the most representative organizations of the personnel. In 1959 the Conseil d'Etat
quashed the appointment of the representatives of
the personnel because the government had appointed
only delegates of the catholic trade union of teachers without ascertaining first whether it was the
only representative organization after a split had
occurred in its ranks. No new appointments have
been made since, with the result that the joint
committees exist only on the books.

A consultative commission of the personnel of
the gendarmerie has been instituted (royal decree
of February 2, 1965), with three sections--for the
officers, for the sergeant majors, and for the lower
ranks. The consultative commission of the armed
forces includes six delegates of the Minister of
National Defense and 12 delegates of the three recognized associations of the personnel, four of them
chosen from the army, four from the air force, and
four from the navy. If the delegates of the minister and those of the personnel have not come to a

unanimous conclusion, points of view of each delegation are set forth; eventual disagreements within
the delegations of the personnel must also be mentioned. This commission is thus less an institution for collective bargaining than an advisory
body of the old type (royal decree of October 20,
1964).

Joint committees have been set up for the gas
and electricity plants; for streetcar lines, trolleys, and buses; and for hospitals and clinics.
A peculiar situation arises here: some gas and
electricity plants are municipal, others are run by
private firms; some streetcar-line systems are run
by private firms, others by cities; and some hospitals are run by local authorities, others belong
to religious congregations, and private clinics are
owned by individual or associated physicians. Although these three branches overlap into the public
sector, their joint committees have been set up on
the basis of the arrêté loi of June 9, 1945, which
concerned the private sector.

The joint committee for the medical profession
consists of 10 delegates of the mutual insurance
societies. The joint committee for the pharmacists
consists of eight delegates of the representative
associations of the pharmacists and eight delegates
of the mutual insurance societies. The joint committees for midwives, nurses, kinesists, opticians,
orthopedists, acousticians, and bandagists are set
up in the same way.

ISSUES OF COLLECTIVE BARGAINING

Any problem arising out of public employment
can be discussed within the joint committees of the
civil service: selection, promotion, compensation,
superannuation, age of retirement, discipline, holidays, family allowances, leaves of absence, fringe
benefits, hours of work, and so forth. Originally
the issues were submitted to the joint committee by
the government. Later, the representatives of the
personnel were allowed to require that issues be
placed on the agenda.

Individual complaints are outside the jurisdiction of the joint committee, but any rule affecting the conditions of employment has to be submitted to the joint committee, whether it is to be
enacted by Parliament, by royal or ministerial decree, or in a less formal way by a circular note
emanating from the administration. The same is
true for the creation of new jobs or the suppression of existing jobs, for the organization of services, and for questions of safety and hygiene at
the place of work.

The problems concerning one ministerial department or one agency are submitted to the joint
committee of that department or agency. Any problem concerning more than one department or agency
is submitted to the central joint committee. The
jurisdiction of the joint committee of the railroad
corporation and of the National Society of Rural
Railways is similar. The jurisdiction of the joint
commission of the gendarmerie is more limited; it
does not specifically extend to the creation and
suppression of jobs.

The joint committees for the field of gas and
electricity, for streetcar lines, trolleys, and
buses, and for hospitals and clinics, are competent
for all problems of wages, hours, and conditions of
work. They have, moreover, an important task to
fulfill; they must determine which are the activities of vital importance for the nation that have
to be performed in case of a strike or a lockout.
If, however, they fail to do so, the government is
empowered to act in their stead. Furthermore, the
joint committee must set up a subcommittee with
equal representation of employers and employees
that will choose the members of the personnel who
are called upon to perform these vital activities
(law of August 19, 1948).

The joint committees of the compulsory insurance against disease and invalidity have to regulate the financial and administrative relations
between the beneficiaries of the insurance and the
medical and paramedical professions. This includes
all aspects of the profession. The fees of surgeons and physicians, for instance, which have been

set on the basis of this collective bargaining,
enumerate all surgical operations, all kinds of
radiographs, and every conceivable kind of medical
examination. Whenever some progress is achieved in
diagnosis or treatment of an illness, the schedule
is modified.

ENFORCEMENT OF AGREEMENTS

The decisions of the joint committee of the
National Corporation of Belgian Railroads, the
first to exist in the public sector, are binding
for the corporation and for all railroad employees.
They can be enforced by the courts; and any individual decision of the board of the corporation
contrary to the rules defined by the joint commit-
tee--in cases of promotion or discipline, for instance, can be quashed by the Conseil d'Etat. The
same is true for the rural railways.

The joint committees of the civil service are
only consultative. In theory, a unanimous decision
of these committees can be disregarded by the government; but, in practice, when the delegates of
the minister and those of the trade unions have
agreed on a matter, the proposals of the joint committee are accepted by the competent authority.
The proposals are enacted by law or by royal or
ministerial decree.

Once confirmed by law or by royal or ministerial decree, the decisions of the joint committees
will be enforced by the courts and by the Conseil
d'Etat. Any royal or ministerial decree relating
to matters pertaining to the jurisdiction of a
joint committee that has not been submitted to the
joint committee can be quashed by the Conseil
d'Etat upon request of any civil servant or employee
to whom it should be applied.

The collective agreements negotiated within
the joint committees for gas and electricity, for
streetcar lines, trolleys, and buses, and for hospitals and clinics are binding for all employers
represented in the joint committee and for all employees of these employers, whether affiliated or

not with the trade unions represented in the joint
committee. The collective agreement can be made
binding by royal decree for all employers and employees of the branch.

The agreements concerning the pharmacists,
the dentists, and the paramedical professions are
made binding by the Minister of Social Affairs.
For the medical profession the system is more complicated. The country is divided for this purpose
into districts. In each district the surgeons and
physicians are invited individually to accept the
agreement. The agreement is binding for all practitioners if 40 percent of them have not declared
by registered letter that they reject the agreement.
As a result of this poll, the present agreement is
binding all over the kingdom, except in a rural
district of the Ardennes with only 30,000 inhabitants, where half of the physicians expressed their
opposition.

TRADE UNION RECOGNITION

Trade unionism originated in Belgium in the
second half of the nineteenth century. Local craft
unions, inspired by socialist ideology, were organized by skilled workmen: bookbinders, glassblowers,
printers, carpenters, masons, and the like. Local
federations frequently were charters of the Knights
of Labor, mostly miners, related to the American
organization of that denomination.

The Belgian Labor Party, which was founded in
1868, tried to establish closer links between the
various unions and in 1898 set up a Trade Union
Commission, which became later the Belgian Federation of Trade Unions. The membership of the Belgian Federation of Trade Unions grew slowly:

1904	20,000
1907	55,000
1910	69,000
1913	127,000
1919	450,000
1945	450,000
1970	775,000

Amalgamation of the craft unions began around 1910
and was achieved after World War I. The number of
industrial unions has been constantly reduced.
Craft unionism has practically disappeared at
present.

In the public sector trade unionism began in
the municipal gas and electricity works and in the
state-owned railways. The combination of state employees was strongly opposed by the government, as
has already been noted above. A general strike of
railway personnel in 1924 led to the discharge of
the union officials from government service.

As a counterweight to the socialist union
movement, catholic trade unions were organized, inspired by the encyclical Rerum Novarum. The Confederation of Catholic Trade Unions was founded in
1912. The catholic union movement, originally
rather tame, has become more and more militant and
often tries to outbid the socialist movement.

Although the socialist movement is dominant in
the Walloon region, the catholic movement has its
stronghold in the Flemish provinces. As the industrialization of the Flemish region progresses, the
catholic trade unions become numerically more important than their rivals. The catholic trade unions
presently have 855,000 members (74 percent in Flanders, 18 percent in the Walloon region, and 8 percent in Brussels).

The catholic unions are also organized along
industrial lines. Their membership in the public
sector is as follows: Central Union of Public Services, 52,000; Union of Railway Employees, 37,000;
and Union of Catholic High School Teachers, 6,000.
The liberal trade unions, which are fostered by the
liberal party, are loosely organized. Their membership, scattered all over the country, is below
100,000.

Recently, a reaction of the rank and file
against amalgamation has become evident in the public sector. Some government employees have a notion
that their interests have been disregarded in the
collective bargaining conducted by what they call
the political trade unions and have split off.
Letter carriers, customs officials, and consular
and diplomatic agents have independent unions,

which in their field seem to be more influential
than are the amalgamated movements.

The Belgian trade union movement is thus divided along ideological lines. The principle of
freedom of association written into the Belgian
Bill of Rights therefore excludes the practice of
the closed shop. There may be plants where it is
practically impossible to be hired if one does not
show the membership card of one specific union, but
the whole legal system aims at a protection of the
minorities.*

In the private sector elections are held periodically for the works councils (conseils d'entre-
prise), whose main function is the drafting of the
working rules (règlement du travail) for each firm
or plant (law of April 5, 1965). There are very
few enterprises where the works councils are 100
percent socialist or catholic.

In the public sector, the principle of plural-
ism has always been admitted. For the oldest joint
committee in the public sector, the National Society of Belgian Railroads, the law of July 23, 1926,
provides that the joint committee be made up of 10
members appointed by the board of the society and
10 members appointed by the organizations encompassing the personnel. On the basis of this text
it was decided by the joint committee that all
unions were eligible for representation provided
that their membership included at least 10 percent
of the total personnel.

In 1962 these rules were amended by the joint
committee. It was decided that to be eligible the
organizations of railwaymen had to be affiliated
with a national and interprofessional organization
with at least 50,000 members and recognized by the
National Labor Board and the Central Economic Council. The aim of this provision was to restrict the
representation of the three main unions--that is,
catholic, socialist, and liberal. The independent

---

*Dock workers in Antwerp, however, are hired
only if they belong to the union. (Magrez, 43).

union of railwaymen brought suit against this new
provision before the Conseil d'Etat, which decided
that such a restriction was illegal.

The government, after having sought the consent of the joint committee, asked Parliament to
amend the law. A bill was introduced and "rail-
roaded" through both houses within a week, despite
the opposition of the liberal party. The law of
April 21, 1965, provides that only those unions are
eligible for the joint committee of the railways
that are open to all crafts and work on the national
level. To justify this amendment of the 1926 law
the government explained that only interprofessional
unions had complete knowledge of the various activities of the personnel and that only nationwide
unions could make a certain balance between their
own aims and those of the trade unions in the private sector and thus enable the railways to work in
the interest of national economy.

For the ministerial departments and the public
or quasi-public corporations the royal decree of
June 10, 1955, provides that recognition is granted
to the unions encompassing all or part of the personnel for the defense of their professional interests that have at least one delegate on the
central joint committee as a result of the election
or that are represented on the central labor board.
The recognition may be withdrawn by the prime minister after consultation with the joint committee.

In 1962 recognition had been withdrawn from
the Independent Federation of Customs Officials
because their secretary had published an insulting
article in the union paper. The Conseil d'Etat decided that this withdrawal of recognition was justified.[6] A similar union was later recognized, but
in 1963 this union asked its members to "work according to rules"; the Minister of Finance considered this appeal as an incitement to sabotage and
withdrew recognition. A month later, however, recognition was restored to the Independent Union of
Finance Personnel.

In the gendarmerie one single professional association is recognized, because its aims and means
are considered by the Minister of National Defense

as compatible with military discipline. In 1964
two noncommissioned gendarmes founded a union affiliated with the Independent Union of the Personnel of National Defense, which hitherto included
only civilian staff. The commanding general decided that membership in a trade union was illegal;
he was upheld by the Minister of National Defense.
The two founders of the union were discharged, after
the joint disciplinary commission had unanimously
advised that there had been a grave act of insubor-
dination.

The noncommissioned officers appealed to the
Conseil d'Etat, claiming that their constitutional
freedom of association had been violated and that
no law forbade affiliation of members of the armed
forces with a union. The high administrative court
rejected their plea, taking into account the Dutch
law of March 15, 1815, which is still in force in
Belgium; this somewhat antiquated text requires absolute obedience from members of the army. The Conseil d'Etat held that military discipline would be
imperiled if members of the gendarmerie belonged to
a union together with civilians.

In the joint commission of the armed forces
only three organizations are recognized (royal decree of October 20, 1964): the Association of Officers on Active Service, the Mutual Association of
Noncommissioned Officers of Belgium, and the Association of Active Soldiers and Corporals of Belgium.
The Minister of National Defense may disown a delegate of these associations if he thinks it advisable.
Said delegate may no longer take part in the discussions of the commission. Before making his decision the minister must relate his reasons to the
committee of the organization and hear its opinion
on the matter.

As far as the provincial and local authorities
are concerned, a law of July 27, 1961, empowered
the King to draft the guiding principles for the
selection, promotion, and compensation of their
personnel "after consultation of delegates of the
most representative associations of their personnel," whereupon a joint committee was established
(royal decree of October 23, 1961). The delegates

of the personnel were to be chosen from among the
three main trade union movements.

The National Union of Municipal Policemen
(Syndicat National de la Police Belge) claimed that
the municipal personnel were mainly organized in
craft unions (municipal clerks, municipal treasur-
ers, firemen, policemen, and so forth) and that the
socialist, catholic, and liberal unions were not
"the most representative organizations" that Parliament had in mind. Official figures of the membership of the contending organizations were not
available. One fact, however, seemed to be clear:
the government had not investigated the relative
strength of the craft unions and the three big
unions. The joint committee for the personnel of
provincial and local authorities never functioned,
and the royal decree was repealed.

The royal decree of August 20, 1969, provides
that the government will consult the most representative organizations directly and that only the organizations that are open to all categories of provincial and municipal personnel are to be considered as such. The Conseil d'Etat rejected a new
plea of the National Union of Municipal Policemen,
which claimed that its membership included 7,500 of
the 10,000 municipal police forces, with the following explanation:

> The standard of membership may be sat-
> isfactory in the private sector or in
> large administrations where the staff
> is submitted to one hierarchy and gov-
> erned by the same rules, but it should
> not be applied to municipal employees
> belonging to numerous categories for
> which Parliament has enacted different
> rules; this diversity in categories
> and rules makes it much more difficult
> to consult the representative organiza-
> tions; in each category the tendency
> prevails to seek the greatest advan-
> tages for themselves without consid-
> eration of the impact on other cate-
> gories, which, however, the government

must consider; the consultation of
the unions can therefore only be
fruitful if the government asks the
advice of those organizations whose
membership includes employees of all
categories, which for that reason are
bound to be fair to all of them.[7]

Local authorities often associate for a special purpose. In 1860 several cities founded a
company to sell bonds and thus finance public works.
Practically all municipalities are shareholders of
this company, called Crédit Communal, which receives deposits from the public; the subsidies that
the government owes to the municipalities are paid
to their account at the Crédit Communal. This institution has become one of the main banks of the
kingdom. The joint committee of banks has jurisdiction over this association of municipalities.
Several municipalities of the province of
Liège founded a cooperative society for road maintenance and building. A royal decree of January 5,
1957, stated that the joint committee of the building industry has jurisdiction over this public corporation as far as their workers are concerned.
The national confederation of the building trades
appealed to the Conseil d'Etat, claiming that the
King had acted ultra vires by submitting a public
corporation to a joint committee of the private
sector.
The high administrative court ruled that no
law prevented a public corporation from hiring
workers in the same fashion as did private employers; in such cases the public corporation was
bound by law to pay compensation in case of accidents and to post its working rules like any private enterprise. Therefore, there was no reason
why the wages and hours of its workers should not
be determined by a collective agreement.[8]
In the medical profession there were several
unions founded in 1962 that led a medical strike.
Some of these unions have become more cooperative,
but others have continued their opposition to the
system of insurance against sickness. They have

asked their members not to use the official document that asks about the fee paid by each patient;
this document is then forwarded by the Mutual Insurance Association to the income tax administration.

Before appointing the members of the joint
committee of insurance (comité médico-mutualiste),
the prime minister formally asked the unions that
instigated this "administrative strike" to put an
end to it. He received only an evasive answer. No
members of these "striking" unions were appointed
to the joint committee. These medical unions appealed to the Conseil d'Etat, claiming that the
majority of surgeons and physicians were affiliated
with them and that the government had violated the
law by refusing to appoint members of representative
associations. They also claimed that the demand of
the prime minister violated the "right to strike."

The Conseil d'Etat decided that the professional organizations had no unlimited right of
representation and that the government was entitled
to exclude from representation those unions that
fought against the legal system by organizing an
"administrative strike"; with regard to the "right
to strike" the decision held that a strike is the
collective stoppage of work, bringing about the loss
of any compensation for the strikers. The refusal
to utilize official documents was no strike in the
usual sense of the word; without examining whether
physicians had the right to cease medical care collectively, the Conseil d'Etat decided that in casu
there was no infringement on the right to strike.[9]

For the joint committees for gas and electricity, for streetcar lines, trolleys, and buses, and
for hospitals and clinics the law of December 5,
1968, defines as follows the representative organizations:

> For the purpose of the present act,
> [these] are considered as representa-
> tive organizations of the employers:
>   1. The interprofessional orga-
> nizations of workers and employers
> established national level and

represented in the Central Economic
Council and in the National Labor
Board; the workers' organizations
must have at least 50,000 members;

2. The professional organizations affiliated with or belonging
to an interprofessional organization
mentioned under No. 1;

3. The professional organizations of employers which, in a given
branch, are declared to be representative by the King, upon advice of
the National Labor Board.

Moreover, are considered as
representative organizations of the
employers, the National Interprofessional organizations recognized
according to the Law of March 6, 1964
organizing the middle class, which
are representative of employers of
crafts, small and middle sized commercial firms and small industrial
enterprises and of persons with
liberal professions or other intel-
lectual profession.

As far as the three above-mentioned joint committees, which belong to the private sector but
overlap in the public sector, are concerned, there
has been little controversy. In 1952 a joint committee had been founded for the artistic crafts,
such as gold and silversmiths, lace manufacture,
embroidery, and the manufacture of sets of artificial teeth. Three years later a joint committee
was founded for hospitals, clinics, sanitariums,
and manufacturers of sets of artificial teeth.
The national union of manufacturers of artificial teeth claimed that the government had exceeded its powers by submitting their profession
to the jurisdiction of two joint committees. The
Conseil d'Etat rejected their appeal, because the
royal decree of 1952, inasmuch as it concerned the
profession of the claimant, had obviously been
abrogated by the royal decree of 1955.[10]

RIGHT TO STRIKE

The right to strike is even at present not
recognized in so many words by Belgian law. When
the Belgian Parliament, before granting independence
to the Congo, drafted a bill of rights for the future republic, however, it inserted in the law of
June 17, 1960, the following article: "The right
to strike is exercised within the frame of the Law
which regulates it and which may in no case abridge
the freedom of work and the free exercise of the
right to property." Neither in the Chamber of Representatives nor in the Senate was the slightest
objection raised against this clause. The right to
strike thus appears nowadays as evident.

The European Social Charter, signed on October 18, 1961, states the following:

> In order to vouchsafe the effective
> right of collective bargaining, the
> Contracting Powers recognize the
> right of workers and employers to
> collective actions in the case of
> conflicting interests, including the
> right to strike, with reservation as
> to obligations which might result
> from collective agreements which are
> in force.

The charter is not self-executing and has to be
approved by the Belgian Parliament. More than a
decade has elapsed, and the charter is not yet on
the Belgian statute books.

Many Belgian laws deal with strikes and lockouts, however. For family allowances, compensation
of industrial accidents, paid holidays, and unemployment doles, strike periods are treated in the
same way as are periods of illness or other causes
of suspension of the labor contract. The Supreme
Court has ruled that the foreman who takes part in
a strike does not ipso facto break the contract
that binds him to his employer.[11]

According to the law of August 18, 1948 (loi
relative aux prestations d'intérêt public en temps

de paix), in case of collective and voluntary stoppage of work or in case of collective discharge of the personnel the urgent repairs to machines and equipment and the urgent works required by unforeseen necessity have to be accomplished. Besides, the vital needs of the population have to be taken care of. These vital needs are determined for each branch of activity by the competent joint committee. Decisions on this matter need not be unanimous, as is required for collective agreements, but are valid when made by a majority of two-thirds.

The joint committees' decisions can be made binding for all employers and employees by a royal decree. The joint committees were required to determine the vital needs of the population in their respective branches of activity within six months. If they failed to do so, the law authorized the King to act in their stead. Availing themselves of this clause, the government decided which were the vital needs in various activities not only in the private sector but also in the public sector. This was the case for postal services and radio, for the production and distribution of gas and electricity, for streetcar lines and buses, and for hospitals and clinics (decrees of the Prince Regent of July 27, 1950; and January 29, May 24, and May 25, 1951, respectively.

For instance, the government decided that bakeries, hospitals, and police stations had to be provided with electric power if a strike occurred in the electricity works. But it is impossible to provide electricity exclusively to a hospital, a bakery, and a police station in a given district. The government decided that, in case of a strike or a lockout in the electricity works, the governor of the province has to send out technicians to cut off from the electric net all plants that are not considered vital.

The highest authority in the province thus becomes the agent of the trade union that started the strike. This curious system has been applied several times since 1951, and, whatever the political outlook of the government has been, none has found another way of enforcing the 1948 law.

As things stand, nobody can claim that strikes are illegal, although no law expressly mentions the right to strike. As a matter of fact, nobody claims it for the private sector. Such, however, is not the case for the public sector. There is almost unanimous consent among lawyers that a public servant may not strike.

Various arguments uphold this theory. First of all, it is alleged that strikes are prohibited by the rules of civil service. These rules were drafted by a royal commissioner, Louis Camu, who is the head of the second largest Belgian bank. In his report to the government he wrote that, "in a democratic state, a strike in public services is an assault against the entire nation." He submitted a statute text that read as follows: "Civil servants may not have any activity which would be in opposition with monarchy, the institutions and law of the Belgian people or the respect due to established authorities. It is forbidden for them to go on strike."

This last, clear-cut sentence, which aroused the hostility of the trade union movement, was deleted. Instead, the royal decree of October 2, 1937, says that the civil servants "may not without previous permission interrupt the performance of their functions."12 This sentence is ambiguous. One may argue that the government altered the text of the royal commissioner because it did not want or did not dare to forbid strikes within the civil service. The decree of October 2, 1937, has been amended time and again, but the ambiguous sentence has survived.

Recently, rules have been drafted for the personnel of the agencies of social security that have many points in common with the rules for civil servants; but the ambiguous text has been omitted. Instead, one finds the following: "The members of the personnel may not, without previous permission, interrupt their activity for reasons of personal convenience" (royal decree of February 14, 1961). Nobody goes on strike "for personal convenience." This new rule, therefore, is a step further from the prohibition of strikes intended by the royal commissioner.

Prime Minister Theodore LeFevre (Christian Social Party) declared the following in the Senate on
July 13, 1961:

> The statute of the personnel of the
> state does not exclude the right to
> strike. I believe everybody agrees
> on this point. A great number of
> jurists and politicians could be
> quoted in this respect. I shall only
> mention one statement, made by the
> honorable Mr. Lilar, Vice-President
> of the Council of Ministers on Feb-
> ruary 23, 1960: "What is the situa-
> tion in regard to the problem of the
> right to strike of civil servants.
> As a jurist I must say that the right
> to strike is not regulated by any
> text." Whenever continental lawyers
> do not find a definite clause in the
> statutes of their executive orders,
> to solve a controversial issue, they
> resort to "general principles of
> law."[13]

The prohibition of strikes in public service
is frequently based on the principle of the continuity of public service. It is in the very nature
of public service that it should not be discontinued. Up to the beginning of the twentieth century
mail was delivered on Sundays as well as on weekdays. Railroads function seven days a week. De-
linquents are prosecuted and tried without interruption all year long.

This dogma of continuity is, however, not absolute. All government offices close on Saturdays
and Sundays. Schools do not function during the
months of July and August. Civil cases are not
handled during the judicial holidays. Interruption
of the distribution of gas and electricity is admitted in case of strikes, with the exception of
vital needs. In France, where the principle of
continuity was also invoked as inherent to the nature of public service, the law of July 31, 1963,

affirms the "right to strike" of civil servants of
the state, of the local authorities, and of public
corporations. Thus, the general principle has
loopholes.

A second argument against strikes is derived
from the traditional concept of the civil servant.
The old Prussian civil service still appears today
as the prototype.[14] The civil servant is required
conscientiously to discharge his office and all the
duties directly appertaining thereto, to obey the
official orders of his superiors insofar as they do
not contradict the laws, and to behave in a manner
worthy of the respect accorded to his office.

It is not the business of an inferior to question the material value of the policy of his superior's orders. When the civil servant does not
obey, it is at his own risk. He becomes liable to
disciplinary penalties if his disobedience is declared unjustified by the higher official or the
disciplinary judge. When a civil servant is in
doubt, he is counseled to obey and make a complaint
afterward.

Civil servants must carry out the duties of
their office with the greatest sincerity and pro-
bity, with all industriousness and care. Civil servants must keep punctually to the hours of arrival
at and departure from work. No legal claim to extra pay can be made by the civil servant if an extension or alteration of existing functions takes place,
as long as the new work corresponds to the training
and capacity of the civil servant. When special
help is demanded during a strike to make up what
the strikers would normally have done, all civil
servants are obliged to obey; even higher officials
are obliged, where necessary, to do purely physical
labor.[15]

Respect of superiors is demanded outside as
well as inside the office, even when the superior
is objectionable in character and demeanor. Officials must not allow insults to pass unnoticed,
lest the service should suffer degradation. In
cases where the official is in doubt about the significance of the insult, he may consult his superior, who may take an action for insult, if this

occurred during the exercise of, or otherwise in
respect to, the official's duties. Such behavior
is enjoined in nonofficial life so that the dignity,
confidence, and respect bound up with the office
shall not be disadvantageously affected.

Every official must in his extraofficial life
have regard for the special obligations that his
official position imposes upon him. The official
must, therefore, so order his general way of life
as to conform to prevalent opinions in virtue, manner, and morals. This duty he owes not only to his
master, the state, to which he stands in a special
relationship of loyalty, but to the whole of officialdom, which ought to suffer in its ranks only
worthy professional colleagues.

In the matter of contracting debts not only is
the official himself watched, reprimanded, and
fined when matters become serious and damaging
enough, but he is expected to stop his wife from
frivolous domestic economy! Games of chance may be
played in good company, so long as one's economic
independence is not thereby jeopardized. No official may take any additional offices or employment
other than those for which he has asked and obtained permission from the appropriate departmental
authority. It is an axiom that all the official's
time and energy must be devoted to the proper fulfillment of official duties. The civil servants
must observe official secrecy.

Similar rules--written or unwritten--prevail
in other countries. As an American author puts it,
they are a kind of state religion:

> They are the commandments which issue
> from the nature of the state and are
> based upon the desire to maintain the
> state. A note of religious solemnity
> is introduced into the whole arrange-
> ment by the institution of an oath
> that civil servants take when entering
> service. In bygone days, such oaths
> were personal--that is, they were
> made to the Prince, King, or Emperor--
> and it was to the personal service of

these that in the olden days Chancellor, Marshal, and other officers
swore devotion. The transformation
of the royal state into the imper-
sonal state has resulted in the oath
being taken to the laws and the constitution.[16]

In Belgium a law of July 20, 1831, provides
that

all officers of the judicial or administrative order, the officers of the
army and, in general, all citizens to
whom a public office or service of any
kind is entrusted, must, before beginning their functions, take the following oath: "I swear fidelity to the
King, obedience to the constitution
and the laws of the Belgian people."

In the ministerial departments this oath must be
taken even by the lowest ranks. Employees of the
provinces, municipalities, and public and quasi-
public corporations take the oath only if they hold
positions of authority.

The duties of civil servants are summarily
enumerated in the decree of October 2, 1937, as
follows:

Civil servants must, in all their
activities, see to it that the interests of the state are vouchsafed.
They must fulfill personally and conscientiously the duties which are imposed upon them by the decrees and
rules of the administration to which
they belong. They must punctually
execute the orders and accomplish
their task with zeal and precision.
They may not interrupt the exercise
of their functions without previous
permission.

They are bound to the strictest
politeness as well towards their superiors, their colleagues and their
inferiors as towards the public. They
must help each other inasmuch as it
is required by the interest of the
service.

They must, in service and in
private life, avoid anything that
might mar the confidence of the
public or impair the honor or the
dignity of their function.

They may not have any activity
which is in opposition with the constitution and the laws of the Belgian
people, which pursues the destruction
of the independence of the country or
endangers the national defense or the
fulfillment of the obligations of
Belgium which guarantee the security
of the country. They may not adhere
nor lend their assistance to any
movement, group, organization or
association with a similar activity.

They may not reveal the facts
which should have come to their
knowledge because of their function
or which have a secret character by
nature or by the orders of their
superiors. This prohibition applies
also to the civil servants whose
function has ceased.

They may not solicit, require
or accept, directly or through in-
terposed persons, even outside but
because of their function, any gift,
gratification or advantage whatsoever.

In practice, these prescriptions are applied
more or less strictly. For instance, no civil servant has ever been prevented in times of peace from
adhering to the Communist Party nor to a movement
advocating the abolition of Belgian independence by

the absorption of the country in a politically integrated Europe. Civil servants may run for elec-
tive office on any ticket, but they should express
their opinions with restraint. If elected to Parliament, however, they have to resign from the
civil service.

With regard to an official's private life, the
Conseil d'Etat has held that the head of a secondary
school was rightly demoted because of debts. It
put forth the following:

> No text says precisely what an offi-
> cial, taking into consideration the
> varying circumstances of time and
> location and the requirements of his
> rank and office, should do or not do
> in his private life in order to avoid
> being considered as impairing the
> dignity of his function or creating
> conditions detrimental to the exer-
> cise thereof.
>
> In the absence of such a code of
> honor, stating the minimal norms of
> a decent life for an official, he
> should in his private life conform
> himself to the opinions commonly held
> in this regard, while the disciplinary
> authority who has no power to set a
> posteriori rules of which the official
> had no knowledge, nor to regulate the
> private life of their officials, can
> only appreciate said conduct accord-
> ing to what they deem to be the mini-
> mal norms of a decent life, to which
> the official must conform in the in-
> terest of the service and according
> to the generally admitted concepts.
>
> According to presently prevail-
> ing opinions and habits, an official
> may certainly contract debts to buy a
> house or durable consumer goods, but
> it is the duty of a correct official
> to pay the debts which he has con-
> tracted except if unforeseen

circumstances [occur]. It therefore
does not behoove an official to live
constantly above his means and consequently in a permanent state of impe-
cuniosity up to a point where he has
to contract debts all the time for
small services or for goods of immediate consumption and to resort constantly to tricks in order to pay
them back. He must see to it that
such debts are paid without coercion
and at least avoid being the object
of humiliating procedures.[17]

In this context, the strike of a civil servant
might be considered more as a problem of ethics
than a question of law, "taking into consideration
the varying circumstances of time and location and
the requirements of his rank and office," as the
Conseil d'Etat said in regard to debts.

A third argument against strikes rests on the
legal nature of the bond that links the public employee to the public employer. It was formerly
accepted that the public employee was hired by the
state, the province, or the municipality in a fashion similar to the hiring of a private employee by
a private employer. Both parties were linked by a
contract that in certain regards differed from a
private labor contract but was essentially similar
in that this contract could only be altered by the
common consent of both parties.

This concept was admitted by the courts and by
the government. For instance, when a city decided
to change the age of retirement of its personnel,
the decision would be declared null and void by the
King. The municipal council has no power to alter
the conditions of employment that have induced a
person to become a municipal employee. An intermu-
nicipal health laboratory was condemned to pay damages to an employee because he had been pensioned
at an earlier age than was prescribed when he had
accepted his job.

The Supreme Court, however, decided that no
contract exists between an officer and the state;

their relations are determined entirely by law and
can therefore at any time be altered unilaterally.[18]
The same principle was proclaimed concerning a municipal policeman.[19] The Conseil d'Etat adopted
the same view:

> The legal status of an employee who
> has been incorporated by way of ap-
> pointment in the permanent staff of a
> public administration is exclusively
> ruled by laws, by-laws and decrees.
> This status can always be changed for
> the future. The changes apply imme-
> diately to the employee, even if he
> entered the service at a time when
> the status was more favorable.[20]

The normal status of a civil servant and of a
municipal employee is thus set unilaterally by the
public authority. The state may, however, as a
matter of exception, decide to hire personnel by
contract. When a Bureau of Economic Programmation
was created by the government, it was decided that
the highly qualified economists would be hired by
contract (royal decree of October 14, 1959).

What about public or semipublic corporations?
When the state railroads were incorporated, it was
expressly stated that the joint committee should
deal "with all questions concerning the labor contract of the personnel" (law of July 23, 1926).
The bilateral concept still prevailed. The Conseil
d'Etat decided, nevertheless, that the National
Corporation of Belgian Railroads was a public authority and that the status of its personnel was of
a public nature.[21] When the law creating a public
or semipublic corporation is silent, the Supreme
Court holds that the status of its personnel is
normally of public nature.[22]

The dominant theory is thus that there is an
intrinsic difference between the public and the
private sector with regard to labor relations. In
the private sector these relations are based on the
common consent of employer and employee, whereas in
the public sector the unilateral decision of the

public employer excludes bargaining. This legalis-
tic doctrine is becoming less and less convincing,
for the will of the individual employer and of the
individual employee plays hardly any role in the
private sector.

The hierarchy of rules determining relations
between employers and employees has been defined in
the law of December 1968 concerning collective labor
agreements as follows:

1.   The imperative clauses of the law
2.   The collective agreements made binding by
the King
3.   The collective agreements not made binding
by the King when the employer is affiliated with
an association that signed the agreement
4.   The written individual labor contract
5.   The collective agreements not made binding
by the King when the employer is not a member of
the association that signed the agreement but
falls under the jurisdiction of the joint committee
6.   The working rules of the plant adopted by
the works council
7.   The suppletive clauses of the law
8.   The unwritten labor contract
9.   The custom.

When one takes into consideration the numerous
laws that have been enacted in recent years, as
well as the detailed provisions of hundreds of collective agreements, the individual free will of the
parties to a labor contract appears to be theoreti-
cal. As the leading expert on labor legislation
puts it, "Hiring a workman has become a gamble. No
employer can figure what it will cost him."[23]
Moreover, relations between the state and civil
servants are being regulated by collective agreements. Since 1962, besides the bargaining that began in 1939 with the joint committees, the government has been negotiating directly with the leaders
of the "common front" set up by the socialist and
catholic trade union federations of public services.
The document resulting from these negotiations was

first timidly called "Agreements of Social Programmation." But Prime Minister Van Den Boeynants, a
meat-packer by profession, let the cat out of the
bag. He called the document "Collective Agreement"
and signed it solemnly under the spotlights of
television. Prime Minister Eyskens signed the second collective agreement with the same decorum. A
third one is being negotiated.

These collective agreements are not within the
scope of the law of December 5, 1968, but they resemble those negotiated at the national level in
the private sector as twin brothers do. However
painful it may be for the exponents of the dualism
of private and public employment, the impact of
pressure groups has the same results on the government as on the Belgian federation of employers.

If the right to strike vouchsafes the effective exercise of the right of collective bargaining,
as the European Social Charter states, will it be
possible to deny the right to strike in the public
sector once the charter is on the statute book?

The socialist trade unions claim that the
right to strike has already been granted in the
civil service. Under the royal decree of July 11,
1949, the trade unions had to submit their rules to
each minister in order to be recognized. The socialist unions in the public services submitted
their rules, which expressly mention strikes as one
of the means of action. The Minister of National
Defense objected that the workmen of the arsenals
were under military discipline and could therefore
not resort to strikes. No other member of the government raised any objection to the clause relating
to strikes in the rules of the socialist trade
unions; these unions were recognized in all ministerial departments, which they claim means that
striking is permitted.

REALITIES

During World War I Belgium was almost completely
invaded by German troops. The German army financed
its occupation by emitting currency, which the

Belgian Government was compelled to exchange after
the armistice of 1918. A tremendous inflation
caused a rise in the cost of living. Salaries had
to be readjusted. The majority of the personnel of
the Belgian State Railways (125,000 men at that
time) joined the socialist union. The unskilled
workers of roads maintenance were especially dis-
satisfied with their wages, and in May 1923 a
strike broke out in Antwerp and soon extended to
the entire country.

The government tried to run the train with
the minority of workers affiliated with the catholic
union and with army engineers. The reserve engineers were mobilized on May 16 by the Minister of
National Defense. For three weeks the wages of
railway workers were discussed in the Chamber of
Deputies. The Labor opposition tried to reach a
compromise, but the government was adamant. The
Minister of National Defense justified the use of
the army by the necessity of transporting the coal
from the Ruhr, which had just been occupied by
French and Belgian troops. The leaders of the socialist railwaymen's union were fired. After the end
of the strike the government relented and granted
some of the demands of the strikers. At the general
election of 1925 there was a landslide in favor of
the Labor Party, and the discharged trade unionists
were elected to Parliament.

After World War II the situation was similar,
with inflation and a rising cost of living; however,
bargaining in the joint committees and the strike
ban under "civil mobilization" enabled a rapid reconstruction of the shattered national economy. A
communist was Minister of Reconstruction and kept
his troops in hand. In 1947 the communists were
ousted from the coalition government. The law of
August 19, 1948, was enacted to guarantee that the
vital needs of the population would be taken care
of in case of strikes and lockouts. In 1948 the
personnel of the post office struck. It was a wild
strike, started by a dissident organization. The
socialist Minister of Communications, Achille Van
Acker, fired 427 postmen. They were taken back
only after several years.

In 1952 there was a "warning strike" of 24
hours in the Telegraph and Telephone Corporation.
The catholic Minister of Communications, Paul
Segers, inflicted a severe reprimand on 56 employees
and a simple reprimand on 92 employees for a total
of over 6,000 strikers. Criticized in Parliament
by the Labor opposition, he declared: "I have
punished only men who had authority over subordi-
nates. I tried to maintain the authority of the
State and to be moderate."

In 1959 the government announced that the prevailing recession required an adjustment of the unemployment doles, an increase in taxation, the
raising of the retirement age in the civil service,
and a reduction of 7 percent of the pensions of all
retired civil servants. The socialist unions and
especially the union of civil servants were vio-
lently opposed to this drastic cure.

A warning strike of one hour was announced for
June 24, 1959, in all ministerial departments and
public corporations. Two days before the planned
strike the Minister of Social Affairs informed the
leading officials of the institutions of social security that no absence was to be permitted on
June 24 except for due reasons and asked them to
send him a list of all men and women who quit their
work on that day. Nevertheless, the token strike
took place. Some leading officials belonging to
the socialist union ostentatiously left their offices with their staff, and then sent in a list of
the strikers with themselves included. The Minister inflicted the lowest penalty provided by the
rules applying to the personnel of these public corporations. The officials concerned appealed to the
Conseil d'Etat on the grounds that their absence
had caused no delay in the activity of their organization, and that during that hour urgent talks had
been carried out. The Conseil d'Etat decided that
the Minister was justified in inflicting a penalty
on the leading officials.[24] In one case, however,
the penalty was quashed because disciplinary power
in one particular organization belonged to the
Crown, rather than with the Minister.

The discussion of the controversial 1959 bill
was protracted. In the parliamentary committee,
the government accepted certain amendments moved on
behalf of the catholic unions. It was decided that
the retirement age would be raised only for employees entering service in the future. The opposition
of the socialist unions was unrelenting. The Union
of Public Services asked that a general strike be
called. The Council of the Belgian Federation of
Trade Unions met and a vote was taken. There were
475,823 votes for the resolution (including 131,190
votes of the public service) and 496,487 against,
with 53,112 abstentions.

The call for a general strike was thus defeated,
but nevertheless, when discussion of the bill began
in the lower house, strikes broke out in several
municipalities of the Walloon industrial area on
December 20th. It occurred in the ore smelters and
the machine factories and spread to the harbor of
Antwerp. Gradually, the entire country was para-
lyzed. The industrial towns of the Walloon region
were in a state of siege, road traffic was blocked
by pickets, retail stores were closed, strike committees distributed meals to the population, and
passes were given to doctors and ambulances. Mr.
Eyskens, the catholic Prime Minister, insisted that
the passage of the bill should be pressed despite
the general strike. It was accepted by both houses .
on January 18, 1961. The strike was called off in
the Flemish region after this vote, petering out a
week later in the Walloon region. The membership
of the socialist unions decreased. At the elections
for the Works Councils in 2,704 plants with more
than 150 employees and a total staff of over 1 million, the socialist unions received only 50.50 percent of the vote, as against 54.85 percent in 1958,
whereas the catholic trade unions increased their
strength from 41.20 percent to 44.21 percent and
the liberal unions from 3.73 percent to 5.29 percent.

The Cabinet was, however, shaken by this social
uproar and also by the disastrous events in the
Congo. Eyskens resigned, and Parliament was dissolved. A defeat of the Labor Party was expected,
but at the general elections of March 26, 1961, the

Labor Party did not lose a seat in the Chamber of
Representatives and gained eight seats in the Senate, whereas the catholic party lost eight seats in
the Chamber of Representatives and nine seats in
the Senate. The liberal party also suffered defeat.
The winners were small parties (communists and
Flemish nationalists).

The catholic and the Labor parties decided to
form a coalition. The Catholic Prime Minister
Lefevre announced that several clauses of the law
that had provoked the general strike would be suspended, especially the reduction of the pensions of
retired civil servants. On December 15, 1961, the
catholic and socialist union movement decided to
constitute a "common front" and to act henceforth
after mutual consultation. The "common front" has
lasted for more than 10 years and is effective in
the public services as well as in the private sector.

Outrages committed during the general strike
were punished by the courts. A municipality was
condemned to pay 1 million francs compensation to a
physician who had been severely hurt by a thrown
stone because he refused to show his pass to pickets controlling the road traffic. The local authority was considered responsible because the local
police had not maintained order in the streets.

A foreman was dismissed by his employer because he had taken part in the strike. The labor
court, however, ruled that he was entitled to damages because a strike suspends the labor contract
but does not break it. As has been seen above,
the Supreme Court upheld this judgment, although
the employer insisted that the general strike was
of a political, not economic, nature.[25]

In the public services the repression was mild.
Only one case was brought before the Conseil d'Etat.
Two garbage collectors in a suburb of Brussels were
suspended by the Board of Aldermen and the mayor
for six weeks without pay. They quit work on December 20, 1960, and resumed work only on January 17.
The main grievance of the municipal authority was
that the two men had prevented garbage trucks from
leaving the municipal depot, thus making the garbage
collection--a vital need of population--impossible.

The high administrative court ruled that the
Board of Aldermen and the mayor had not exceeded
their power by punishing the two strikers, who had
obstructed the continuity of a public service.[26]
The ambiguity of the "right to strike" in the minds
of members of the various governments and the peculiarities of the disciplinary procedure are two
factors in this leniency.

Another consequence of the general strike of
December 1960-January 1961 was to bring about overall negotiations between the "common front" of public employees' unions and the government. The prime
minister and the Ministers of Public Employment,
Labor, and the Budget (two catholics and two socialists) met a delegation of the "common front" on
three occasions (January 1, 17, and 18).

An agreement of social programmation was signed
on March 1, providing for an increase of some fringe
benefits, called "home allowance" and "residence allowance." A general increase in wages was also decided upon in principle, an advance payment of
1,000 francs ($20) was granted, and the reduction
of the pensions of retired civil servants was stopped.
Two working groups were appointed to improve the pensions scheme and the wage scales. The agreement was
endorsed by the general joint committee.

In 1963 difficulties arose in the Ministry of
Finance. A competitive examination was to take
place on June 29 for the promotion of clerks from
the third to the second category; 5,000 men had been
called to Brussels for the examination. The Independent Union of Finance Personnel claimed that the
essay on an administrative problem would favor the
younger clerks, who had bookish knowledge, and eliminate the experienced older clerks, who had acquired
their knowledge by long practice. Tear gas bombs
were thrown into the huge hall where the candidates
were to write their essay, and the examination had
to be canceled.

Two leaders of the dissident union were suspended, and on July 15 a wild strike ensued. On
July 19, 3,000 strikers marched through Brussels.
The Minister of Finance agreed that half of the promotion would be granted on the basis of seniority

and the other half as a result of the competitive
examination. The strike was called off on July 25.
On October 14 agitation started again, and the dissident union asked its members to "work according
to rules" but met with little success.

The same year trouble began within the health
insurance system. During World War II delegates of
the employers' organization and the three trade
union movements had met secretly and agreed that an
extensive social security system should be created
in Belgium along the lines advocated by Sir Walter
Beveridge. The system was to include compulsory insurance against disease and invalidity; however, it
was to be based on the mutual insurance societies
that already existed.

The mutual insurance societies were voluntary
associations subsidized by the government. They
were federated in five confederations: socialist,
catholic, liberal, neutral, and professional. The
socialist societies had created clinics in various
regions and favored teamwork among the physicians
they employed, whereas the other societies adhered
to the traditional system of medical care, merely
paying amounts to help their members who suffered
illness or accidents.

The arrêté loi of December 28, 1944, enacted
during the Battle of the Bulge, laid down the principle of compulsory insurance against disease and
invalidity based on the existing mutual insurance
societies. The details were worked out in various
royal decrees, which were frequently amended to
cope with the constant deficit of the system. During the first period of the insurance there was
fierce competition between the socialist and catholic organizations, each advocating its conception
of medical care and trying to have it adopted by
the government. But as the years went by this an-
tagonism subsided, and in 1963 the government
thought that the time had come to have the insurance system regulated by an act of Parliament.

The government negotiated with the General
Association of Physicians, whose leaders were old
and successful practitioners who apparently had no
contact with the rank and file. The bill submitted

to the Chamber of Representatives was very detailed
and was extensively discussed in the commission for
social insurance first and then in a full meeting
of the Chamber. The physicians founded various
trade unions that disowned the agreement of the General Association of Physicians with the bill. In
July several short local strikes were organized.
The workers' organizations, however, expressed their
support of the bill.

The physicians refused to accept the limitation
of fees, the supervision of medical care by the advising physicians of the National Insurance Board,
the red tape, and, most of all, the requirement to
deliver a receipt to every beneficiary of the insurance. They claimed that the system led to "over-
consumption of medical care"; and they objected to
the individual health booklet that would show to
any physician the treatment that had hitherto been
prescribed by his colleagues.

When the law of August 9, 1963, was published,
the unions bluntly asked that all clauses concerning the practice of medicine be abrogated. Negotiations were resumed with a few medical unions that
wanted a compromise, and various clauses were amended
by a law of December 24, 1963. But the majority of
physicians persisted in their total hostility. They
claimed that a physician was paid less than a plumber
was. The fee for a visit at the physician's office
was 50 francs ($1); the fee for a visit of the phy-
sician at the patient's home was 75 francs ($1.50);
and the fee of a specialist was 100 francs ($2). On
January 28, 1964, a strike notice was given for
February 3.

The leaders of the employers' and workers' organizations offered to mediate. A truce of two
months was accepted by the physicians' delegates.
Prime Minister Lefevre, Minister of Social Affairs Leburton, and the delegates of the physicians',
the employers', and the workers' organizations met
several times; the last meeting lasted 30 hours but
was in vain.

The strike began on April 1, 1964. The physicians closed their offices and clinics. In each
town a system of urgent help was organized by the

physicians' unions, which directed all patients to
the public hospitals for the least ailment as well
as for severe cases. By overcrowding the hospitals
the physicians' unions hoped to force the government into submission. The government opened the
military hospitals for civilians, and field hospitals were set up.

Many physicians left Belgium and went to neighboring towns in Holland, France, and Luxembourg.
Others went "underground," as the resistance movement had done under the German occupation. The government mobilized 3,642 reserve Army physicians.
Only three failed to answer the call. They were
prosecuted as deserters, but the prosecution was
later dropped by the attorney general because the
three were able to show valid reasons for their absence.

Negotiations were resumed on April 11 between
the government and the physicians' delegates but
broke off after 14 hours of discussions, whereupon
the physicians' unions announced that the emergency
service would be discontinued. On April 12 a royal
decree requisitioning all physicians connected with
private or public hospitals was published in a special issue of the official gazette (Moniteur Belge).

This decree was based on the law of August 19,
1948, and on the royal decree of July 27, 1950, according to which hospitals were of vital need to
the population. Failure to comply with the requisi-
tion was punishable under the penal law. On April
16 the rectors of the four universities offered to
mediate. The next day the strike was called off.

On June 25 an agreement was reached. It provided for some changes in the administration of the
National Insurance Board. The number of delegates
of the representative organizations of physicians
were to be in proportion to their membership. The
medical secret was to be fully guaranteed; the physician would have the free choice of the treatment
of his patients. Underprivileged patients (widows,
orphans, invalids, and beneficiaries of old age pensions) would not be limited in their choice of a
physician.

The patients would receive from the physicians all documents required to be reimbursed by the mutual insurance societies. An agreement between the representatives of the physicians and those of the mutual insurance societies would set the fees for the various treatments, and the physicians would individually pledge to respect these rates. The increase in the cost for medical fees in 1965--budgeted at 1.4 billion francs--was to be borne by the government. The agreement was ratified by Parliament (law of July 6, 1964).

Another strike began in the public sector on December 31, 1964, paralyzing the port of Antwerp, the third most heavily used in the world. This harbor is under the management of the municipal authority. The harbor master (capitaine du port), the harbor police, and the dock operators are municipal employees. The city countil determines their wages, under supervision of the government.

It is the set policy of the Ministry of Internal Affairs that salaries of municipal employees should not exceed the salaries of comparable employees of the state. Whenever the personnel of the Antwerp harbor asked for better wages, the city was willing to pay them in view of the economic importance of maritime traffic, but the government vetoed such measures, which would have distorted the general scale of salaries in public service.

Since fast service was essential to the shipping companies, it had become a custom that shipmasters would tip the underpaid harbor employees. This system was satisfactory to everybody but was very unethical. The government decided that it should stop. The catholic trade union called for a strike, which lasted until January 7. Negotiations took place between the government, the city, and the unions. The socialist union asked for a general raise for the entire personnel of the city of Antwerp. No agreement was reached.

On November 16, the catholic trade union resumed the strike, but the government requisitioned the personnel (ministerial decree of January 6, 1965).[27] Work was resumed on November 18. Because of the strike 150 ships were diverted to other ports.

Altogether, the traffic of Antwerp was severely hit
by the action of 700 employees. Although 18,550
ships had entered the harbor in 1964, the total
dropped to 18,065 in 1965.

In several branches of the public sector there
is a growing tendency to entrust certain activities
to private firms. The trade unions object to this
practice, which leads to a reduction of the personnel employed by the state or by the public corporation. In the production and distribution of electricity the workers of the power plant at La Louvière
struck on October 23, 1967, as a protest against contracting out repair jobs.

The strike gradually extended to the other
power plants. On November 8, 82 percent of the workers and 15 percent of the clerks were on strike.
The management entered into negotiations with the
trade unions. An agreement was signed in December
defining the kinds of jobs that could be entrusted
to private firms. Whenever such contracts are to
be made, the works council is supposed to be consulted.

On June 4, 1970, there was a one-day strike
of all teachers in public and private primary
schools. The grievances were numerous. The teachers in the municipal schools were concerned by the
devaluation of their standing. In the past the
teacher was a respected person in the village or
the town. He stood out by his education and his
way of dressing, and his salary allowed him to live
comfortably. Now the shopkeepers and the skilled
workmen earn more than the schoolteacher; they have
better cars than he can afford. He feels shabby.

In the Catholic schools there is another complaint. The state has to pay the salary, but the
payment is deferred for months and sometimes for
more than a year. In recent years the number of
pupils has grown considerably. More teachers had
to be engaged. The salaries vary according to the
number of hours and the kind of teaching. One hour
of sewing is rated less than one hour of mathematics.
Private schools are not as strict as public schools
concerning the qualifications of their teachers.
The Department of Public Education must therefore

verify for each new teacher whether he has the required diplomas.

Besides, subsidies are paid according to the
number of pupils in a school. If the enrollment
decreases, one teacher or several are omitted from
the subsidy. The situation varies from one year to
another. The government has appointed more clerks
to handle this red tape, and computers are used to
calculate teachers' salaries. Despite great efforts, the Department of Public Education has not
yet been able to cope with the expansion of the
schools. The one-day strike was meant as a warning.
Negotiations were conducted between the government
and the two main unions of teachers and resulted in
various improvements in the remuneration of teachers.
The total cost will be 700 million Belgian francs in
1972 ($14 million).

DISCIPLINARY PROCEDURE

As has been noted, public employers are rather
lenient in the repression of strikers. With the
exception of the wild strike in the Brussels post
office in 1948, when 427 employees were fired, the
competent authorities have abstained completely
from punishment or have punished only the strike
leaders. This is due to several causes. First of
all, the superiors, who have to institute disciplinary procedure, are often in sympathy with the strikers. Second, when a strike occurs, there generally
is a valid reason for the discontent. Third, the
disciplinary procedure is cumbersome.

In the civil service a royal decree of December
17, 1923, has instituted a unified procedure. A
disciplinary council has to be consulted before a
penalty is inflicted. The civil servant is heard.
He can be assisted in his defense by a colleague or
a former official. Witnesses can be summoned. The
competent authority is not bound by the opinion of
the disciplinary council, but the minister generally
follows this opinion.

The royal decree of October 2, 1937, decided
that the disciplinary council (chambre de recours)

would consist of two trade union delegates and two
officials chosen by the minister. The president, a
member of the judiciary, casts the deciding vote if
there is a divided opinion. This system still pre-
vails.

The trade union delegates readily vote in
favor of repression when a civil servant has been
grossly negligent or dishonest or if his private
conduct has been intolerable. But when the offense
is participation in a strike, the two trade union
delegates will normally take sides with the accused
employee, unless the two main trade unions have
taken different positions in the strike. This an-
tagonism between the socialist and catholic trade
unions is infrequent, since the two organizations
have a "common front."

But whatever the verdict may be, it occurs
several months after the strike. In the meanwhile,
the excitement has subsided. The grievances of the
strikers have in one way or another been remedied.
The government coalition may even have changed.
There is thus not much purpose in initiating a disciplinary procedure, the outcome of which is so un-
certain.

If the civil servant is finally dismissed, suspended, or reprimanded, he may appeal to the Conseil
d'Etat. The high administrative court does not
verify whether the competent authority has been too
severe, but only whether due process of law has been
applied; and in this regard the Conseil d'Etat is
very finicky. For a minor technicality the penalty
may be quashed.

In 1965 the automatic telephone system was constantly disturbed. An independent organization of
telephone operators had invited its members to "work
to rule"; it even appeared that telephone engineers
were tampering with the automatic equipment. The
socialist Minister of Communications, Edward Anseele,
Jr., decided to stop this sabotage. The president
and the secretary of the independent organization
were dismissed without being given a chance to appeal to the disciplinary council. This high-handed
procedure was effective, and the disturbances ceased
a few days later. The two dismissed engineers

appealed to the Conseil d'Etat. The outcome of the
case could be foreseen. After five months the discharge of the engineers was changed into a "severe
reprimand," and the case was dropped.[28]

Many jurists consider the prevailing disciplinary system highly unsatisfactory. The authority of
the state is undermined. They advocate an independent disciplinary tribunal that would have full
powers to punish, as exists in the Federal Republic
of Germany;[29] however, no bill has been introduced
for such purpose. Public or semipublic corporations
have adopted disciplinary procedures that are similar to the system used in the civil service.

Municipal employees may be suspended for at
most six weeks by the Board of Aldermen and the
mayor; heavier penalties are inflicted by the municipal council. The civil servant must be heard in
his defense. When the hearing takes place in the
municipal council, the opposition will normally take
a stand for the striker, and even members of the
majority may waver. The employee who had been suspended for more than three months or dismissed can
appeal to the provincial authority. In any case
the Conseil d'Etat may be asked to verify whether
due procedure has been applied.

CONCLUSION

Collective bargaining has become a normal practice in the public sector of Belgium. From a theo-
retical point of view collective bargaining is in-
compatible with public service. U.S. President
Franklin Delano Roosevelt made an important statement on the subject in a letter to the president of
the National Federation of Federal Employees on
August 16, 1937:

> All government employees should real-
> ize that the process of collective
> bargaining, as usually understood,
> cannot be transplanted into the pub-
> lic service. It has its distinct and
> insurmountable limitations when ap-
> plied to public personnel management.

>The very nature and purposes of Gov-
>ernment make it impossible to repre-
>sent fully or to bind the employer in
>mutual discussion with Government em-
>ployees' organizations. The employer
>is the whole people, who speak by
>means of laws enacted by their repre-
>sentatives in Congress. Accordingly
>administrative officials and employees
>alike are governed by laws which es-
>tablish policies, procedures, or rules
>in personnel matters.

Collective bargaining has nevertheless been
accepted in the federal government of the United
States in an Executive Order of President John F.
Kennedy of January 1962. In Norway an act of July
18, 1958, provides that the salaries and working
conditions in the public services are determined by
agreement between the state and the trade unions.
This agreement is binding for the state and for the
employees. In Sweden an act of June 3, 1965, states
that the salaries and fringe benefits, as well as
the hours of work, are determined by a government
commission and the trade unions of civil servants.
Inasmuch as the agreements have an impact on the
finance of the state, Parliament must ratify the
agreements, but this is done without discussion.

In France the law of July 31, 1963, limits the
right to strike of public employees in the service
of the state, of the local authorities, and of the
public corporations. Whenever the personnel makes
use of its right to strike, the concerted cessation
of work must be preceded by a notice given to the
hierarchic authority by the trade union organization. The notice must mention the reason for resorting to a strike. This notice does not impede
negotiations with a view to the settlement of the
conflict.

The Belgian practice is thus in harmony with
legal bargaining procedures in democratic countries.
This evolution may appear surprising and even shock-
ing to those who consciously or unconsciously consider the state as the sovereign power whose will
is supreme and whose authority should be accepted
without discussion.

How and why has collective bargaining been accepted? The explanation is to be found in the economic evolution. Originally, civil servants were a
small and privileged minority within the nation.
This minority accepted special rules and submitted
to a special discipline because it enjoyed material
advantages and social prestige.

Public employees had stable employment in a
society where unemployment was a constant threat to
workers in private enterprise. Public employees retired with a pension, whereas workers had to rely
on their savings when age compelled them to stop
remunerative occupation, and, if they had been un-
able to save, they had to ask support from their
children or from public charity. Public servants
often wore a uniform and were better dressed than
people who had to buy their own clothing. Even the
modest street sweeper wore a sort of military cap,
which showed that, despite his menial job, he belonged to a different sort of people than those who
had the same skill but worked in private employment.

But in the course of the twentieth century,
owing to the pressure of organized labor, the situation of workers in private enterprises has been
constantly improving. Social security has granted
protection against the risks of accidents, illness,
unemployment, and old age. In many countries the
security of tenure has increased in the private sector.

Moreover, the twentieth century has witnessed
an extraordinary growth of public services. The
number of civil servants has increased considerably,
and, at the same time, the state has assumed power
over an increasing number of industries through the
mechanism of public corporations. These public corporations have hundreds of thousands of employees
who serve the state and are under the supreme ultimate direction of the government with regard to
general policy.

As the number of people directly or indirectly
subjected to the authority of the state increases,
the state becomes less capable of giving them the
privileged status that was previously implied by
public employment. In fact, public employees often

lag behind the personnel of private enterprises in periods of rising cost of living and rising productivity.

In Belgium salaries of public employees are automatically increased according to the rise in the cost of living, but only after a certain period. The cost of living is measured by an official index number, but this index takes no notice of the changing way of life of the average citizen, or does so only after many years. In the private sector higher wages are granted as a result of increasing productivity. But nobody has yet been able to figure out the productivity of a ministerial department or of public schools.

The main concern of the government is to see to it that remuneration in the public service catches up with remuneration in the private sector. The government does this only when it finds out that it cannot fill the vacancies in its offices. In the affluent society public employees are more or less condemned to struggle for their lives because of the rampant inflation.

The present economic policy in most industrial countries is to secure full employment in the private sector. This seems to be possible only by the erosion of the currency. Paradoxically, servants of the state lag behind because unemployment must at all cost be prevented in the private sector. Under such circumstances public bargaining appears to be the only remedy.

POSTSCRIPT

On February 18, 1971, the Belgian Government submitted to the Chamber of Representatives a "bill to organize the relations between public authorities and the trade unions of the personnel of such authorities."[30] The bill applies to the personnel of all state offices and services, including schools and auxiliary services of the courts, public and quasi-public corporations, provinces, and municipal authorities, according to the conditions and limits determined by the King.

The bill does not apply to the personnel of
Parliament and the Cour des comptes, the members
and clerks of the courts, the holders of a function
in the Conseil d'Etat, the members of the armed
forces, the professors of the state universities,
or the state security. The bill does not apply
either to the personnel of the National Corporation
of Belgian Railroads, for which collective bargaining is already organized by law, nor to the public
and quasi-public corporations for which joint committees have already been set up.

No rules may be established by the competent
authorities concerning admission, promotion, discipline, leaves, retirement, relations with the trade
unions, and the organization of social services
without previous negotiation with the representative
unions in the committees set up for this purpose.
No bills relating to the above-mentioned objects may
be submitted to Parliament before such negotiation.

The King shall set up the following committees:
(a) the committee for national public services;
(b) the committee for provincial and local services;
and (c) the committee for the whole of all public
services, which will deal with matters common to
the personnel of national, provincial, and local
services. The King shall also set up 25 special
committees for specific branches of government services and public or quasi-public corporations and
determine their jurisdiction. The King shall determine the composition and functioning of all committees of negotiation.

Only representative trade union organizations
shall sit on the committees of negotiation. Deemed
representative are those trade unions that are organized on a national level, defend the interests
of all categories of the personnel of the public
services, are affiliated with an organization represented in the National Labor Council, and have a
dues-paying membership of at least 10 percent of
the occupied personnel concerned by committees mentioned under (a), (b), and (c), above. For the 25
special committees other trade unions shall be
deemed representative if they defend the interests
of all categories of the personnel concerned by the

special committee and represent at least 15 percent
of the personnel.

The conclusions of any negotiation will be
written into a unanimous agreement of the delegation of the authority and the trade union delegates
or will set forth their respective positions. The
Conseil d'Etat, which was consulted about this bill,
remarked that the unanimous agreement could not be
legally binding for the public authorities, but
that only a political responsibility to enact the
rules that have been agreed upon existed for the
public authority, whose delegate had agreed.

Concerning the representative character of the
trade unions, the Conseil d'Etat recalled the objections that the Committee on Trade Union Rights of the
ILO made in its 93rd report concerning the monopoly of representation that had been established by
the National Labor Council Law of April 21, 1965.

3

GREAT BRITAIN
Arthur I. Marsh

PUBLIC SECTOR

The public sector in the United Kingdom* provides jobs for almost 5.9 million civilian employees, about 70 percent of whom are members of trade unions. About two-fifths of all trade unionists in the country are to be found within its ranks; almost one worker in every four is either a civil servant, a local government employee, or a worker in a public corporation. (See Table 7.)

Broadly speaking, the public sector has grown up in the order given in Table 7--that is, what is now known as a central government was first on the scene, and local government and public corporations were added later. Official lists giving the makeup of these subsectors often reflect their origins. Under central government are to be found the Royal Household, the Duchies of Cornwall and Lancaster (the former the estate of the eldest son of the Sovereign since 1337 and the latter Crown property since 1399), the Houses of Parliament, the College of Arms, and other ancient institutions, as well as

---

*England, Wales, Scotland (together making up Great Britain), and Northern Ireland. In the discussion that follows, particular attention is paid to Great Britain, and variations that exist in Northern Ireland are not dealt with.

TABLE 7

Employment in the Public Sector, United Kingdom, 1956-69

Year	Central Government (thousands)	Local Government (thousands)	Public Cor- porations (thousands)	Total Public Employees (thousands)	Total Working Population (thousands)	Percentage Employed in Public Sector
Average						
1956-60	1,631	1,662	2,003	5,296	23,814	22.2
1961-65	1,340	1,913	2,124	5,377	24,933	21.6
1966	1,405	2,134	1,969	5,508	25,477	21.6
1967	1,458	2,233	1,941	5,632	25,066	22.4
1968	1,488	2,306	2,077	5,871	24,883	23.6
1969	1,487	2,363	2,041	5,891	24,841	23.7

Note: Excluding Her Majesty's Forces.

Source: Economic Trends, October 1968, June 1969, and June 1970.

more modern users of civilian labor, such as the
Ministry of Defence, the great offices of state, the
Treasury, the Foreign and Commonwealth Offices, the
Home Office, the more recent Departments of Employment, Health and Social Security, and Trade and Industry, and a host of others employing almost 1.5
million workers in 1969.

Local government, accounting today for about
2.4 million employees, has followed a similar path.
The charters of older towns emerged from royal patronage or from struggles for independence from the
Crown or from local barons. In the nineteenth century local administration was developed to meet the
demands of industrialization through ad hoc bodies
of improvement commissioners and local boards of
health and education; then, as a result of the great
local government Acts of Parliaments of the 1880s
and 1890s, local administration developed into bor-
ough, county, and urban units, which still persist
today.

The spread of employment includes authorities
(such as water boards)--which are associated with,
but not identical to, local councils--and stretches
from environmental health to police and fire protection and from education to inebriates' homes, work
in graveyards, street maintenance, and town and
country planning.

In the process of development local authorities, especially after 1945, lost some of their
functions, especially gas and electricity, to public corporations and seem likely to lose more in
the future. The public corporation has, particularly since World War II, become the chosen device
for management of large national industries and institutions, including coal, railways, telegraph and
radio, the Bank of England, the major airlines--
British European Airways and British Overseas Air-
ways--and, more recently, iron and steel,* the post
office (formerly a national government department),
and a major part of the omnibus industry.

---

*Now nationalized for the second time since
World War II.

The public corporation was an invention of the
1920s and early 1930s, devised to provide a new
form of public ownership, with wider coverage and
more commercial character than local authorities
(of which there are currently almost 2,000 in the
United Kingdom), but without the disadvantage of
being a government department subject to day-to-day
parliamentary accountability. Today public corporations are the employers of more than 2 million workers, the largest groups being in the post office
(417,000), coal (380,000), railways (275,000), steel
(254,000), electricity (228,000), gas (120,000),
national freight (66,000), the state airlines
(43,000), atomic energy (31,000), and docks (11,000),
with smaller numbers in other sectors.

The public sector in Great Britain is thus an
employment area of great complexity. It has interests, some small and some large, in all the major
types of employment in the economy, whether these
are concerned with public utilities, other services,
mining, manufacturing, agriculture, or construction.
(See Table 8.)

CHARACTERISTICS OF COLLECTIVE BARGAINING

In so complex a situation as that of the public sector in Great Britain, all generalizations
are hazardous. Four can be made with some certainty,
however. First, public-sector employers generally
support and encourage trade union recognition, as
well as the right of their employees to organize
and be members of trade unions, leaving only pock-
ets of employment in which, for one reason or another, the establishment of trade union representation raises difficulties.

Second, with very few exceptions, public servants enjoy the same basic legal and conventional
relationships within the industrial relations system as do workers in the private sector. Third,
the public sector is, like British industry in general, multiunion in character. Fourth, the collective bargaining machinery has mostly, although not
entirely, been derived from a common stock--the

TABLE 8

Employment in the Public Sector by Industry Group, United Kingdom, June 1969

Industry Group	Total Public Employees		Central Government		Local Government		Public Corporations	
	Number	Percent	Number	Percent	Number	Percent	Number	Percent
Total employed	5,891	23.6	1,487	6.0	2,363	9.5	2,041	8.2
Agriculture, forestry, and fishing	12	3.0	12	3.0	-	-	-	-
Mining and quarry	382	85.8	-	-	-	-	382	85.8
Manufacturing	396	4.4	87	1.0	4	-	305	3.4
Construction	157	10.5	20	1.4	132	8.8	5	0.3
Public utilities	1,405	70.9	7	0.4	143	7.2	1,255	63.3
Other services	3,539	36.0	1,361	13.8	2,084	21.2	94	1.0

Note: Number and percentage of national employment in each group; numbers are in thousands.

Source: Economic Trends, June 1970.

systems of joint relationships and attitudes recommended by the Whitley Committee, which reported in 1917 and 1919 on methods of securing a permanent improvement in relations between employers and workmen.[1]

Trade Union Recognition

A major impediment to the encouragement and full recognition of trade unions in collective bargaining in the public sector is frequently to be found in the doctrine of the "sovereign employer"--in the contention that, if the legislature is supreme, no bargaining is possible, since the actions of the representative of the people cannot logically be found or restricted, even by those of its governmental agents.

Such a doctrine has had no serious impact on public-sector industrial relations in Great Britain since the early 1920s. The practice of insisting that civil servants should proceed with grievances and claims by presenting "memorials" to their Lordships of the Treasury was superseded as early as 1919 by the official acceptance of a scheme whereby decisions on pay and conditions, made by collective agreement, should be reported to the cabinet and thereupon become operative.[2]

In truth, the system of party and cabinet government in Great Britain made such a solution relatively simple, since it was, and is, unlikely that any agreement made by the Treasury (now the Civil Service Department for negotiating purposes) would ever be rejected by Parliament. It cannot, however, be said to have solved all problems associated with governmental acceptability of freely negotiated settlements for its own servants or for those in the nationalized sector, especially during the 1960s.*

But the scene was set very early in Great Britain for a spirit of confident acceptance of

---

*See pp. 162ff., below.

trade unionism by government, which has led officials to advise new recruits to the civil service
to join their appropriate unions on the grounds
that the existence of fully representative associations not only promotes good staff relations but
also is essential to effective negotiations on conditions of service.[3]

Such a policy has set the tone for the whole
public sector. Although the central and local governments have been anxious, on questions of pay and
conditions, to follow rather than to lead,* their example on recognition has greatly encouraged its development elsewhere in public life. Most of the areas
of employment in Great Britain reported in a research
paper to the Lord Donovan Royal Commission on Trade
Unions and Employers' Associations, 1968, as having
no recognition problem were in the public sector.[4]

Having commented on the high level of trade
union membership in public employment, the writer
of the research paper concerned noted that even in
the private sector most white-collar recognition
had, in his view, come about directly or indirectly
as a result of government policies.[5] Such respect-
ability as British trade unionism enjoys is at
least partly due to government acceptance. Where
governments will go, the public sector will follow,
and sometimes the private sector will too.[6]

Government attitudes have not resolved all recognition problems in the public sector; nor have
governments sought to extend their own civil service
recognition arrangements to other areas of the public sector.** Where recognition itself is concerned,

---

*See pp. 149ff., below.

**Nonindustrial civil servants are those whose
conditions fall within the jurisdiction of the
National Whitley Council; industrial civil servants
are served by other councils and usually belong to
noncivil service unions. Nonindustrial civil servants were prohibited by the Trades Disputes and
Trade Union Act, 1927, from belonging to trade
unions outside the civil service and from having

trade unions have principally found problems in the
National Health Service and on the edges of the public sector. There has also been some difficulty
with particular groups of public-sector employees
in devising acceptable forms of machinery for
settlement of pay or for negotiation.*

Relatively low membership and effectiveness in
the National Health Service has been attributed by
trade union leaders partly to the existence of professional associations for nurses and other staff,
which has inhibited negotiating activity, and partly
to inadequate systems of representation and procedure.[7] Some unions have also reported difficulties
to the Donovan Commission in satisfying government-
established and -supported research councils of
their recognition qualifications.[8]

Such difficulties might be experienced by
unions anywhere when organizing on the fringes of
professionalism, and over time this has usually
proved to be no barrier to organization, for example, of teachers or university staff. It has not
been customary, either in the public sector or
elsewhere, to lay down precise criteria or procedures for trade union recognition, although this
situation may be modified with the advent of the
Health Administration's 1970 Industrial Relations
Bill.**

---

any political objects or associations with any political body. This act resulted from the general
strike of 1926, during which some civil service
unions had collected voluntary subscriptions for
the strikers; it was repealed as the first act of
the Attlee Administration in 1946, and its conditions have not been reimposed.

*For doctors, dentists, and university teach-
ers, for example; see p. 144, below.

**The 1970 Industrial Relations Bill, at pres-
ent before Parliament, seems likely to become law
before the end of 1971. It lays down procedures
for the determination, where application is made,

But the Treasury, for nonindustrial civil servants, grants national recognition to "recognized
associations" solely on numerical strength and may
withdraw this recognition if membership figures
change. Departments may also recognize associations
for their own staff, which may be the same or different from those recognized nationally, and the
same conditions for recognition apply. There have
been instances in which recognition has been unilaterally withdrawn. Such unions, recognized for
particular grades, do not recruit outside the nonindustrial civil service. These conditions of
recognition apply nowhere else in the public sector,
although they have been continued by the Post Office,
itself formerly a government department.*

Legal Restrictions on Public Sector

The abstention of the law in the British industrial relations system is a characteristic that has
often been described.[9] The origins of this situation lie in the reluctance of Great Britain's
nineteenth-century forebears either to subject the
country to a body of administrative labor law or to
allow the common law to intervene where the courts
seemed likely to compromise voluntary relationships
between employer and trade union. In particular,
collective agreements, except when otherwise intended by the parties, have been presumed not to be
legally enforceable,[10] and trade unions acting in
contemplation or furtherance of a trade dispute
have been protected from action for civil conspiracy and tort by the 1906 Trades Disputes Act.

---

for the establishment of both agency shops and bargaining units with sole bargaining agents (which
may be joint). Small parts only of the public sector appear to be exempted from the operation of the
bill.

*The Post Office, following this tradition,
unilaterally withdrew recognition from one small
union in 1970.

This negative approach to the legal status of trade unions and collective bargaining ended with the enactment of the Heath government's Industrial Relations Bill,* but its general effect has been to allow industrial relations structures and procedures to develop by voluntary agreement, and this has militated against the placing of special restrictions on government servants in their relationships with the state as an employer.

In general, therefore, civil servants are not prohibited from taking strike action; nor is there any law expressly giving them the right to strike. Until the late 1960s few workers in central or local government would have contemplated such action, and few unions in these sectors had strike funds or strike policies of any kind.

The Treasury might remind civil servants that striking, if not illegal, was a disciplinary offense and that pension rights might be forfeited, that there might be limits beyond which governments could not surrender their freedom of action in collective bargaining, and that at some point the doctrine of the "sovereign employer" might apply, but these were formal rather than substantial cautions.[11]

Only three specific pieces of legislation that modify this situation--the Conspiracy and Protection of Property Act, 1875; the Electricity Supply Act, 1919; and the Police Act, 1964 (the Police [Scotland] Act, 1956, in Scotland)--currently exist in the public sector. Under the first two acts criminal liability rests upon workers in gas, water, or electricity undertakings who <u>willfully</u> break their contracts of employment having reasonable cause to believe that the probable consequence of a breach will be to deprive the inhabitants of service;

---

*The bill provides, inter alia, that written collective agreements shall be conclusively presumed to be legally enforceable, unless they contain a provision to the contrary, and creates a number of unfair industrial practices, with penalties attached, the whole being under the jurisdiction of labor courts in the form of industrial tribunals and a National Industrial Relations Court.

under the first only (sec. 5) it is similarly (and
generally) a criminal offense to break a contract
of employment willfully, knowing that the probable
consequence of the breach will be to endanger life
or cause serious injury to persons or valuable property.

Neither of these criminal sections has been
the ground for any major prosecution since the
early 1920s,* and the present government specifically eschewed their use during a nationwide dis-
location of electricity supply, as a result of an
industrial dispute, for a week in December 1970, although it did declare a state of emergency.[12] Perhaps it is not surprising that the Industrial Relations Bill before Parliament proposes to repeal
Section 4 of the Conspiracy and Protection of Property Act and Section 31 of the Electricity Supply
Act, leaving public utilities in exactly the same
position about strikes as are all other sectors of
industry.

The police (although not the firemen) have
long been thought of as falling into a different
category. A wave of discontent among policemen in
September 1918 was followed a few months later by
a Police Act that made it a misdemeanor to "cause
disaffection" or to induce any member of the police
force "to withhold his services or to commit a
breach of discipline." It also banned policemen
from joining trade unions and created, instead, a
Police Federation as a consultative and advisory
body representing various ranks of the service.

In 1953 the Police Council was established as
a negotiating body on all matters affecting pay and
service, a development that was confirmed by the
1964 Police Act, which also affirmed the ban on
police membership in trade unions and its approval
of representative police federations. The federations have shown themselves to be doughty campaigners

----

*The Gas Council, in evidence to the Donovan
Commission in 1966, mentioned that "only one sum-
mons has been taken out, and that by the Attorney
General."

for the policemen's lot, however anomalous their
position may be, and are far from being passive
recipients of government salary decisions.

Multiunionism

Great Britain has almost 500 trade unions, of
which 150, mostly larger unions are affiliated with
the National Trades Union Congress (TUC) and comprise nine-tenths of all trade union members. Since
the repeal of the 1927 Trades Disputes and Trade
Union Act in 1946, civil service unions have been
free to undertake such affiliation, and seven associations encompassing 318,000 civil servants are
currently doing so.

Such a small response may well seem disappoint-
ing, but it includes substantially all nationally
recognized associations except those serving administrative and executive-class civil servants, whose
activities are of a kind that are rarely even unionized in Great Britain; and since 1970 they have excluded the two major post office unions (the Union
of Post Office Workers and the Post Office Engineering Union), as well as other post office unions,
with an aggregate membership of almost 340,000.
Relatively few departmentally recognized associations outside the Inland Revenue, Customs and Ex-
cise, and the Department of Employment offices are
affiliated.

Even though more than 70 TUC-affiliated unions,
including the seven civil service unions already referred to, have membership in the public sector,
Parliament has shown little inclination to make
special arrangements to debate or discuss their interests. This may, in part, be a result of diversity. Discussions resulting from the recommendations of the Donovan Commission were unique not
only in being the first to discuss the public sector as a whole but also in demonstrating the extraordinary range of representational and collective
bargaining situations to be found within it.[13]

But there has also existed in the TUC a suspicion that trade unions in the public sector, and in

central and local government in particular, might
be tarred with the brush of management sponsorship.
No other group of unions could have been tartly
warned by the acting general secretary of the TUC
not to come running to the TUC too late when reorganization threatened because they had dallied
too long with managements that pretended to be
their friends,

> but loved management . . . or staff
> associations . . . limited to an area
> where they think there is greater loy-
> alty, and where they think that they
> can apply greater pressures than they
> can in respect of trade unions in
> general.[14]

If suspicion of patronage dies hard, it remains
true that relations between trade unions and employers in the public sector have traditionally been
close and that they have had little need for assistance from the TUC in resolving their multiunion problems. The instrument at hand in accounting for both
of these situations has been that of Whitleyism.

Influence of Whitleyism

The patterns of collective bargaining and of
relationships in the public sector in Great Britain
are those of Whitleyism. Their form is that of the
joint body at industrywide and often at lower or
departmental levels; their spirit has traditionally
been that of the Whitley Committee itself in developing, along with or in addition to collective bargaining, a strong admixture of workers' participation, of "self government in industry."*
To the public sector Whitleyism has therefore
been both a bargaining model and a background for
positive cooperation between employer and employee.

---

*A phrase frequently used to summarize the
social intentions of the Whitley reports.

Originally conceived as a universal formula for good relations, it evolved over a period of time into a form particularly acceptable in central and local government and in nationalized industries. The evolution has been a long one, and its future may be a subject for discussion in some parts of the public sector.*

The story has often been told of the Lloyd George coalition's reluctant acceptance in 1919 of the formula for the civil service that it had accepted for private industry.[15] By 1939 there were 12 Whitley councils for government departments, some for industrial and some for nonindustrial civil servants. There were also 10 such councils for local authorities, although comprehensive negotiating machinery for local government was a by-product of World War II.

In 1955 Marjorie McIntosh noted that of the 37 negotiating committees functioning in local government at that time, 29 had been set up in the previous 10 years.[16] Early joint committees included Burnham committees (joint labor relations committees) on the pay of teachers, originally established in 1919 and still in operation today in a modified form.

In the area of public utilities Whitley-type machinery was established in docks, electricity supply, gas, railways, and water supply during the initial surge of Whitleyism after World War I. In 1944 the original machinery for joint negotiation in docks was changed into the present National Joint Council for the Port Transport Industry, and to this was added in 1947 a dock labor scheme in which the supply of labor was made subject to joint control by management and the unions.[17]

In water supply a national joint council dates from 1919 and that for municipal road passenger transport from the same date.** In 1919 a railway

---

*See pp. 169f., below.

**The original streetcar-line joint industrial council assumed the title National Joint Council for Municipal Road Passenger Transport in 1937.

strike resulted in collective bargaining arrangements that were incorporated in 1921 into a conciliation scheme[18] with councils composed of officials and elected employees with functions as designated in Clause 16 of the 1919 Whitley report, a
system that was revised in 1935 and again, after
the 1947 nationalization, in 1956.

It was characteristic of Whitleyism that, as
originally conceived, it made no distinction between
collective bargaining and consultation, although the
somewhat equivocal wording of the Whitley reports
has for many years been widely assumed to suggest
the contrary.[19] Joint consultation, as a formal
device separate from negotiation, appears to have
originated during World War II, and postwar attempts
were made by the Ministry of Labour to make this
standard practice in British industry with little
overall success.[20]

The drive for joint consultation coincided,
however, with the period of nationalization of
major British industries after World War II, and
the statutes establishing such industries included
clauses making joint consultative machinery mandatory. Hence, electricity and gas, both of which
had developed early joint industrial councils under
the original influence of Whitleyism and been nationalized in 1947 and 1948, respectively, have
both developed separate consultative machinery, and
this has been extended to the coal industry (1947),
to civil air transport (1946), and to others.

The public sector, therefore, appears today as
a mixture between an older integrated view of Whitleyism and a more recent view seeking to separate
negotiating and consultative functions, resulting
in some difficulties of terminology. In the civil
service, for example, joint Whitley relationships
are sometimes referred to as "consultation" or even
as "joint consultation,"[21] although it is clear
that, after the older Whitley style, no distinction
has ever been made between negotiation and consultation and that the latter is only part of a common
process to which may be added, for good measure and
to smooth relationships, an element of informal
consultation also.[22]

In electricity, by contrast, consultation is held strictly to exclude, in local advisory committees, salaries and terms and conditions of employment.[23] In civil aviation the wording of the relevant agreement on local panels is such that, although management regards them as purely consultative, trade unions may claim that they have a bargaining role.[24]

Although there is considerable interest in these distinctions and within them also the essence of an underlying conflict over the nature of management in the public sector that has begun to show its head more and more acutely in recent years, it is evident enough that Whitleyism has been historically attractive to the public sector precisely because of its ambivalence over the negotiation/consultation issue.

If the essence of the public servant is to serve the public, this is the function of <u>all</u> public servants, irrespective of rank. Some may have higher status and broader functions than do others, but they all exist to further the public interest. Hence they ought to develop close relations, and, if this involves bargaining, it ought to be tempered by consultation. Relationships between higher and lower civil servants are not, in this sense, <u>managerial</u>; they are, rather, <u>administrative</u>. The aim of all ranks is to administer the rules in the public interest, and, in doing this, there is no room for conflicts between them where these can be avoided.

Whitley-type machinery has been singularly well adapted for this purpose. Whitleyism, as one writer has recently pointed out, "is undoubtedly a clear and orderly system of bipartite decision-making which found ready application in a governmental system with a single employer, readily identified, and a clear and integrated administrative apparatus."[25] Outside the public sector Whitleyism might weaken from lack of common interest between employer and employee due to lack of uniformity in the tasks to be performed or in the grades or types of worker to perform them, or it might founder on the demands of the employer to assert his managerial

rights or on the determination of unions to impose
their will. Where there is no room for such conflict, Whitleyism ought to flourish.

And so it has. If its development has taken
time, this has been the result not of lack of appropriateness as a system but of immaturities in the
situation. In earlier days relations between private coal owners and men in the coal industry made
Whitleyism impossible; public ownership in 1947, a
long-sought objective of the miners, revolutionized
the situation. In local government progress might
be inhibited for some time by the existence of hundreds of local authorities, each seeking to retain
its own independence and standards or lack of them.
Sooner or later, they would see a common interest
in subscribing to machinery and collective agreements ensuring national uniformity.

There might be difficulties arising out of
weaknesses of unions in one part of the public sector or another, or of numbers of different unions
to be brought under a single negotiating body.
Given time, Whitleyism has also proved adaptable,
by its sympathetic attitude toward recognition and
its emphasis on joint representation, to deal with
these difficulties also.

The spirit of Whitleyism has also stretched
out into those sensitive areas in which governments
are direct or indirect paymasters of large groups
of workers whose management is outside their control; it has fallen short only of those groups for
whom no negotiating machinery is, for one reason or
another, appropriate. The latter have been made
subject to review bodies, which give advice to the
relevant minister, and have chiefly applied to doctors and dentists, boards of nationalized industries, the judiciary, and the armed services.

University teachers were, until recently,
treated in a similar way but have now developed a
more orthodox bargaining machinery; other teachers
had a Whitley-type system as early as 1919. The
machinery is still, however, established by the Secretary of State for Education and Science, currently
under the 1965 Remuneration of Teachers Act, although he must implement any agreement that the
Burnham committees make.[26]

WAGE AND SALARY DETERMINATION

Machinery of Negotiation

First, each Whitley body is <u>joint</u>, in the sense that it has in it representatives of both trade unions and employers. The equality of the parties is symbolized in the convention that each has joint secretaries, one from each side, and in some the chair alternates from one side to the other (as, for example, in civil air transport), although it is more usual for the employer (or official) to provide the chairman and the union or unions to provide the vice-chairman. Second, most of the bodies are also <u>standing</u> in character. Unlike many such committees in the private sector, they meet regularly, rather than on demand, and have a continuing agenda indicative of the continuity of their interest in the service, or part of the service, that they cover.

Third, the committees or councils have areas of jurisdiction covering grades or types of worker within each service or industry. Most commonly there are different councils for industrial and non-industrial or manual and staff employees, but these may be further differentiated by rank or by function, differentiation varying from one context to another. Most differentiation exists in central and local government, both by function and by grade; in nationalized industries it is usually, but not always, simpler, basically following the manual and staff distinction. In some cases manual and staff or industrial and nonindustrial grades are covered by a single trade union; in others they are covered by a number of unions, working together in greater or lesser degrees of cooperation.*

---

*The late Sir Leslie Cannon, president of the Electrical, Electronic, and Telecommunication Union, commented in evidence to the Donovan Commission on the low level of interunion cooperation that can sometimes exist. The outstanding case of a single trade union for manual workers is that of the National Union of Mineworkers in the coal industry;

Growing as they did from Whitleyism in the
civil service--the heart of the public sector--
negotiating bodies, as they evolved, were highly
conscious of the importance of avoiding strike action. There are very few, therefore, that lack
provisions for conciliation and/or arbitration in
the event of deadlock, the latter event in most
cases being subject to the agreement of both sides.*

The constitution and rules of procedure for
the National Joint Council for Civil Air Transport
provide, for example, that, where all possible
avenues of negotiation have been exhausted, a conciliation committee shall be set up or the matter
shall be referred to a conciliator appointed by the
Department of Employment. Failing settlement
through this procedure, Clause 17 of the council's
constitution provides that the difference shall,
subject to agreement by both sides--with neither
side obstructing the other--be referred to the Industrial Court,** in which event the decision of
the court shall be final and binding on the parties
to the difference.

The "final and binding" force of arbitration
is, of course, in the British system moral only,
and the phrase in the civil air transport agreement

----

that union represents all the workers in the national conciliation scheme, although deputies, over-
men, and shotfirers have their separate representative machinery, as do the clerical and management
staff.

*Except in the coal industry, where the words
"conciliation" and "negotiation" are, for historical
reasons, synonymous; the former is normally used to
mean what in the United States would be called
mediation.

**The Industrial Court was established as a
permanent arbitration body under the 1919 Industrial
Courts Act and is voluntary in character. It is not
a court in the legal sense, and the 1970 Industrial
Relations Bill changes its title to that of Industrial Arbitration Board.

"with neither side obstructing the other" reflects
some of the fears that negotiating parties frequently have about arbitration. Some are more confident,
and some less. In atomic energy, for example, a
majority vote of _either side_ can result in arbitration. In coal mining, in which the normal device at
the national level is a National Reference Tribunal
of unusual composition,* reference to arbitration
can be prevented, since 1961, by either side _ob-
jecting_.**

In all parts of the public sector, with the exception of coal mining, arbitration exists at the
national (or industrywide) level only. In coal,
where collective agreements have historically been
made at pit and district level and in which no
logic is seen in allowing issues to pass beyond the
level at which the relevant agreement was made, pit
umpires and district referees are also appointed ad
hoc from panels nominated by both sides.[27] In some
sectors, especially the nonindustrial civil service
and in rail transport, only national arbitration is
used, but this is provided by a permanent body specially set up for the purpose--in the former case
the Civil Service Arbitration Tribunal and in the
latter case the Railway Staff National Tribunal.[28]

Where their own employees are concerned, governments have traditionally shown more caution
about being bound by arbitration than have the

----

*Three people in no way connected with mining
are appointed by the Master of the Rolls (a judge
of the Supreme Court who appears to have this as
his sole direct industrial relations function); one
acts as president and has a casting vote. When the
tribunal meets, each side appoints an assessor to
help it in obtaining the facts but takes no part in
making the award itself.

**The earlier arrangement had the effect of
making a "constitutional strike"--that is, one arising after procedure had been exhausted--formally impossible, since reference to the National Reference
Tribunal was unconditional.

employees themselves, although in recent years the
boot has tended to move to the other foot.* As late
as 1969, however, a national trade union official
could note with disapproval that the workers' side
in the National Health Service was not allowed to
proceed to arbitration unless the Minister of
Health ruled that the issue concerned represented
a major problem involving a large number of staff
and could recall the splendid days when the union
could use the Industrial Disputes Tribunal.[29]

Ministers of Health have often made heavy
weather of arguments of public policy where arbitration is concerned, and this has become general
since the Heath Administration came into office in
1970 with a policy of "de-escalating" wage demands.
Its current sensitivity may be judged by the government's decision in February 1971 not to renew
the appointment of the chairman of the Civil Service Arbitration Tribunal, Hugh Clegg, on the
grounds that he had allowed himself to be nominated
by a trade union as a member of an ad hoc arbitration body set up in connection with an industrywide
stoppage of local government workers.**

Such touchiness would not have surrounded the
operation of civil service arbitration even by the
end of the 1950s. After early hesitations over the
role of arbitration in civil service Whitleyism,
the government of the day finally put it on a permanent footing in 1925 through the Industrial Court

_____

*See p. 165, below, for recent developments
along this line.

**The arbitration in question was chaired by
Sir Jack Scamp and related to dustmen and other
local authority manual workers. The government is
said to have been affronted by both the amount and
the tone of the award, which appeared to chide it
on the lack of an incomes policy. It is significant that the unions preferred an ad hoc tribunal
to an arbitration body established through official
government provision.

and then in 1936 through the Civil Service Arbitration Tribunal itself. Certain subjects--such as salaries above a specified level, superannuation, and the granting or withholding of established status--were excluded from arbitration, and two further conditions were imposed: that the government "will give effect to the awards of the Court . . . subject to the overriding authority of Parliament" and "must also reserve the right to refuse arbitration on grounds of policy." The first condition has never been invoked, and the second only to exclude the issue of equal pay for women, which was later conceded in seven installments from January 1955.

Trade union suspicion of arbitration is of longer standing than is that of government and has its origins in the development of concepts of incomes policy. A first brush in 1961, when the Chancellor of the Exchequer took it upon himself to postpone the operation of awards of the Civil Service Arbitration Tribunal until the end of the "Pay Pause," has now grown into a widespread belief that arbitration has ceased to be "free," which has scarcely been discouraged by the dismissal of Professor Clegg.

Even the teachers, who appear to be protected under Section 4 of the 1965 Remuneration of Teachers Act both by the need for agreement on arbitrators and by the provision that their award can be upset only by a vote in each house of Parliament on the ground that this is required by "national economic circumstances," have remained unassured and are presently attempting to continue negotiations rather than adopt the arbitration path, which the government appears to prefer.

Principles of Pay Settlement

Civil Service

The "fair wages principle" in public life in Great Britain dates from a resolution of the House of Commons of February 13, 1891, the object of

which was to ensure that workers employed on government contract work received wages no less favorable
than those paid by good employers in the trade.   It
had no statutory force; nor have the more comprehensive resolutions of 1909 and 1946 been given such
force.* Nor was it originally intended to have
<u>direct</u> application to employees of the state itself.
It was, nevertheless, directly applied to the state's
manual employees in 1910 and has provided the historical basis for the development of a system of
"fair comparison" that has dominated the settlement
of civil service pay since the 1940s.**

The problem of governments in steering a steady
course between their responsibility to pay their
servants adequately and their obligation to manage
the taxpayers' money prudently and economically is
often referred to in British literature on the civil
service. Fair comparison has appeared to be the
only acceptable way out of this difficult dilemma.
Practice has, however, proved more difficult than
principle, and formulae have been more difficult to
devise and to apply than precept.

A formula devised in 1931, that of the Tomlin
Commission, offered no clear guide to civil service
pay determination, was often ambiguous, and became
a source of great dissatisfaction to civil service
unions. It went as follows:

---

*The 1946 resolution includes clauses requir-
ing contractors to observe "fair" conditions of
work, as well as "fair" wages, and also to recognize the freedom of their workers to be members of
trade unions. Contractors are also responsible for
the observance of the resolution by any subcontrac-
tors that they employ. The terms of the resolution
have also been embodied in a number of acts that
make it a statutory duty of the authority or authorities named to observe "fair" wages and conditions;
these include road haulage, film-making, renting
and exhibition, civil aviation, television, and the
British Sugar Corporation.

**The situation as it has developed for govern-
ment industrial workers is described later in this
section.

> Civil Service remuneration should re-
> flect what may be described as the
> long term trend, both in wages, sal-
> aries and in the economic condition of
> the country. We regard it as undesir-
> able that the conditions of service of
> Civil Servants when under review should
> be related too closely to factors of a
> temporary or passing character.[30]

Such "long term trends" could hardly be defined.
Negotiations tended to be based on evidence about
outside pay but to be diverted into arguments about
the validity and relevance of the information produced by either side.

The Priestley Commission, which reported in
1955, took a more detailed view of the formula and
machinery required.[31] It recognized two principles,
a primary principle of fair comparison with "current
remuneration of outside staffs employed on broadly
comparable work taking account of other conditions
of service" and a secondary principle of internal
relativities that would be used as a supplement to
the primary principle, particularly where fair comparisons proved impossible to establish.

It also recommended the establishment of a
Civil Service Pay Research Unit as a fact-finding
body, independent of the negotiating parties, to
collect facts and to establish "outside analogues"
to civil service jobs, leaving the parties to evaluate the information, argue about money, and fill in
those grades for which analogues could not be found
(for example, tax inspectors and tax officers), referring their disagreements to the Civil Service
Arbitration Tribunal. The Pay Research Unit was
set up in 1956.

On this basis, the officials and staff people
in the civil service have elaborated a system of
periodic pay reviews on the basis of the Pay Research Unit's investigations for classes with outside analogues, developing these into pay adjustments for "child grades" attached to these "parent
grades." General upward adjustments for civil servants as a whole are provided for by general agreements in addition to these reviews.[32]

The more recent Royal Commission on the Civil
Service (the Fulton Commission), which reported in
1968, generally approved the fair comparison principle but advised the adoption of "broad banding"--
that is, the absorption of the many hundreds of existing grades of civil servants into a limited number of general grades--and the adoption of job evaluation in dealing with civil service pay.[33] The full
consequences of these decisions are yet to become
evident.

Fair comparison for industrial civil servants
has followed a different path. The Whitley councils that were established have been bound by the
1910 "fair wages" decision of the Asquith Administration. Some craft workers have been "trade rated"
and paid according to agreements negotiated in private industry. The majority, however, have been
paid rates adjusted to follow average movements in
outside rates and, since 1940, on a national basis.
Two craft rates, one for London and the other for
the provinces, were fixed by averaging the minimum
time-work craft rates paid in 22 outside industries
(21 for London), and two "M" (for Miscellaneous)
rates for laborers were similarly settled by averaging rates paid in 34 outside industries (32 for
London), these four rates being adjusted every six
months.

A 1966 report of the National Board for Prices
and Incomes revealed the already obvious failure of
these mechanisms to achieve fair comparisons for industrial civil servants.[34] "Rates," on the average,
were being equated, but not "earnings." A smaller
proportion of industrial civil servants were getting
payments based on results schemes than were their
counterparts outside, and the shortfall in pay resulting from this and other causes was only in part
made up by supplementary or "lead" payments.

The proposal of the board was that existing
practice should be abandoned and that the system
should be thoroughly overhauled by grouping industrial civil servants according to types of work
done--engineering, chemicals, dockyards, building,
and so forth--and later initially by basing pay on
actual levels (not basic rates) for a 40-hour week

of outside timeworkers in similar activities.
Thereafter, each industrial group could conduct its
own separate pay negotiations, not by statistical
comparison with outside basic rates but according
to its own needs assessed in the light of government incomes policy and including pay resulting
from productivity agreements.[35] Industrial civil
servants, many of them previously grossly underpaid,
gained considerably from the initial regroupings
and reforms carried out in 1967, and various productivity deals have been made since that time. Whether
in the longer run the new arrangements will provide a
durable basis for fair comparisons remains to be seen.

Other Public Employment

     Fair comparison as a doctrine has been less
persuasive outside the civil service than inside
it. Both governments and the various public authorities concerned have approached the situation with
a good deal of ambivalence, arising partly from dis-
like of some aspects of comparability put forth by
the National Board for Prices and Incomes, partly
from straightforward considerations of cost, and
partly because of a disinclination to handle pay in
terms of productivity measurements, commonly thought
to be difficult in the public sector. Outside the
civil service proper, therefore, pay settlement
seems more like a patchwork quilt than an orderly
fabric of principles--a patchwork established by a
number of authorities, commissions, and negotiating
bodies, all operating against the background of
changing governmental policies on prices and incomes.
     The whole situation has been complicated by the
difficulty of evaluating and understanding the role
of government in collective bargaining in nationalized industries. The _form_ of the public corporation
is designed to relieve management of day-to-day parliamentary interference and the custom for the minister in charge of each relevant department to refuse to answer managerial questions, including those
relating to wages and salaries. But the responsible
minister also has, under each nationalization act,

the power to "give directions of a general character as to the exercise and performance by the Board
of their functions in relation to matters appearing
to the Minister to affect the national interest."*

The minister can also dismiss, force the resignation of, or refuse to renew the contract of any
board member he pleases. For some years it has been
impossible to maintain the fiction that nationalized
boards are free to determine pay and conditions as
they please. Recalcitrant boards and chairmen have
evidently learned their lessons, and fewer and fewer
seem inclined to go it alone.**

A number of commissions and public bodies have,
overtly or otherwise, tackled the fair comparison
problem. In 1960 the Willink Commission expressly
rejected the method of fair comparison but related
the pay of a police constable to an average of the
minimum rates of skilled craftsmen, to which it
added 45 percent to take account of the supplementary earnings that such an average craftsman might
be expected to take home each week and a further 25
percent to compensate the policeman for the dangers
and inconveniences of his job.[36] The logic of these
calculations was not revealed.

In the same year the Pilkington Commission argued that the work of doctors and dentists could
not be compared with that of workers in any other
profession but made sideways comparisons with the
professions competing for the kinds of recruits expected in medicine and dentistry.[37] This showed
that doctors and dentists were relatively overpaid,
but increases in their remuneration were nevertheless

---

*These words appear in the Coal Industry Na-
tionalization Act, but other acts include similar
provisions.

**Examples are the case of Steven Hardie,
chairman of the Iron and Steel Corporation, in 1952,
and of Lord Hall of the post office in 1970. The
resignation of Lord Robens, chairman of the National
Coal Board for 10 years, also in 1970, may not have
been unrelated to this situation.

justified on grounds of the disadvantages to be found in their working conditions.*

Also in 1960 the Guillebaud Committee--the Railway Pay Committee of Inquiry--found somewhat crude but relatively straightforward comparisons easier. It discovered 137 comparable jobs, 87 percent with pay above the railway rate--and 6 percent above at that, the median rate being 10.2 percent above--and did a similar exercise for various grades, in the end awarding 10 percent to salaries staff and 8 percent to conciliation grades (that is, nonsalaried manual workers, with some exceptions).

In the five years that followed there was continual argument between the railway unions and the government on whether the Guillebaud comparisons should be applied in subsequent negotiations. Ultimately, the National Board for Prices and Incomes, faced by the April 1965 White Paper on prices and incomes policy and its 3.5 percent norm,[38] roundly condemned the "Guillebaud Formula" and stood on the practice of productivity agreements.[39] The National Union of Railwaymen issued strike notices, and a stoppage was averted only by the intervention of the prime minister.

Nurses and university teachers, each bearing a problem of fair comparisons, have also been referred to the National Board for Prices and Incomes. No form of fair comparison emerged in the first case, and, despite large increases in nurses' pay, the

---

*The commission proposed a permanent review body, similar to the Standing Advisory Committee for higher civil servants, to review the pay of doctors and dentists from time to time. The proposals of the Kindersley Committee that resulted were subsequently rejected by the Wilson government, leading to resignations and a crisis that was only resolved by the advent of the Heath Administration in 1970, which pledged to assist the doctors (to whom it gave two-thirds of the Kindersley award, with a promise of more to come). Such expedients have not eased the difficulty of imposing tighter criteria on other groups of workers.

matter continues to be a source of controversy.[40]
University teachers were first, in 1964, referred
to the National Incomes Commission,* which rejected
the suggestion that academic salaries should be determined by fair comparison but expressed itself
satisfied that a salary increase was justified because "over the years there has been a decline in
the position occupied by university salaries in the
overall pattern of relativities."[41]

Thinking to establish at least some regular
method of settling university teachers' claims after
the disbanding of the National Incomes Commission,
the government turned them over to the National
Board for Prices and Incomes as a standing reference in 1967. The board's first report on the matter in December 1968 was not popular with university
teachers.[42] The board subsequently commissioned a
comprehensive study of university teaching from the
Higher Education Research Unit of the London School
of Economics as a guide to its decisions.

In April 1970 the board made an interim award
of 9 percent, suggesting that this was generally
made on a comparison basis but that no permanent
link of this kind was intended. On its recommendation collective bargaining machinery of a more normal kind was subsequently established.[43] Neither
nurses, university teachers, nor school teachers
have, it seems, found it possible to join doctors
and civil servants in the fair comparison league.

Incomes policy pressures apart, pay settlement
in other parts of the public sector has mainly been
concerned with issues of productivity and/or low pay.
Such considerations were encouraged as a reason for
higher remuneration in the 1965 White Paper on
prices and incomes policy mentioned above. The effect has been to put considerable pressure on some
parts of the public sector to improve working

---

*The commission had a brief existence between
1962 and 1965 as an instrument of the Macmillan Administration's wage policy. It was boycotted by
the TUC, reported on three wage settlements, and
acted as arbitrator in this one case only.

methods, to use work study, and generally to adopt
more "managerial" attitudes toward their functions
than was formerly the case, especially where low
pay and low productivity have been associated with
the other.

The National Board for Prices and Incomes has
arraigned local authorities, the National Health Service, and the water supply as both low paid and inefficient and has made sweeping proposals for justi-
fying better pay by more determined and economic
management.[44] In the same reference the gas industry was less severely taken to task but was considered capable of improvement. Of all the nationalized industries coal and electricity have shown the
most startling technical improvements and have been
less subject to pressures either on grounds of low
pay or of efficiency, although the coal industry
has been faced by a decline in the demand for coal
that has led to periodic tensions between the National Coal Board and the National Union of Mineworkers, and in 1969 pressures for higher wages in
electricity eventually led to a major work stoppage.[45]

CONFLICT AND COOPERATION IN PUBLIC SECTOR

Traditional Pattern

George Hildebrand has characterized four main
elements as special features of collective bargaining in the public sector in the United States: prohibition or inhibition of the right to strike, the
nonmarket relations of the public services, the
lack of management power to come to final agreement,
and a strong tendency "to treat the legislative
process that governs the employment relationship as
reserved territory, to be excluded as much as possible from collective bargaining."[46] Although it
would be impossible to deny that in one way or another all these features affect the public sector
in Great Britain and have sometimes caused problems,
their impact has historically been a relatively
muted one.

Reasons for this situation are not difficult
to find. In a country without a written constitution and with government firmly tied to party majority it has been relatively easy to moderate the doctrine of "reserved territory" or of the "sovereign
employer"; in a country with the broadest possible
view of the right to strike it has been correspond-
ingly difficult to impose on the public sector conditions not required of workers elsewhere in the
economy.

This is not to say that trade unions, particularly those in central government, have never been
made to feel the uncomfortable tightness of the public purse, or the force of ministerial pride, or
the hidden hand of government policy; nor is it to
say that civil servants have been unconscious of
the inhibitions about strike action placed upon
them by their office or of struggles to assert the
union position against administrative or political
hostility. By and large, however, such tensions
and conflicts have traditionally--and within the
lifetime of a generation of trade union leaders up
to the 1960s--been relatively mild ones.

An important clue to this situation lies in
the encouragement or, at worst, passive resistance
of most of the public sector to trade union membership and representation. The background of Whitleyism and its assumptions of mutual cooperation and
joint participation have produced fertile ground
for easy relationships. It has also tended to mold
public-sector unions in its own image.

Historically there has been no question of
making public-sector unions resemble those in the
private sector. Where membership has overlapped
from one sector to the other--as in the case of the
Transport and General Workers Union and the General
and Municipal Workers--public-sector traditions
have prevailed with members in the public sector
and private-sector traditions with those in the private sector, and it has been relatively uncommon
(although not unknown) to find groups prone to aggressive behavior or bargaining. Where these have
existed, the effect of public-sector tradition has

tended to moderate trade union tactics and worker
unrest.*

A conscious desire to <u>produce</u> smooth relationships seems also to have emerged from Whitleyism.
There are few parts of the public sector in which
employer-employee relationships have suffered from
lack of careful attention. The casualness that
characterizes much of private industry in this respect tends to be absent. "Personnel management,"
if this is defined in terms of recruitment, training, grading, payment, and pensions, has been consciously superior, as has the tendency to analyze
problems, to attempt to plan solutions, and to encourage cooperation between worker and employer.

Standards of industrial relations behavior that
have emerged from this situation have become associated with a kind of nice-minded scrupulousness
that is less common in the private sector than in
the public sector. The nonmarket relations referred
to by Hildebrand have the effect that he suggests of
inducing public response to the costs of providing a
public service; they are also often asserted by private industry to cushion the public sector against
the vagaries of the customer, against the competition that would lead it to be tougher and less cozy
in its relationship with workers. Such relationships become, it is sometimes alleged, a kind of
tacit conspiracy between union and employer to the
detriment of the consumer. Such a situation would
not be possible if the public sector was more ex-
posed to reality.

It could, indeed, be said that the activities
of the "official" side may be more akin to <u>adminis-
tration</u> than to <u>management</u>, to keeping the ship of

---

*Success has been greater in some industries
than in others. Coal mining, since nationalization
and despite a drastic run-down of capacity and manpower, has tended to develop improved relations,
particularly since the abandonment of piecework.
London transport cannot be said wholly to have
solved its labor problems, and least of all the
docks industry.

state afloat rather than using it to scour the seas,
to minding the shop rather than exhibiting enterprise, to seeking tidiness rather than profit or
commercial success. The demand on the public sector for a more commercial attitude is, in fact, one
of the changes that has begun to challenge the traditional pattern of relationships in recent years.

Challenge to Traditions

Some part of the changing and, in some ways,
evidently deteriorating situation in public-sector
labor relations can be associated with a general decline of belief in the viability of the British industrial relations system generally. The spirit
that produced Whitleyism and that supported volun-
tarism as a means of settling differences and developing worker-management relations through collective
bargaining was characteristic not only of the public
but also of a large part of the private sector.
Opinions may differ on the reasons why in some industries the old formulae have failed to pass the
tests of the 1960s.
The view of the Donovan Commission was that
the general emphasis placed upon regulation by industrywide bargaining, characteristic of British
industrial relations, has proved insufficient and
has led to the development of a second world of
"fragmented" or "fractional" bargaining at the workplace, out of control of either management or trade
unions, and giving scope for the unconstitutional
stoppages so typical of the British scene in the
1960s. Assumptions of centralized trade union authority have proved unrealistic; management has
been attempting to obtain control by passing on responsibility to employers' associations. More positive approaches are therefore needed, especially
from employers, in stimulating greater formality of
agreements and procedures and more realistic levels
of bargaining, particularly at plant and company
level.
The Donovan Commission did not claim that a
degeneration of relationships of this character had

generally taken place in the public sector. With
some exceptions, this would certainly have been un-
true. But industrywide bargaining could certainly
be criticized there also, on at least two counts.
First, it could be claimed that insistence on industrywide bargaining only was creating a situation of
strain for the operation of policies of fair comparison; second, it could be argued that bargaining
at this level <u>only</u> was leading to ineffective and
inefficient use of manpower. Both claims could expect powerful support from considerations of incomes
policy and the advocacy in the 1960s of productivity
bargaining.

The notion that in times of inflation as well
as deflation, of full employment as well as unemployment, it is the obligation of the state to assume responsibility for achieving an economically
and socially acceptable rate of income generation
has become a commonplace in the Western world. In
Great Britain rising price levels, accompanied by
balance-of-payment problems, led to an attempt at a
wages policy by the Attlee Administration as early
as 1948. This was reborn as a "Pay Pause" under
the Macmillan Administration in 1961-62 and reached
its most sophisticated phase under the Wilson Labour
Government as a prices and incomes policy from 1965
to 1969.

Discussion of the intricacies of these developments can be found elsewhere.[47] Their effects on
the public sector can be described simply. Successive White Papers and the reports of the National
Board for Prices and Incomes in general deplored
arguments that wage increases should be determined
on grounds of comparability; increases beyond a
"norm"--at most 3-3.5 percent and sometimes zero--
could only be justified on grounds of absolutely
low pay, distribution of manpower, or in situations
in which the employees concerned, for example by
accepting more exacting work or a major change in
working practices, make a direct contribution towards increasing productivity in the particular
firm or industry. And successive governments felt
obliged to apply "wage restraint," "pause," or
"norm," as well as insistence on productivity

bargaining, first of all to the public sector, both as an example and as the area over which, directly through the Treasury or more indirectly through ministerial responsibility, it had greatest control.

The traumatic effect of such policies on labor relations in the public sector can be inferred from previous discussion of the principles of public-sector pay settlement. Why, public-sector unions demanded, should their areas of the economy be singled out for special treatment? How were fair comparisons to be worked out in such circumstances? And, in some senses most significant of all, what did the search for "productivity" mean? Did it imply that private-sector management practices were to be applied?

The growth of major industrial relations tension in the public sector has undoubtedly been a direct result of incomes policy. In the civil service several unions that had not previously thought it necessary to adopt militant attitudes and that, indeed, possessed no strike funds, thought it necessary, as confidence in arbitration declined, to develop a strike policy. Among these unions was the Civil Service Clerical Association (CSCA), an organization that had never before contemplated even the possibility of industrial action.[48]

The strength of Whitleyism, the CSCA declared in its more than usually militant mood, lay not, as the officials would have it, in the strength of an "idea" or the promotion over the years of "a single viewpoint and spirit" but in the desire of governments to avoid conflict with their employees; but this did not mean that governments could not, nor that they would not, at the end of the bargaining process "exercise the ultimate sanction." "In rejecting the conventional view that strike action is never needed, in rejecting spurious theories about industrial harmony and therefore the passive role which some people would wish trade unions to play," the Executive, in advocating a strike policy was not, it declared, arguing that strike action was an alternative to collective bargaining; it was saying that militancy involved a "participating membership" and an organization that could act with "maximum possible vigour and aggression when necessary."[49]

Despite the mood of greater militancy, public-sector unions have remained cautious about the application of industrial action. One reason for this has been reluctance, evident enough in the CSCA policy discussion, to play fast and loose with long-standing relationships with government, in the knowledge that, in the last resort, ultimate power lay with political authority. Since the general strike of 1926 the British trade union movement has shown no inclination to take on the state in strikes certain to be labeled political and extremely doubtful of success. Nor in the absence of a militant tradition have many public-sector unions been certain of the support of their own members in such a challenge.

Some public-sector unions, like the Post Office Engineering Union, with the forces of technology and considerable negotiating skill on its side, have thought in terms of intermittent stoppages and periods of noncooperation rather than outright confrontation. Teachers, a group that has practiced such tactics from time to time in the past, found itself increasingly involved in direct action in 1969 and 1970, and it is no doubt true that in the National Union of Teachers, as among other "bureaucratised professionals, discontent has become sufficiently deep as to overcome reservations among some sections about loss of status by industrial-type strike behaviour."[50]

The reciprocal of the feeling of undue pressure from incomes policy and the proximate justification for direct action has been the impression that manual workers in the private sector have been making hay in augmenting their earnings, despite appeals for restraint and government disapproval, and that they have succeeded in this as a result of their greater militancy. Some low-paid professional sections, such as nurses, have had much public (and even governmental) sympathy on these grounds. Others have had more sympathy from review bodies, which government (or even public opinion) has always found acceptable. The proposal of the Kindersley Committee for a 30 percent salary increase for doctors and dentists during a particularly severe

period of incomes restraint in 1970 brought the
wrath of the Labour Government upon the award, and
an open clash was prevented only by a change of administration and the development of a new review
arrangement.

Although in some respects relatively new and
somewhat alarming on the British scene, public-
sector stoppages have until recently contributed
very little to the national strike figures. Stoppages on the docks have been familiar enough for
many years; conflict in the coal industry has, especially since the adoption of a national power-
loading agreement in 1966, been drastically reduced.*
Railway stoppages have not been unknown. But such
national stoppages as those that have occurred in
local government, in electricity, and in the post
office at the beginning of the 1970s have been of
an unfamiliar character, and one that, if it continues, will presage a completely new relationship
between the public sector and the state.

These strikes were, of course, associated with
the determination of the Heath Administration to
lower to 8 percent, or at most to 9 percent, the
results of wage negotiations at a time of steep
rises in the cost of living and of claims for increases of three or even four times those percentages. In the case of the local government "Dirty-
jobs" strike and the strike in the post office, the
situation was further complicated because workers
widely recognized as low paid--refuse collectors,
other unskilled workers, and postmen themselves--
were the principal groups of trade union members
involved.

The government, the unions alleged, was not
only encouraging public employers to stand against

---

*The agreement replaced pit bargaining about
piecework prices with inclusive shift rates to power-
loading teams as each face was mechanized. In the
years after World War II 62.5 percent of all stoppages in Great Britain took place in the coal mining
industry, which accounted for 22 percent of total
man-hours lost; by 1969-70 this had been reduced to
4.9 percent and 11.9 percent, respectively.

their demands; it was also, by rejecting the Wilson Administration's notions of equity arising from incomes policy, perpetrating a monstrous unfairness upon those workers least able to help themselves. In the case of the power workers, who had worked to rule between December 7 and December 14, 1970, the situation was no better, because here the government appeared to be attacking those who had been more cooperative in raising productivity than any other group in the public, or even in the private, sector.

The government's unconcealed hostility to the award of the Scamp Committee in the "Dirty-jobs" strike--an increase of between 14.5 percent and 15 percent on earnings--did nothing to reassure public-sector unions on the independence that the government was willing to concede to arbitrators and did further harm to the image that arbitration had already gained as a possible instrument of wage and salary restraint--a situation that, together with the work of the Pay Research Unit, is reflected as a fall in the number of appeals addressed to the Civil Service Arbitration Tribunal.

A further element in the uneasiness of public-sector unions about incomes policy in Great Britain has been the emphasis, already referred to, of approving pay settlements higher than the "norm" where productivity bargaining can be shown to be involved, a practice that received the formal blessing and appropriate guidelines for its operation from the National Board for Prices and Incomes in 1967 but that had been a part of the board's thinking since 1965.[51]

One of the earliest board references had the effect of conceding that administrative staff and clerks in electricity supply had to be kept in line with manual workers who had gained from a productivity settlement.[52] But in January 1966 the board found itself highly critical of the Guillebaud comparability arrangement on the railways and much more in favor of a policy of productivity deals.[53] It was later to probe the same question and to produce a similar answer in relation to busmen; industrial civil servants; manual workers in local

government, the National Health Service, gas and
water supply, and atomic energy.[54]

Sentiments such as these were understandably
unwelcome where, as in the case of the railways,
they appeared to replace an acceptable formula for
pay settlement with one that appeared to suggest
that in return for higher pay greater efficiency
should be imposed on a declining industry with a
declining labor force; they were less unwelcome
where, as in the case of industrial civil servants
and local government manual workers, they appeared
to open up possibilities for higher earnings. But
even here there were causes for anxiety among public employees.

First, it was questionable whether some public
authorities were sufficiently well organized in
their labor relations to administer the kind of productivity schemes that the National Board for Prices
and Incomes had in mind and questionable, therefore,
what period would elapse before workers could benefit from such arrangements. Wage and salary re-
structuring might for a time be used as a justification for higher pay, but in the longer run the
chips would be down, and some groups of workers
could expect very little.[55]

Second, the advocacy of a trend toward "scientific management" in the public sector seemed to
suggest that an attempt was being made to change
the "style" of public services from administrative
to managerial, of altering their ethos from that of
making contributions toward the general good to
that of partaking in the competitive, work-measured
and profit-conscious world of the private firm--a
world from which members of public-sector unions
had deliberately cut themselves off in taking their
present jobs.

In part, such an impression may have been mis-
taken in that the introduction of managerial techniques into the public sector in Great Britain is
far from new. The application of work study methods
to office work originated as long ago as 1919 in
the investigation section of the Treasury and became
known as "O and M" (Organization and Methods) in
1941. In one form or another scientific management

had spread to every part of the public sector by the time the National Board for Prices and Incomes was established.[56] There was, however, a question of attitude, a new aggressiveness in the tone of the reformers of the 1960s that suggested that they would be content with nothing less than a complete adoption of criteria of efficiency and a breaking up of close relationships between staff and officials in public employment.

The 1955 report of the Royal Commission on the Civil Service conveyed such an impression more, perhaps, than any public document in the 1960s, criticizing managerial weaknesses in this part of the public sector and casting doubts upon the effects of Whitleyism. Although it created an atmosphere that was democratic and trouble free, Whitleyism acted, the commission thought, as a powerful constraint on managerial authority: "Management is sometimes less active and determined than it should be; arguments are allowed to go on too long, and rigid procedures are accepted where flexibility should be insisted upon." Observers may have been forgiven for thinking that the doctrine of public responsibility was being replaced by one of managerial prerogative, a thought that was not lost on public-sector unions.

Given the impact that attempts to stabilize the national wages and salary bill have had upon the public sector since the early 1960s, it is not surprising that its strike record has deteriorated, nor that a mood of defensive militancy has grown, nor that in some parts of the public service there is discontent about managerial trends in an area where service by administration has historically been the rule. It remains to be seen how this situation will develop in the future.

FUTURE OF LABOR RELATIONS

If it is hazardous to attempt to summarize the experience of a public sector of great complexity in a chapter of this kind, it may be even more hazardous to divine its future. The policies of

governments on prices and incomes are far from predictable. Indeed, in 1971, as a result of the
breakup of the apparent Labour-Conservative consensus of economic and social policy, they were
less predictable than they have been for many years.
Added to doubts about incomes policy and managerial
style is also the question of the extent to which
the "hiving-off" of parts of government departments
and profitable sectors of public corporations will
be encouraged to proceed.

It is also difficult to project into the future
the possible reactions of labor, and particularly
organized labor, to the public-sector situation.
One reason for this is the background of stability
in labor relations that most parts of public employment have enjoyed over a considerable period of time;
another is the long-standing expertise that governments have acquired in handling public-sector relations.

It is unquestionable that the system of industrial relations that developed in Great Britain--
from the Royal Commission of 1867, through the Commission on Labour of 1891-94 and the Whitley Committee of 1917 and 1919, to the management-government-
union relationships of World War II--has been seen
at its best in the public sector. There can be very
few countries that have seen so smooth and so uninterrupted a development of collective bargaining
machinery and of joint understandings between the
parties; nor can there be many that have been so
little interrupted by overt conflict.

Although there exist in some parts of the public service problems of developing trade union representation, these are problems of evolution rather
than principle; although there are inefficiencies
and complaints about remuneration, the machinery
exists to deal with them. Even more important, no
inherent inclination exists on either side, despite
the increasingly aggressive talk of recent years,
to attempt to settle disputes by trial of strength
rather than by open discussion. Insofar as explo-
sive differences exist, these are the result of ex-
ternal rather than internal forces and arise principally from the commitment of governments to regulate
incomes levels and to encourage productivity.

The issue at stake is the survival of Whitleyism, and the most important consideration is the
absence of a viable alternative. Interestingly, in
the implementation of the far-reaching proposals
for the reform of the civil service advocated by
the Fulton Commission very little has survived in
practice of the advocacy of managerial functions.
The newly constituted Civil Service Department,
with responsibility for this reform, has preferred
to count its blessings in having powerful and ar-
ticulate employee representation and "has deliberately set out to make the National Staff Side a
full partner in the enterprise." Indeed, as a
spokesman for the Civil Service Department recently
pointed out, it had no other choice.[57] The same
situation evidently holds true in some areas of the
public sector where relationships have deteriorated
considerably, notably in the post office. Unfor-
tunately, no detailed study has been made of the
situation in this industry, although it appears to
contain most of the elements of <u>internal</u> public-
sector problems.

The substance of such internal problems appears
to lie not in the unwillingness of the officials to
exercise their managerial rights but in their disinclination to take constructive initiatives.*
Such a disinclination, institutionalized into Whitleyism, has the effect of confirming the least active and progressive part of the labor force in a
habit of unimaginative action and thought and of
irritating those who favor progress.

The situation combines low pay, low productivity, and reluctance to accept technical change,
with deteriorating relationships. It also has the
effect of making the industry or sector peculiarly
vulnerable to governmental intervention. It is no
accident that it is railways and the post office--
the first formerly and the second currently in this
position--that have been subject to the most extreme
pressure for board members to toe the government line.

---

*A criticism leveled against British manage-
ments generally in the industrial relations field.

Evidence suggests that in resisting government intervention the public sector--whether in the central government, the local government, or the public corporations--has a primary interest in making Whitleyism work. It is noticeable that those parts of the public sector in which there has been the most active cooperation between the parties have been the least subject to government pressure. It may be difficult in some cases to transform "administrative Whitleyism" into a form that allows for greater initiative, but the effort appears to be well worthwhile.

It still remains possible that government handling of labor relations in the public sector will be so dogmatic or so inept that it will be impossible for internal adjustments within particular parts of the service to be made before a further deterioration of relationships develops. Recent experience with the present government may appear to underline this danger, but it is questionable whether any government could continue for long to induce crisis situations in areas directly or indirectly subject to its own jurisdiction. At worst, as those in the public sector know well, such actions are likely to be intermittent, and there is a strong incentive for government to set an example of smooth, rather than rough, operation.

It seems likely, therefore, that the forces making for historical continuity in the development of labor relations in the public sector in Great Britain will prove stronger than will those leading to breakdown. The characteristics of collective bargaining are too firmly based to be eroded by transient problems; British experience in juggling with the problems of wage and salary determination where public servants are concerned is too great to allow gross errors to be made. And it seems likely that the challenges to tradition that have grown up during the 1960s will find that tradition firm, yet flexible enough to adapt to changing needs. Indeed, there appears to be no other choice.

4

**FEDERAL REPUBLIC
OF GERMANY**
Dieter Gaul

HISTORICAL DEVELOPMENT OF
COLLECTIVE BARGAINING

Labor laws dealing with the legal protection
of workers in subordinate positions are especially
subject to social and political factors and tensions. From their beginnings in 1848 they have defined an area of jurisprudence in which employers
and employees have participated both individually
and collectively through a variety of organizations.
For this reason bargaining laws can also be viewed
as laws governing the ways in which organizations
of employees (trade unions) and of employers (employers' associations) or individual employers have
entered into social contracts. The law of collective bargaining thus concerns such collective
agreements rather than individual ones.

It is the objective of the laws governing the
organizations in the various trades to achieve
self-regulation for the workers employed in it,
subject to such legal limits as may have been provided and including specifically the laws governing
the public order. This has led to considerable
autonomy within the organizations of industry.

Around the middle of the nineteenth century
there were groups of workers in the metal, textile,
and mining industries that endeavored through mutual help in emergencies to take over undue burdens
falling on individual workers and thus make them

socially acceptable. But this joint activity of workers, which took the form of emergency provisions only, cannot be regarded as industrywide organization in the current sense. These organizations lacked the will to act collectively against the employers or employers' organizations to secure improved working conditions or the will to initiate any systematic joint representation of worker interests.

During the following decades Germany did not favor the trend toward the formation of trade unions of the present type. The form of government of the recently recreated empire, the strong personality of Chancellor Bismarck, and the social laws introduced by him were responsible for the fact that not until the end of the nineteenth century could trade unions be created that could really collectively espouse the improvement of the working conditions of their members. The trade association of the printers did special pioneering work, which led as early as 1873 to a wage agreement; in 1896 it was renegotiated.[1]

At the beginning of the twentieth century the development of industrial or trade organizations was still proceeding very hesitantly; there was little progress in shaping working conditions by means of contracts between employers and employees. The free trade unions were still affected by the spirit of the antisocialist laws of October 19, 1878, which prohibited all associations with social democratic objectives, provided for the confiscation of their funds, and thus meant a return to the earlier police state.

During World War I, which required the mobilization of the whole work force, conditions changed with the passage of the Voluntary Service Act. In this law the trade organizations were for the first time given the right to nominate the members of arbitration tribunals.[2] It was only on May 22, 1918, that the prohibitions of Section 153 of the trade regulations were suspended. These had threatened penalties for anybody who might have tried to induce anyone through force or threats to join an organization or prevent him from leaving it.

Finally on November 12, 1918, a wage contract settlement was given legal force by the Council of the People's Representatives. It provided as follows: "There are no restrictions on the right of association or assembly; this applies also to civil servants and public workers. Conflicting municipal regulations and special legislation for agricultural workers are cancelled."

The German National Assembly, which created the new constitution, also ratified the wage rate regulations of November 12, 1918, by means of the temporary law of March 4, 1919. For the first time freedom of organization was granted legally in Article 159 of the Weimar Constitution of August 11, 1919. This clause provided that "In order to maintain and develop the economic environment freedom of association is granted to all individuals and occupations. All agreements and measures limiting or interfering with this freedom are illegal."

This phase of evolution shows a remarkable growth of trade unions and of their importance; at the same time the employers' associations remained organized by industry, on the basis of their historical background. For example, the masons were united in their trade union "building, stone, ground" (bau, steine, erden). They sought to regulate the working conditions of their members by collectively bargaining for wage contracts regardless of whether their members worked in the construction, metallurgical, or chemical industries.

In the same way the trade unions of the textile industries took care of the interests of their members; similarly the trade unions of the metallurgical industry represented the interests of their constituents, such as mechanics, turners, and welders. Today in the Federal Republic of Germany establishmentwide bargaining is practiced in which the establishment is defined as a working unit, often called a factory, but not identical with the firm; this concept did not exist then.[3] Rather, the trade organizations took care of the interests of their members regardless of the industries in which they worked.

Because of this, for example, masons working in the chemical industry were paid according to the

wage contract of the masons—that is, according to
a different one from the chemical workers of the
same firm. Mechanics in the chemical industry were
treated according to the contract covering the
metal trades. One or two printers in the printing
shop of a large firm had to be treated according to
the graphic arts contract. Although this led to a
certain unity in the conditions of employment in
individual occupations, it also led to the need to
treat the staff of a single establishment according
to widely varying contracts, with respect to both
formal and material content; this was considered
undesirable.

     After the National Socialists came to power,
the employers' associations, as well as the trade
unions, were dissolved as early as 1933. The parties that had concluded the existing collective
bargaining agreements were, therefore, eliminated
and with them the possibility of autonomous agreement with respect to the working conditions of
their members. The tasks of the associations were
temporarily taken over by government agencies.
Later the Law for the Regulation of National Labor
replaced the wage agreements. The Reich Trustee
for labor, a state official, had the unilateral
right to issue regulations. State regulation thus
replaced free collective self-determination.

     Only after the end of World War II could free-
dom of organization be reintroduced. Law No. 40 of
the Allied Control Commission, passed on November 30,
1946, abolished the law for the regulation of national labor, but there was no uniform new regulation. Rather, there were in the various states
quite different regulations because the four occu-
pying powers—the United States, Great Britain,
France, and the U.S.S.R.—followed different legal
developments. It was not until the occupation
zones of the United States, Great Britain, and
France were united into a single economic and administrative area that conditions were created for
a common development of legislation.

     This development was completed by the issuance
of the Law of Wage Contracts of April 4, 1949,
amended on January 11, 1952, which is still in force.

This law granted to the trade unions, single employers, and employers' associations the right of regulating rights and duties for themselves and their members by means of wage contracts and agreements governing work content, termination of employment, and other operating or administrative questions.

COLLECTIVE BARGAINING RIGHTS AND THEIR IMPORTANCE

Collective bargaining law contains, first of all, the norms of the state laws, the state constitutions, and the federal constitutions, together with regulations dependent upon them. Second, it comprises individually negotiated agreements between partners in employment that govern not only collective matters between trade unions and employers or employers' associations but also local issues. This right of autonomous trade or industry organization includes the participation of representatives of workers of an establishment or public agency in decisions made by the employer or public administrator (right of personnel representation).

The main focus here is collective bargaining in public employment, and, therefore, it is necessary to concentrate on the activity of the trade union as negotiating partner of the employers' organization of public service. Such other organizations as the staff councils of state, county, and municipal governments will remain in the background.[4] The self-determination in labor with respect to trade unions and employers' associations is at the core of bargaining rights, but it is still bound by a sequence of higher jurisdictions. Therefore, it is necessary to be aware of the ranking of these different sources of law.

The highest source of jurisdiction is the constitutional law for the Federal Republic of Germany issued on May 23, 1949. Articles 20 and 28 regulate the federal structure of the republic and hence the distribution of authority for legislation, administration, and jurisdiction between the federal and

the state governments. Article 25 establishes the
legal link between the Federal Republic of Germany
and the body of international law; it states that
the general rules of international law are also
part of German law.

Articles 1-19 of the constitutional law are
the so-called freedom rights, these being the
rights that citizens enjoy in their relationship
with the state; these rights derive in large measure from the historical achievements of the French
Revolution. Thus, the sphere of freedom of the
citizen is so defined that he may not be limited in
the free development of his individuality, except
under special circumstances as provided by law.

These rights comprise equality before the law
in Article 3, protection of freedom of religion and
conscience in Article 4, the special protection of
marriage and family according to Article 6, the
guarantee of privacy for letters, postal services,
and telephone calls in Article 10, the freedom to
move about or to settle in Article 11, the freedom
of choosing a profession in Article 12, the invio-
lability of the individual home in Article 13, the
protection of property in Article 14, and, most
important for the purposes at hand, the freedom of
organization--that is, to form unions for the maintenance and promotion of working and economic con-
ditions--in Article 9.

The federal laws and those that the states are
authorized to establish and that are valid only
within them are all subordinated to the federal
constitutional law, as supplemented by the state
constitutions. In the absence of a uniform code of
labor law the German civil code is still valid for
the legal relationships between the partners in employment. It includes special protective laws concerning working hours, work schedules, and protection against dismissal, as well as laws governing
the employment of persons in special categories,
such as pregnant working women, disabled workers,
and juveniles up to the age of eighteen.

These and other legal standards, however, regulate working conditions only in a general way, by
providing minimum conditions and constraints on the

characteristics of collective bargaining contracts.
Legislators are hardly able to create rules for the
duties of both partners within a particular work
contract. The economic, social, and physical conditions in the various parts of the economy and in
public administration vary too much for that.

This is where wage contracts begin their
sphere of validity, in that they establish rules
for certain industries within the framework of the
law on freedom of organization; they take into account the special needs of the particular business.
The agreements are subordinated to federal and
state law but are tailored more particularly to the
employment conditions of the negotiating partners.

When such contracts are not agreed upon for a
single establishment or public authority (which is
permissible), they cannot adequately cover the
working relationships within specific establishments or plants. Accordingly, there is an Agency
Law for Personnel of August 5, 1955, and a Shop
Organization Law of October 11, 1952. These laws
make it possible for a shop or staff council to
take part in codetermination of the organization of
the service.

Although the basic wage contract gives an
overall framework for the relationships between the
various classes of employment, there is also collective bargaining for a single plant or public
authority. The basic wage contract assumes a position of minimum standard in the course of this two-
stage bargaining. The supplemental agreement for a
single establishment or authority may add to the
provisions of the basic wage contract and, as far
as permitted, may fix more favorable conditions for
the employee.

Finally, there are individual employment contracts that may be entered into with salaried staff
as well as wage earners in the sphere of private
enterprise as well as public service. In the ranking of the legal framework governing employment
such arrangements have fourth priority after constitutions, law, the wage contract, and the establishment contract. The individual contract can
specify more favorable conditions for the employee;

the higher ranking legal and contractual rights and
duties cannot be impaired for the employee.

Central Importance of
Basic Wage Agreement

In view of the central importance of the trade
union as the legitimate representative of the interests of employees and, thereby, as an agency of
social regulation,[5] it is understandable that the
basic wage agreements are the primary source for
defining the rights and duties of public as well as
private employees. This is so for workers and office personnel in public employment, but civil servants are subject to special laws.

A civil servant has a special relationship; he
is not a natural person entering into a business
contract, subject to the norms of private law, but
rather he receives a letter of appointment that
starts a service relationship bound by public law.
This establishes a superior constraint on the relationship. Because of this close connection between
the state and its officials, the state grants representation of worker interests to trade unions not
only for employees and workers in public authorities
but for civil servants as well. The result of this
social endeavor of the trade unions finds its expression in laws rather than in basic wage agreements, as far as civil servants are concerned.

A considerable number of employees and workers,
however, are employed in public service, and their
working conditions are influenced and determined by
basic wage agreements. Therefore, in public employment as well the social partners--that is, the
trade unions and the employers' associations--have
a central importance for the definition of working
conditions whether directly in a basic wage agreement or by promoting new laws.

The trade unions and the single employer or
employers' association are the partners in contracts
governing conditions in the sphere beyond a single
establishment. Insofar as such unions of employees
or employers are based on civil law and have a

democratic basis aimed at guarding the collective
interests of employees or employers, respectively,
they are true organizations able to enter such a
contract.

Their organizational work must last over the
long term and include the furthering of the common
interests and the improvement of the working conditions of its own members as against the contractual
partner; if necessary, the objective must be pursued by industrial action. It is thus a special
feature of the trade union that only employees
(workers) may join as members in order to avoid
organized adversary groups within the trade union.
This principle of freedom from organized adver-
saries also holds for the employers' associations.

When it is realized that certain occupational
groups do not have the right to strike or to engage
in job action against their contractual partner because of legal or other considerations, it is clear
that the readiness to strike cannot be regarded as
a criterion of a trade union. This is so, for example, for civil servants, who are not allowed to
strike, because such a method of conducting a confrontation with the employer would conflict with
the principle of their official subordination to
the state or other authority, such as a municipality. At times this poses boundary problems, when,
for instance, a professional group--such as doctors
or chimney sweeps--has to carry out both private
and public duties. In this case a right to strike
exists only insofar as it does not affect the performance of the public duties.

The corporate form of an alliance of employees
or employers is that of an association in the sense
of the German civil law. Such an association or
union is established by the decision of its members,
who have to define the purposes and bylaws and
choose a governing body as well as management. In
the Federal Republic of Germany it is usual nowadays for trade unions and employers' associations
to choose a form of organization not subject to
registration by the local district court. Thus,
such a union is not a legal person.

The difference between a union in the form of
a legal person and one not so qualified lies in the

realm of liability. When an association qualifies
as a legal person, an individual member may be liable for actions and omissions of the organization,
over and above his membership contributions. Conversely, a registered group not qualified as a legal
person is liable as an organization, while the members are exempt from personal liability.

In view of the large importance of the trade
unions to the state structure and economy of the
Federal Republic of Germany and considering the
formal difficulties of coping with a constantly
changing membership, the federal labor courts or
district courts take the registration for granted,
as if the trade union were a legal person, which in
actual fact it is not, as noted above.

Only a written contract agreed upon by one or
more trade unions on the one hand and one or more
employers' associations on the other is considered
a basic wage contract.[6] The basic wage contract
thus belongs to the sphere of civil law, and this
applies also to the contracts negotiated by the
federal government, states, counties, or municipalities and the union of public employees. In this
case the employers--that is, the public authorities
concerned--act toward the trade union not as a
higher or "sovereign" power but, rather, on a basis
of equality like any other citizen or organization.

Thus, the relationships set forth in the basic
wage agreement are not made part of public law but,
rather, civil law, and they are in this way part of
the free right of agreement established for the
private sphere. They are, however, distinguished
from other contracts with respect to jurisprudence
and jurisdiction, in that the interpretation of a
basic wage agreement uses the principles of validat-
ing laws rather than interpreting a civil contract.
In cases of doubt the courts do not ask what the
intent of the contractual partners had been.

The Federal Constitutional Court has developed
special principles with respect to this problem.
The determining factor is the written text agreement and the intent expressed in it; any definition
objectively expressed in the contract is thus decisive. Only if the interpretation of the written

wording leaves room for doubt is it possible to use
intent as a means of arriving at a resolution of
the question considering the structure of the contract and the evident purpose.

Because of the importance of such collective
agreements, legislation requires them to be in
written form. According to German federal law a
contract in the civil sphere may be agreed on in
any way as to both content and form; therefore,
oral agreements are as valid as written ones, but
for some special legal spheres--such as the pur-
chase of real property or agreements to eliminate
competition--the written form is explicitly required.

Since the basic wage agreement is similar to a
formal law and gives standardized regulations for
its area of application concerning the duties of
its partners, the need for security under law
prompted the legislature to require the written
form. This requirement is set forth in paragraph 6
of the Law of Basic Wage Agreements, which also requires that the agreed-upon contracts have to be
registered with the Federal Ministry of Labor or,
if they are valid only within a state, with the
State Department of Labor.

This procedure does not represent state influence on the internal administration of the contractual partners. They are absolutely free, as
provided in the legal framework, to use their own
discretion in forming the legal regulation of working conditions in their activity as they wish. The
register of basic wage agreements is only meant to
make public their details to anyone interested in
their legal evolution and content.

The basic wage agreement defines and regulates
the working conditions of those involved and, in
addition, the mutual obligations of the partners.
Therefore, a basic wage agreement consists of a
normative part as well as a part defining these responsibilities. The normative part fixes standards
that define directly the performance duties of both
contractual partners. This means the determination
of salary and wage groups, as well as their rates
of pay--that is, it sets the basis for job

evaluation. After this, the normal working hours
are fixed, together with schedules for overtime and
premium pay for it. In this part are also found
any additional rates for heavy work, vacation pay,
and minimum vacation time.

The part setting forth the responsibilities
includes provisions for both parties to refrain
from strikes or lockouts during the period of the
contract, for employers to accept promotional activities by the unions, and for abstention from
political activities within an authority or establishment. Finally, a basic wage agreement may contain regulations for operating procedures and organizational structure, such as the establishment
of arbitration and conciliation committees, which
are authorized to reconcile disparities of views
with respect to the contract itself or problems
arising out of it; this is to avoid possible litigation.

The contractual partners thus have far-reaching
legal competence for the regulation of their relationship, although it is limited to working conditions in their broadest sense and cannot transcend
the legal constraints.

By virtue of the general rules governing associations the contracting parties in a basic wage
agreement can only exercise their authority to
enact mutually binding rules of conduct insofar as
they are authorized to do so by the membership.
Moreover, neither trade unions nor employers' associations can rest their legitimacy on a requirement
of forced membership. Rather, membership must be
based on voluntary entry.

On this circumstance rests the authority of
the contractual partners to establish minimum conditions of employment binding on these persons.
Thus, a basic wage contract has a personal sphere
of validity. The wording in some contracts to the
effect that it should be valid for all public servants, employees, and workers in public employment
is not exact. Rather, it binds only those who are
members of the trade union for public service and
transport and who confirmed their acceptance of
their basic wage agreement by this membership.

In addition to this personal sphere of validity, the unions also exercise such control with respect to trade skills and professions. Since 1945
the trade unions in the Federal Republic of Germany
have been organized on an occupational basis, so
that they are also called industrial unions. The
employees thus represented by a professional trade
union, such as the Union of Public Service and
Transport Workers and the German Association of
Civil Servants, are endeavoring to standardize their
working conditions collectively. Until 1933, however (as is still usual in Great Britain today), a
uniformity of wages was aimed at--that is, it was
valid for most of the executives, employees, and
workers employed by the business. The occupational
characteristic of a basic wage agreement is thus decisively dependent on the membership qualifications
of the trade union or the employers' association.

Furthermore, every basic wage agreement is
valid within a certain given area; at maximum, the
agreement is valid for the whole territory of the
Federal Republic of Germany, but the contractual
partners may use their own discretion in limiting
the validity to a smaller territory by considering
special differences in costs of living when setting
salaries and wages.

Finally, the contractual partners can limit
the applicability of the agreement to a restricted
number of employees within one authority or enterprise if this does not interfere with the requirement of collective order. Thus, the contracting
parties--the trade unions and employers' associa-
tions--are allowed to specify the limits of personal,
occupational, and territorial validity. They are
not, however, allowed to make individual regulations, since they are only competent to undertake
collective regulation.

Constitutional Freedom to Organize

The framers of the constitution granted to
workers or civil servants the right to form trade
unions to secure their group interests in Article 9.

Here the individual right of a single person is extended to a collective action by a group that is
sanctioned by the constitution. This serves as the
basis for the authority of unions and employers'
associations to regulate working conditions.

Article 2 GG of the federal constitution ex-
presses the freedom for an individual to make decisions and develop his personality within his own
sphere at his own discretion. This right exists as
long as the interests of a third party are not
harmed. It is, therefore, necessary also to recognize constitutionally the right to stay out of any
organization. For some years this question was in
dispute, but a short time ago the Federal Labor
Court handed down a decision that the negative
right to organize is also guaranteed by the constitution. Therefore, the single citizen not only has
the right to join an existing trade union or to
form such a union with others but also is authorized
by the constitution not to use this right and to
keep aloof from collective action.

This last point creates certain disadvantages
in the execution of collective bargaining agreements. Most of current economic regulation is associated with pluralistic ways of thinking. Only
the trade union is authorized to appeal for strike
action, but the individual has no right to take
such sociopolitical measures. Certain legal standards, such as the Federal Vacation Law and the
Sick Pay Law, can be altered by the basic wage
agreement, but only the member of a trade union can
rely upon the application of these provisions without making a special agreement of his own with the
employer. Finally, the freedom from having to join
an organization has to be paid for by less security.

LEGAL ASPECTS OF INDUSTRIAL DISPUTES

The constitution of the Federal Republic of
Germany does not expressly grant associations, such
as trade unions and employers' associations, the
right to act in the interests of their members by
strikes or lockouts. Such means of furthering

industrial disputes are, however, sanctioned in some of the state constitutions.

Legal writings and precedents leave no doubt that Article 9 GG, with its guarantees of freedom of association, does, nevertheless, grant the right to attain improved working conditions by means of a strike. It is said that the freedom of association contains an immanent additional right to enforce the interests of one contractual party against the other by strike or lockout as well.

A strike is a planned and collectively executed work stoppage by a sizable number of employees, with or without notice, within one occupational group or one enterprise that also has the objective of continuing work after the purpose of the strike has been attained. A strike is characterized by the identical conduct of many employees with a view to a conscious and common purpose. A strike is a means of struggle directed against the contractual partner, the employer or employers' association, in order to force him to make certain concessions related to employment. A strike can begin only after a vote of all the workers affected--that is, those organized in a trade union. The vote is on the question of whether or not a given purpose is to be attained by a strike.

A legitimate strike has to serve to improve working conditions and must not be misused for other purposes, especially political ones. In such a case the collective work stoppage would mean a breach of contract, and the employees taking part would be acting unlawfully. The employer then has the right of giving the strikers a notice of dismissal or suing them for damages. This is the consequence of a "wildcat strike." A strike can be directed legally only against the contractual partner; it thus cannot be directed against a political institution, such as Parliament or other legislatures.

Furthermore, only the trade union itself can authorize a strike and not the elected representatives of employees in a public authority or the local personnel association or the shop stewards' council in a factory. This is because, according to the existing legal standards, such bodies are not merely representing employees according to the Shop Organization Law but also have to act in the interests of the well-being of the authority or enterprise.

This legal orientation is unfamiliar to American thinking on labor law. It is only the trade union that functions as the pure representative of worker interests, without also being bound by the interests of the enterprise. Nevertheless, since it is a constitutionally recognized regulatory power, the trade union has to consider the legal and economic constraints of the Federal Republic of Germany so as not to function in a destructive manner. Apart from this, the goals of the trade union may transcend the interests of the establishments.

Finally, the strike can only be the very last resort of an occupational organization. It should always be considered that the close economic linkages within the national and the international economy, the division of labor in production not only within one enterprise but within the entire domestic or even international economy, may cause a strike to have far-reaching, even disastrous, effects. This was not the case in former times, when more factories carried their production process from raw material to finished product. This results for the trade unions in a much higher obligation to exercise a sense of responsibility in the utilization of the strike weapon; it can be said with full satisfaction that since 1945 they have been conscious of these obligations toward the national economy.

Of course, it cannot be ignored that every industrial struggle, every work stoppage in the form of a strike, constitutes interference with a functioning economic activity and thus damages the national economy. This may well be a desired effect. It is only the damage imposed on the contractual partner by the strike that appears in the judgment of the parties involved to be a means of exacting the desired concessions on the improvement of working conditions.

Every strike must, however, be kept within the framework of constitutional and other legal orders.

No striker is allowed to carry out illegal acts and
then justify them by his participation in the
strike. A strike does not grant any other right
but that of stopping work and thereby suspending
the striker's duty toward his job; in this way the
default does not constitute a breach of contract.
It is illegal to coerce others by pressure to stop
working, to damage anything, or to cause physical
injury; such acts are punished by the usual criminal
law, even when they occur during a strike.

As a means of conducting an industrial dispute,
the lockout by the employer is the equivalent of
the strike. A planned lockout of a number of employees serves to reach some resolution of conflict
in connection with subsequent reemployment of these
workers.[7] Just like the strike, the lockout is a
collective measure against the contractual partner
by virtue of involving a majority of employees.
Matters of individual rights cannot be the motive
of such a lockout. Whereas the strike generally
represents an aggressive action against the employer
or the employers' association, the lockout is usually
a defensive action. It is rare that an employer
tries by means of a lockout to achieve some kind of
working conditions that he could not reach by way
of negotiation.

Every industrial struggle, whether strike or
lockout, has to conform to legal standards and to
acknowledge the duties deriving from them. Hence,
antistrike and antilockout obligations ("nonaggression clauses") must be kept during their period of
validity. Similar nonaggression clauses appear in
other German business law--in contracts between
licenser and licensee in patent agreements. In the
American legal system such agreements would come
under the purview of the strict antitrust laws,
under which they would have to be examined for legality.

In the laws governing basic wage agreements
this concept is called "the duty of maintaining the
peace"; such an arrangement may be expressly agreed
on between trade union and employers' association.
It is also, however, implied for the duration of
the contract between the two partners. Of course,

trade unions and employers' associations are always able within the applicable legal restraints to re-shape or even cancel the agreement if both are willing to do so. A contract can end by expiring, by a mutual agreement to cancel, or by giving no-tice of abrogation. It is impossible for one of the partners to force any change against the will of the other before the end of the contract.

According to German law, which is in turn based on legal precedents going back to Roman times, a contract cannot be changed unilaterally by one partner. Thus, the duty to maintain the peace un-der a basic wage agreement means that neither the trade union nor the employers' association is au-thorized to try to obtain an alteration of the con-tract during its period of validity by means of a strike or a lockout.

In assessing the objectives that trade unions as well as employers' associations try to achieve by means of industrial struggle, it may at first be thought that working relationships—that is, work and wages—are abolished during the period of struggle. Continuity of employment still exists, however, because the contractual partners are in the process of altering working conditions by fighting but intend to continue their relationship afterward. In legal writings and precedents this sequence of legal relationships is unanimously ac-cepted; industrial struggle does not touch the legal employment relationship but only suspends the duties to work and pay wages.

There do exist doubts, however, with respect to the effects of a lockout. The employer certainly wants to prevent his employees from working by this means; he has the right to stop payment of salaries or wages; he wants his employees to resume work af-terward. This desire to cooperate again in the interests of the enterprise when the struggle is over could lead to the view that a lockout has the effect of a temporary suspension. Considering, however, that "suspending" a worker who is striking anyway does not have the effect of forcing him to stop work, such an interpretation of a lockout makes no practical sense. The striker has a right

to stop work collectively within the framework of
legitimate industrial struggle and thereby loses
his claim to salary or wages. He does not acquire
additional burdens if he is locked out too.

Unless the employer declared that a suspension
of duties was his purpose, a lockout must have
valid objectives other than such a suspension. [8]
Two Senates of the Federal Labor Court had different views of this legal problem, and they have applied to the Supreme Senate of the Federal Labor
Court for a decision, which has not been provided
at the time of this writing.

The above-mentioned principles apply without
limit for all employees and workers in public employment and in federal, state, and local administrations. They do not, however, apply to civil
servants, who are appointed to their office by special documents. The employment of workers and
salaried employees cannot be looked upon and evaluated as a mere set of mutual duties. Every work
contract is also characterized by elements of individual rights. [9]

The position of a civil servant differs from
other kinds of employment by a relationship that
resembles the obligations of faithful service to
government, which was called "fealty" in the Middle
Ages. It also includes obligations for the welfare
of the employee by the employer. These relationships are emphasized by the fact that the civil
servant is appointed to his position for life, that
he can only lose his rights by disciplinary proceedings, that he cannot otherwise be given notice
of dismissal, and that he has a claim to retirement
pay, for which, however, he pays by receiving a
lower salary than does the industrial employee in a
similar position.

The welfare duties of an industrial employer
toward his employee correspond to the much stronger
similar relationship of the public authority toward
the civil servant. The obligation for the civil
servant to follow orders means relatively greater
subordination, not only in function but also in
person; this is why the civil servant is sometimes
called "a servant of the state."

In view of this subordination of the civil
servant to the sovereign power of the state and its
interpretation in jurisprudence and legal decisions,
a civil servant cannot be granted the right to
strike against the state or a public authority.
The position of the civil servant as a representative of the state on the one hand and as its subordinate agent on the other enforces a situation
that, however medieval this may appear, does not
permit a direct struggle against state, county, or
municipality.

This legal evaluation stems from the idea that
the state interprets its welfare duties in such a
way as to do its best to preserve the interests of
the officials entrusted to its care. Whether this
assumption is justified must be doubted. These
doubts are confirmed by the attempts, for example,
of postal employees to improve their working conditions by a strict and formal conformity to the
rules, whereas airport controllers and the police
tried to do the same thing by measures resembling
strikes.

PUBLIC SERVICE

The public service of the Federal Republic of
Germany includes civil servants, judges, workers,
and other employees. The expression "public service" only means that a person works for a public
body, which has sovereign powers within the federal
sphere, state, county, or municipality. Therefore,
the expression "public service" does not derive in
the first instance from labor law but, rather, from
public law, and it concerns the sphere of the "sovereign power" rather than the working person.

Article 33, Paragraph 4, of the federal constitution says that the execution of sovereign
functions has to be delegated to members of the
public service, these persons being subject to public service and loyalty; here, certainly, the basic
parameters of civil servants are defined. The
status of the civil servant is subordinated to public law, which requires the civil servant to remain

loyal and the employer to care for and protect his
employee.[10]

The working relations of a civil servant are
usually based on a lifetime of service and are established constitutionally by presenting the document of appointment to the civil servant. He, in
turn, commits himself to place his time, working
power, indeed his whole personality, permanently,
exclusively, unconditionally, and absolutely at the
disposal of the interests of the office conferred
upon him. Work in the public service does not necessarily consist of taking executive actions, but
it does so often, or in most cases. But this is
only the case if the tasks of public service show
clearly the characteristics of subordination to
public order and exercise of sovereign power.

Still, when one considers the diversity of
state or community activities, it becomes evident
that the boundaries between public and private activities are fluid. The owner of a house and property has the obligation to accept the service of
municipal refuse disposal and has to pay the taxes
or fees for the job; this obligation is subordinated
to the sovereign power of the community. The individual citizen cannot at his own discretion evade
this obligation or make private arrangements for
the performance of this service. The actual work
of refuse disposal, however, is really done in a
"private" way; the municipal worker employed by the
sanitation authority is not armed with "sovereign
power."

The boundary between activities within public
and civil law is especially clear when one examines
the tasks of a chimney sweep. If he enforces safety
regulations, especially when he performs inspec-
tions for the Department of Building, examines new
buildings, and requires building changes to enhance
fire safety, he is acting as a representative of
the sovereign power in accordance with public law.
If, however, a house owner asks him for expert advice with respect to some building or if the chimney sweep does some brick-laying work as a part-
time job, these are certainly purely private trans-
actions.

Of course, the civil servants working within a public authority, a provincial association, a community, or a city administration are usually engaged in public duties in relation to the citizens. If, however, a community, acting through its mayor or other chief executive, and he in turn represented through a civil servant, buys or sells real property, this is a mere fiscal activity, and the relationship between the community and the partner in such a transaction belongs to the civil law. Here superiority or subordination does not exist, but, rather, both partners are equal and have equal rights.

If it is borne in mind that acting on behalf of the sovereign power is the dominant work content of civil servants, it becomes understandable that within the legal sphere of the Federal Republic of Germany the rights of civil servants are mainly regulated by formal laws. There are the federal and state civil service laws, together with their disciplinary regulations and also regulations governing career ladders, provisions for interruptions and terminations, job descriptions and salary schedules, vacation pay and leaves of absence, and, finally, retirement pay.

As a result of these historic developments employees and workers in private industry have defined their minimum working conditions in basic wage agreements, whereas for civil servants these are set forth in laws. These laws are of a collective character, but in the Federal Republic of Germany a law is not termed a collective regulation and there is a clear distinction between laws, collective bargaining contracts, basic wage agreements, and agreements governing particular establishments.

It cannot be predicted today whether or not these legal forms will continue--that is, that all relationships concerning the civil service have to be by way of laws and the legislation process. Rather, the growing importance of trade unions in the republic's jurisprudence economy and social order may lead to change, such as eventually creating a "skeletal law," leaving everyting else to be regulated by collective agreements. The decision

will depend on political developments and may be
decisively determined by the extent to which trade
unions, as professional organizations, are able to
make their influence felt in government and legislative assemblies in the form of legislative initiatives.

It is noteworthy in this connection that more
than half the members of the present German Bunde-
stag are also members of trade unions, a circumstance that is constitutionally compatible with
their mandate as members. In the same way the position of the civil servant does permit him--based
on Article 9 of the federal constitution (freedom
of organization)--to join a trade union or organization of civil servants that follows objectives related to the professional status of its members.

Judges occupy a special position within this
framework. Although the civil servant generally
functions in an administrative office in the federal, state, or municipal sphere, the judge belongs
to the third major branch of government. According
to the delegation of powers conferred upon them by
public law, they exercise their juridical function
in parallel with the two other branches of govern-
ment--the legislative and administrative areas. As
in Montesquieu's doctrine of the separation of
powers, judges are to be considered as part of the
public service but not as civil servants.

This does not, of course, exclude their being
treated as civil servants when it comes to their
rights of remuneration. They are appointed to
their office in line with the rules governing civil
servants and receive a document of appointment in
accordance with public law. Salaries, leaves, disability assistance, and retirement pay follow the
principles of civil service law.

In contrast to civil servants, however, a
judge is not subject to the instructions of an official superior while exercising his juridical
functions. The decision made by a judge can only
be evaluated or changed by presenting the necessary
legal remedies through stages of appeal, which in
Germany are the county or magistrates' courts,
state court, and then state court of appeals or

else the state court, state court of appeals, and
then federal courts. This independence of the judiciary from administrative instructions is explicitly set forth in the constitution.

Since, however, the judges receive their salaries in accordance with the regulations for civil
servants, the principles previously mentioned are
also valid for them. It is still legal practice in
the Federal Republic of Germany to fix the salaries,
personal rights, and duties of judges even outside
of their judicial activities by means of formal
laws, such as a special code for judges and salary
schedules.

Whether this practice will still hold in the
future with respect to the salary aspect of judicial
appointments cannot be predicted any more than with
civil servants. The pay of judges is comparable to
that of other civil servants in jobs that require a
university education, but the professional organization of judges has striven for an independent salary
schedule formally distinct from that of civil servants; sociopolitical influences are bound to affect
future parliamentary discussions, which are bound
to be finally decisive.

Other principles are valid for office workers
in public service. Their legal relationships are
generally regulated by basic wage agreements fixing
minimum working conditions. The contractual partners in these agreements are individual public authorities or special organizations of such authorities, forming the employers' associations on the one
hand and the public service, transport, and traffic
union on the other hand.

An office worker or salaried employee in this
sense is one committed to taking over a position
whose duties are subject to contractual definitions.
The position is confined to office work. The difference between the civil servant and the office
worker is that the latter is not officially appointed
to his position but, rather, has a private work
contract in the sense of the German civil code. He
is, in turn, distinguished from the worker because
his activity is predominantly not physical labor.

Just as in the case of the industrial worker,
the nomenclature is not decisive, although it can

give an indication of how the job is to be evaluated.
Only the working requirements objectively defined
are decisive. If an activity is defined by salary
groupings, the relevant basic wage agreements or
public regulations, like insurance, must treat the
affected employees as office workers. An example
might be a civil engineer employed in the building
department of a municipality. He may perform his
activity as a civil servant or as an office employee,
according to the nature of the basic work relationship.

A worker is employed in a subordinate position,
and his duties are mostly physical. [11] As in the
case of the office worker, the literal definition
of the occupation is not decisive. Rather, it depends on whether he belongs to the legal old age
and disability insurance scheme. Further, he may
belong to an industrial worker group by virtue of
being governed by a respective basic wage agreement,
which is the case especially in newly developed occupational specialties. In general, industrial
workers are grouped into unskilled, semiskilled, and
skilled workers and then craftsmen.

It must be recognized that during recent years
sociopolitical trends in the Federal Republic of
Germany have led to a considerable moderation of
the formerly sharp differences in the regulations
of office and industrial workers. All groups are
equally protected by the laws against dismissal,
the disability and maternity laws, and the laws for
protecting young workers. There are still different
regulations with respect, for example, to length of
notice of dismissal and the allowance of rest periods after convalescence. It is noteworthy, however, that under a law for continued wage payments
of January 1, 1970, six weeks of continuing wage or
salary payments are granted to office and industrial
workers alike. There is still, however, a distinction between office and industrial workers in the
provisions on old age insurance, as well as in the
basic wage agreements themselves that have been
agreed upon between the public service, transport,
and traffic union and the employers' associations.

The growing mechanization, automation, and
technical refinement, however, which has recently

become evident in public service as well, has led
to a blurring and imprecision in the historically
evident boundaries between office employees (mostly
mental activity) and workers (mostly physical labor). [12] From this historical background it is understandable that the messenger is considered an
office worker, although his work requires fewer
mental demands than does the work of a mechanic in
a research and development department. It is
equally doubtful whether a card-punch operator in
an electronic data-processing department deserves
the appellation "office worker" more than does a
foreman in a machine repair workshop who exercises
some managerial functions.

These considerations show that the historic boundary between office employees and workers is kept
for sociopolitical and, in part, financial reasons
where there are problems in distinguishing between
the two, which must, in turn, be decided by collective agreements. Future developments will answer the question whether this boundary will endure
or whether there will be principles of work evaluation that are based on the work content itself,
such as the necessary expert knowledge, the degree
of physical strain, the responsibility, and the
influence of the environment. These may become decisive for the legal regulations of working conditions.

In 1971 at least a draft of the second install-
ment of the recodification of labor law for the
Federal Republic of Germany was expected. This is
not yet an omnibus bill that would eliminate the
distinctions as irrelevant, but the trend toward
equal treatment under law of office employees and
workers will be considerably furthered by it. It
may, therefore, be expected that the right to in-
spect personnel records will be recognized and that
the recognition of contractually established prohibitions against competition between workers will
be equally as valid as that for office employees.
This would not only abolish the still existing different treatment of employees in commercial and
technical positions but would also justify a far-
reaching equalization of treatment between office
employees and workers.

Moreover, it is not only in separating activities of office workers from those of industrial workers that difficulties arise in modern production. As soon as public organizations work in private spheres or private enterprises fulfill public tasks, it becomes quite clear that a distinction between the two can be derived neither from the activity itself nor from the persons taking part. In a given case it may be possible to determine whether a certain activity represents an exercise of governmental power or lies within the private sphere, but neither the authority concerned nor its representative can be described as acting only publicly or only privately.

In the Federal Republic of Germany this functional mixture in the activities of a public authority has led to the decision by a number of institutions having public as well as private functions to submit the rules governing the treatment of their officials, employees, and workers to the law of public service. There are, for example, a variety of organizations of technical inspectors that are organized in the form of private associations but have public functions in such activities as the inspection of elevators, chimneys, or electric motors.

This group also includes the associations of sewage disposal authorities, the medical associations, the academies of art and sciences, technical institutes, the administrations of foundations, the associations of savings banks, old age pension funds and banks, the employers' liability insurance fund, museums, research centers, religious institutions, the German Federal Railways, the Associations of Home Economic Schools, state insurance companies, public liability insurance companies, the Prussian State Bank, bar associations, and the universities.

This shows clearly that, on the one hand, the public service is subject to the collective bargaining laws for government employees but that, on the other hand, additional institutions are similarly situated because they perform mainly a public rather than a private function.

If, according to the area of validity of the relevant basic wage agreement, it is not binding on

such groups and institutions, they do not use this
approach in their relationships with the employees
(arts. 3 and 4 of the Law of Basic Wage Agreements).
The partners in these working relationships cannot,
however, be prevented from agreeing on contracts
that collectively regulate working conditions.
There does exist a legal difference in the effectiveness of these contracts as contrasted with
basic wage agreements, as will be made clear later
in this chapter.

Organizational Structure of
Trade Unions

The formation of trade unions is based on Article 9 of the federal constitution, which gives
legal legitimacy to freedom of association. Thus,
a trade union can be formed if a sufficient number
of interested persons get together with the joint
objective of achieving professional or occupational
representation and improvement of working conditions, if necessary by industrial struggle.
    According to the value judgments of the civil
code, the trade unions should take the legal form of
a registered membership corporation, but in practice most German trade unions generally remain unin-
corporated. As noted above, the principle reason
why trade unions refrain from incorporation is the
burden of constantly having to register a changing
membership with the local registration court and
having to pay the necessary fees for this. Further,
the courts, including the supreme courts, have
granted to the trade unions the advantages of limited liability that incorporated associations enjoy;
thus, judges do not compel individual members to be
liable beyond their membership contribution.
    In order to represent the interests of union
members effectively, if necessary by a strike, the
union has to assure by means of appropriate bylaws
that only persons really working can join it as
members. This furthers the principle of freedom
from internal opposition or conflict of interest.
For the employers' association these principles are

also valid. In practice, the realization of these principles is not always strictly enforced, because otherwise membership could not be granted to union officials who joined at an earlier time while still actually working.

Since 1945 trade unions in the Federal Republic of Germany have been organized on an industrial basis--that is, within a trade union only members of one industrial grouping are included. This has the objective that within one industry only one trade union is faced by a single employers' association. In public service civil servants, office employees, and workers are organized in the trade union for public service, transport, and traffic, as well as the Federation of German Civil Servants and the German Federation of Office Workers.

The Federal Republic of Germany has a principle that is unwritten but has nevertheless become common law--that establishing unity of wage structure. This is a departure from the legal order in other countries, such as Great Britain. This means that within a given establishment only those basic wage agreements should hold that correspond to the activity of the great majority of those employed there.

An establishment is a working technical and organizational unit in which one employer or public authority works for a single specified purpose. This can be the management of a municipal theater, a riding academy, or a gas works. The concept of "establishment" thus differs from that of "firm" in the private sector. From the viewpoint of public authorities the city of Cologne owns an establishment in the form of a municipal electricity plant, as well as several others of similar category, such as the municipal transit system, the airport, and a real property administration. The city thus corresponds to the firm in the private sector, such as Opel AG with its plants in Rüsselsheim, Bochum, and elsewhere.

The principle of unity of wage structure does not apply to all plants of one firm or all plants or institutions of a town or state but only to single such institutions, like the museum or the theater. If a town has a theater in which it employs not only actors but also technical and commercial staff, they are all subordinated to the principle of unity of wage structure; the employees and workers may be governed by different rules, but on the whole they must be treated equally. If, for example, repair mechanics and electricians are employed by the theater, they are not governed by the basic wage agreement for the metal-working industry but, rather, by that for the theaters of the town--that is, most likely, the basic wage agreement for public service.

Organization of Employers' Associations

According to Article 3 of the Law of Basic Wage Agreements a single employer and also a town are able to agree on collective bargaining contracts for any single plant. During recent years, however, most such negotiations have taken place with employers' associations, which, like unions, either remain unregistered or, if registered, like unions, are private membership corporations. They are authorized by their members to agree upon contracts with those employees governed by the basic wage agreement for public service.

BINDING CHARACTER OF BASIC WAGE AGREEMENTS

Since all working agreements are determined by the legally binding provisions of the basic wage agreement, these have central significance for the law governing such agreements. According to Article 3 of the Law of Basic Wage Agreements a binding relationship is established only when both contractual partners are directly connected by way of membership with the trade union or employers' association to which the basic wage agreement applies.

Neither the employers' association nor an employer or trade union is authorized to fix collective standards in favor or disfavor of a third party--that is, "an outsider." The current law does not recognize compulsory membership for trade unions or employers' associations, as was the case during the Nazi period, with its Law for the Regulation of National Labor of 1934 (abolished in 1946 by the Allied Control Commission). Any other interpretation would be contrary to the principle of "negative" freedom recognized by the constitution.

Basic wage agreements have immediate and immutable features in accordance with Paragraph 4, Item 1, of the Law of Basic Wage Agreements. The immediacy means that basic wage agreements in public service create binding minimum rights without the need for any other special agreement. They are like the law governing single working agreements, which bars contracts more unfavorable than the basic wage agreement.

The related principle of immutability of wage scales leads to the possibility of more favorable agreements in a single working contract, but agreements less favorable to the employee are ruled out. Such an arrangement is possible only if there is legislation that expressly allows an arrangement of basic wage agreements more unfavorable for the employee. There are some areas, such as the determination of sick pay or regulations with respect to the Federal Vacation Law, that may be expressly altered in a wage agreement relative to what the law provides.

Another characteristic is the principle of "best terms." In the last analysis the basic wage agreement establishes rights of protection and regulation, and, therefore, its provisions in public service set up minimum working conditions but not maximum ones, such as those in the wage freeze in Germany in 1939. Thus, a single working contract may grant more favorable conditions for the employee, such as longer vacations or a higher salary or hourly wage than required by the basic wage agreement.

In this way the contractual partners in public service also have the opportunity of granting better working conditions by recognizing better performance by an individual or group--that is, merit beyond expectations. Beyond this, such arrangements can also serve to equalize shortages in the labor market or higher costs of living in various cities or towns.

Collective bargaining can ultimately establish only a general framework for regulation, which has the advantage of establishing clear performance duties under law. It cannot make allowance for the peculiarities of a single case. For this, general regulations are not adaptable enough. Collective regulation stresses principles of order and the requirement of legal security over the effort to reward special performance on the part of civil servants, employees, and workers in public service. In comparison with the private sector, such adjustments in the public service can take place only within narrow limits.

Civil service law, in general, prohibits the favoring of one official over another in the same position because legislation prescribes the respective range of salaries for the various activities. In practice, exceptions are sometimes made by promoting a civil servant when his functions alone would not provide a real basis for such a promotion or by a higher job rating for a given activity. Formally, the principle is preserved that every civil servant has a claim to the salary to which his position entitles him. A higher job rating, however, can lead to improvement of the financial situation.

With office employees and workers in the public service such difficulties do not exist in a formal sense because the basic wage agreement, viewed as a source of legal regulation, has more flexibility than the law itself has. Still, public service requires a rather rigid application of the wage and salary structure. Special qualifications of individual employees cannot readily be considered because the budgets of the states, counties, and communities prescribe fixed expenses with detailed job descriptions for the office employees and workers. Therefore, there is little leeway for adjustments of contract provisions, even though the possibility of making such arrangements should legally exist according to the principle of "best terms" as given in the Law of Basic Wage Agreements.

Another characteristic of basic wage agreements in the public service establishes the possibility

of "special contracts." It may happen that within
a community or, for that matter, on the federal
level a collective bargaining contract may include
the workers in an electric power station and in a
municipal transport undertaking. Then the question
arises, which basic wage agreement should be applied. In such a case the principle of "best terms"
cannot be applied, and it does not matter which of
the two basic wage agreements might be more favorable for the employees. Rather, the existence of
specialization is decisive here, with the more nar-
rowly written contract taking precedence over the
general one.

Finally, basic wage agreements can be made generally binding, even within the public service.
Whereas Paragraphs 3 and 4 of the Law of Basic Wage
Agreements establish their validity for the private sector, Paragraph 5 does the same with respect
to public service in the Federal Republic of Germany. The prospective contractual partners have to
make application to the Federal Minister of Labor,
who may then issue a declaration making a contract
legally binding; he may do so whenever a public interest is involved and at least 50 percent of the
employees are covered by the agreement.

This does not constitute interference with the
freedom of the partners to a basic wage agreement.
They still have the opportunity of canceling or
changing it at any time. The sole function of the
Federal Minister of Labor is limited to extending
by executive order the coverage of the basic wage
agreement to those persons who as nonunionists (or,
similarly, nonmembers of the employers' association)
would not be covered.

TACTICS AND OBJECTIVES OF TRADE UNIONS

The Law of Basic Wage Agreements is, in the
last analysis, a law of professional or occupational
organizations. The trade union is the contractual
partner that tries to improve the working conditions
of its members, if necessary by a strike. As previously mentioned, the basic wage agreement grants

obligatory and immutable working conditions in favor of the employees. Naturally, the trade union
tries at all times to make the provisions obtained
as firm and as binding as possible. The difference
between actual and contractual working conditions
is kept as small as possible.

    In the face of these endeavors it might be
said that employers would not really sacrifice anything by giving in to such requests. This is not
correct, however, because conditions granted by an
individual agreement can always be altered by mutual
consent. In times of full employment it may not be
easy to reach such an agreement, perhaps only if
the enterprise itself is in a critical situation.
The legal way of entering into a contract remains
open, but it would be effectively lost if all claims
were immutably regulated by the basic wage agreement. All this makes it clear why any improvement
over and above minimum conditions often means serious conflict, even if no real improvement in actual
pay results.

    From the point of view of the trade unions,
their claims are best made in times of boom, when
employers are especially dependent upon the active
cooperation of their employees. The need for special efficiency depends upon the economic situation,
but in the sphere of public service it is also determined by political decisions. It is not easily
possible to raise electric or gas rates, prices for
theater tickets, or admission charges for municipal
swimming pools at a time when the employees happen
to be tactically well situated. Possibly the upward income trends may be inflationary, and for political reasons the public service employers are
very cautious with respect to measures that would
raise prices.

    Trade unions are also of the opinion that a
high level of employment and vacancy rate means a
more favorable time for bargaining with the employers or employers' associations than periods of unemployment. The trade union tries to make sure
that its demands are endorsed by friendly political
parties and timed as favorably as possible. A
trade union in the public service must win public

understanding because eventually many people may be
charged more money in order to produce higher wages
for a small number of employees.

Naturally, negotiations should be the main
means of realizing the sociopolitical aims of the
trade unions. Thus, they will always try to reach
a contract by mutual agreement with the public service employers' associations. Beyond this, there
is the possibility of striking, but this is often
mitigated by arbitration agreements. These provide
for an independent arbitrator, trusted by both parties, who can devise a suitable compromise solution.

SUMMARY OF CIVIL SERVICE RULES
AND SALARY SCHEDULE

The legal rights of civil servants have a long
history. As early as the end of the sixteenth century, German officials received fixed salaries,
whereas in other countries a perquisite system prevailed. This system of payment was based on assess-
ments of perquisites or fees, and the individual
official was paid a proportion of them. It is
clear that such a system, although it is still used
today in a few areas, such as the consular service,
does not provide equality of pay with respect to
performance or function.

It was not until the 1820s that authorities
succeeded in establishing a fixed schedule of salaries. These were graded, with the highest official
receiving the highest salary and decreasing in a
sliding scale in accordance with the rank. The laws
issued at that time provided for two kinds of salary increase: Either the official was promoted to
a higher rank or he was advanced in the same salary
class.[13] On the whole, both principles are still
valid today, even though payment according to efficiency is only aimed at, but not yet achieved.
There are two schools of thought. Some look upon
the salary as mere wages (the theory of efficiency),
whereas others consider the salary of an official
to be remuneration for his putting his whole personality at the service of the state (the theory of
subsistence).

As noted previously, states and communities, as well as the federal government, tried to evade the rigidity of this system by raising the job evaluations for the same position without actually asking for the appropriate higher qualifications. To consider this comprehensive regulation of the legal position of the civil servant, the civil service law of the state of Nordrhein-Westfalen of June 1, 1962, which is based on the federal civil service law can be taken as an example.

This first part of this law comprises regulations concerning the letter of appointment and related formalities, provisions for transfers to other locations or activities, and provisions for resignations, release from service, retirement, or loss of civil service rights. The second part explains the principles concerning the legal position of a civil servant acting on behalf of the sovereign power, such as entering service, significance, content and limits of official actions, official secrets regulation, prohibition against secondary jobs, prevention of bribery, regulation of working hours, a dress code, and the consequences of non-fulfillment of duties.

Another chapter tells of the rights of the official to protection while on duty, jubilee bonuses, liability for damage, job descriptions, and service record. Another section deals with pension rights, old age insurance, care for widows and orphans, and disability insurance. Finally, there are some special provisions for certain offices, such as civil servants in the state legislature, honorary civil servants, officials of the communities, the association of municipalities, and public bodies. In this last sphere, rank order is especially emphasized.

The large number of basic wage agreements that are in force limits this description to a brief overview. The basis of the legal relationships of public employees is the basic wage agreement for employees in the federal civil service of February 23, 1961, with many later amendments in various areas of competence and salary groups. There are 12 chapters, with a total of 74 sections, generally

regulating all legal rights of employees in public
service.

Chapter 1 defines the validity of the contract.
Chapter 2 contains the formalities necessary for
acceding to the contract, the written document,
extra agreements, and periods of probation. Chapter 3 contains general rules for a medical examination, the duties of disclosure when entering service, secrecy, prohibition of corruption, rules on
secondary jobs, and transfers. Chapter 4 deals
with working hours, Saturday work and work before
holidays, overtime, or absences. Chapter 5 gives
the regulations on terms of office.

Together with Chapter 7, Chapter 6 has a central importance because it contains all details
concerning the classification into salary groups
and pay grades, as shown in Table 9. In general,
the employees in public service receive a basic
allowance that is arranged in 17 salary groups or
grades, each of which also shows a sliding scale
according to the age of the employee. Chapters
8-12 deal with the regulations for fringe benefits,
travel expenses, old age pensions, survivors' insurance, leaves of absence, vacations, and terminations of employment.

The basic wage agreements for industrial workers, like those for office employees, also include
detailed regulations, including salary groups and
wage schedules. They display a growing trend toward changing the historical grouping of workers
into unskilled, semiskilled, and fully skilled
workers. An increasingly fine differentiation has
taken place, based on the principles of job evaluation. It is not a matter of the expert knowledge
of a single worker being decisive. The gradation
of wages is based on the difficulty of the work.
The job evaluation is based on the professional
skills needed for a proper execution of the work,
physical and mental strain, responsibility, and
such environmental influences as noise, dirt, danger of accidents, and special handicaps.

It is to be expected that such circumstances
will be considered even more in future developments.
Beyond this, the basic wage agreements have sections

TABLE 9

Basic Monthly Salaries for Office Workers Employed after Completing Ages 21-49,
Federal Republic of Germany
(in DM)

Salary Group (grade)	Salary Increment Within Grade	21	23	25	27	29	31	33	35	37	39	41	43	45	47	49
I a	77		1,684	1,761	1,838	1,915	1,992	2,069	2,146	2,223	2,300	2,377	2,454	2,531	2,605	
I b	74		1,497	1,571	1,645	1,719	1,793	1,867	1,941	2,015	2,089	2,163	2,237	2,311	2,385	
II a	68		1,327	1,395	1,463	1,531	1,599	1,667	1,735	1,803	1,871	1,939	2,007	2,075		
II b	62		1,237	1,299	1,361	1,423	1,485	1,547	1,609	1,671	1,733	1,795	1,857	1,884		
III	58	1,179	1,237	1,295	1,353	1,411	1,469	1,527	1,585	1,643	1,701	1,759	1,817	1,872		
IV a	53	1,069	1,122	1,175	1,228	1,281	1,334	1,387	1,440	1,493	1,546	1,599	1,652	1,705		
IV b	42	978	1,020	1,062	1,104	1,146	1,188	1,230	1,272	1,314	1,356	1,398	1,440	1,446		
V a	37	856	893	930	967	1,004	1,041	1,078	1,115	1,152	1,189	1,226	1,263	1,297		
V b	37	856	893	930	967	1,004	1,041	1,078	1,115	1,152	1,189	1,226	1,263	1,265		
V c	35	798	833	868	903	938	973	1,008	1,043	1,078	1,113	1,148				
VI a	27	748	775	802	829	856	883	910	937	964	991	1,018	1,045	1,072	1,099	1,122
VI b	27	748	775	802	829	856	883	910	937	964	991	1,018	1,039			
VII	22	681	703	725	747	769	791	813	835	857	879	901	917			
VIII	20	619	639	659	679	699	719	739	759	779	794					
IX a	19	593	612	631	650	669	688	707	726	743						
IX b	18	564	582	600	618	636	654	672	690	703						
X	18	512	530	548	566	584	602	620	638	650						

dealing with the formalities for agreeing on them,
the duties of the worker, the right to inspection
of personnel records, the duty of the authority to
give testimonials, leaves, and severance provisions.

FUTURE TRENDS

Collective bargaining agreements are already
of central importance not only in the sphere of
private business but also in public service, together with the laws concerning civil servants.
The perceptible political tendency within the Federal Republic of Germany is to develop further the
right of representation for the personnel, including
shop organizations, and, in addition, the right of
codetermination. This would let the employees take
over a higher responsibility not only in industry
but also in public service by making them take part
in decisions. All this should lead to maintaining
or increasing the participation of employees in
shaping the rights and laws of labor themselves.
Further, supranational economic relationships,
such as those in the European Common Market, cannot
fail to influence legal developments within Germany.
The International Labor Office (ILO) and the social
objectives set forth by organs of the United Nations,
as well as religious institutions, exert further
influences on collective bargaining. The present
chapter can only show the present status and indicate some probable trends; it can only offer a hint
for the more distant future.

PUBLIC EMPLOYEES IN ITALY

Definitions

Public employment can be defined as "the legal relationship whereby an individual professionally serves, for compensation, assuming specific rights and duties, a public entity to achieve its institutional purposes."[1] The public entity could be either the state itself or any subdivision or agency thereof.*

Public employees--that is, persons bound by a relationship of public employment--can be divided into numerous categories, depending on the type of public entity by which they are employed or the nature of the functions performed. Such distinctions are reflected in the legislation governing public employment, which can vary considerably for each category.

A complete classification of the various categories of public employees would exceed the scope of this chapter, which shall limit itself to those categories of greater general interest engaging in collective bargaining and strikes. Distinction

---

*The state itself is a public entity, but this term will be used exclusively to indicate public entities other than the state.

must first be made between state employees and employees of other public entities.

State Employees

The principal category of state employees is
constituted by civil servants, whose status is governed by Presidential Decree No. 3 of January 10,
1957, promulgated pursuant to Law 1181 of December
20, 1954, delegating to the government the power to
enact new legislation on the status of civil servants and other state employees.

The 1957 decree, which with its 386 articles
is the principal authority governing public employment, is nonetheless not applicable to all state
employees. Other important categories--such as
judges, teachers, and employees of public agencies--
are subject to special laws governing their employment.

It is noteworthy that, although employees of
independent government agencies (railroads, post office and telecommunications, state monopolies, and
so forth) are governed by special legislation, they
are still considered state employees. Their status
is, therefore, considerably different from that of
employees of government corporations (which will be
covered below), notwithstanding their being engaged
in similar activities--that is, production or services.

State laborers constitute a separate category,
which is differentiated from that of civil servants
inasmuch as their work does not involve any managerial, administrative, and clerical services but
simply the performance of manual labor. Their
legal status is regulated principally by Law 90 of
March 5, 1961. There are also career servicemen,
whose employment has regulations very different
from those applicable to civil servants.

Employees of Public Entities

Employees of public entities can be divided
into three general categories: employees of local

entities, employees of government agencies, and employees of state corporations. Local entities are
those subdivisions of the state with activities limited to a certain area of the national territory.
Principal among these are the regions, the provinces,
and the communes. The regions have been recently
created by Law 281 of May 16, 1970, which also governs the status of regional employees. Communal
and provincial employees are governed by Articles
220 and following of the Communal and Provincial
Law of 1934, supplemented by the separate regulations of each entity.

Governmental agencies are public entities created directly by the state for the accomplishment of
certain public functions or services that are national in character. Among these are, for example, the
principal social security and welfare entities like
the National Social Security Institute (l'Istituto
Nazionale della Previdenza Sociale, INPS), National
Institute for Workmen's Compensation (l'Istituto
Nazionale per l'Assicurazione degli Infortuni sul
Lavoro, INAIL), National Health Insurance Institute
(l'Istituto Nazionale Assicurazioni Contro le
Malattie, INAM), and Maternity and Infancy Welfare
Organization (l'Opera Nazionale Maternità e Infanzia,
ONMI). Employment in these organizations is gov-
erned, in addition to the laws establishing them, by
regulations of each separate organization and, there-
fore, can vary considerably from one to the other.

State corporations, known as "public economic
entities," operate for profit and are organized on
an equal and competitive basis with private enterprises having similar purposes. Among these are
investment, commercial, and savings banks; the National Electric Power Authority (ENEL); and the Industrial Reconstruction Corporation (IRI) and its
many subsidiaries (Finsider, Fincantieri, Finmeccan-
ica, Finmare, and so forth).

Employees of state corporations cannot compare
with other public servants, because the master/
servant relationship resembles that existing in
private business. Collective bargaining is admissible for employees of state corporations, as opposed to the categories previously cited. Another

basic difference is that disputes arising out of
the employment relationship are submitted to the
jurisdiction of the courts with regard to employees
of state corporations and to special administrative
judiciary bodies in the case of other public employees.

Two categories of private employees have a
status similar in certain aspects to that of public
employees: employees of private enterprises that
are licensed by the state to engage in public utilities and conveyances and personnel of private corporations in which the state owns the controlling
interest. Concessionaires of public services are,
in fact, subject to government control, which in
certain cases extends to the regulation of the employment status. Furthermore, as will be seen
later, the general-interest nature of such services
seems to permit restrictions on the right to strike.

The corporations controlled by the government
are obviously those of which it is the sole or major
shareholder. Said control, however, does not affect
the employment status, which remains private in nature. The organizing of these corporations in connection with collective bargaining is affected instead, as will be seen in the treatment of public
employers' associations, below.

Statistical Data

A listing of the number of public employees
according to category could be useful for a clearer
picture of the problems that will be covered, as
well as for a better understanding of the divisions
made above. It is not possible to obtain precise
data covering all the fields of public employment.
In particular, although there is an accurate publication by the Ministry of the Treasury on employees
in national government administrations, accurate
figures on employees of other public entities are
not available.[2]

On January 1, 1968, state employees numbered
1,381,670[3] out of 18,813,000 persons employed in
Italy in industry, agriculture, and services, including the government,[4] divided as follows:

Civil servants (employees of ministries and their extensions, other than those listed below)	253,115
Judges	7,394
Teachers	401,081
Career servicemen in the armed forces	307,302
Laborers	54,074
Special status personnel	22,677
Employees of independent state authorities	336,027
	1,381,670

Employees of independent state authorities can be further subdivided as follows:

State Monopoly Administration (Amministrazione Monopoli dello Stato), production of salt and tobacco	17,862
National Road Authority (Azienda Nazionale Autonoma delle Strade, ANAS)	12,233
Post Office and Telecommunications Administration	127,613
State Telephone Authority (Azienda di Stato per i Servizi Telefonici), for international calls only; domestic telephone calls are serviced by SIP, a state corporation	13,142
National Railroad Authority (Ferrovie dello Stato)	165,177
	336,027

There are no accurate figures available with respect to employees of the communes and provinces (approximately 600,000), the other government agencies, and the state corporations.

No figures are available on the five regions
established in the past by special laws (Sardinia,
Sicily, Val d'Aosta, Trentino-Alto Adige, and
Friuli-Venezia Giulia) and obviously none with respect to the regions newly created by Law 281.
Since the resulting decentralization of administrative functions will leave the national government
with a surplus of personnel, it is now contemplating
the transfer of civil servants to regional governments.

UNION ORGANIZATION IN GENERAL

A knowledge of labor law with respect to public
employment cannot be had without a clear understanding of union organization in general. An outline of
the historical development of union organization and
the general principles currently underlying said organization is therefore in order.

Because of its extensiveness, the topic of
union organization will be dealt with in two parts.
First, the legal and organizational structure of
unions will be covered in general, and the principles applicable to both private and public sectors
will be highlighted. Then, particular attention
will be given to those aspects peculiar to unions
of public employees. In subsequent sections, below,
concerning collective bargaining and strikes, a summary on the general situation will introduce the
special treatment of matters related to the status
of public employees.

General Principles and Structure

The Italian system of union representation
stems from the 1948 constitution, Articles 39 and
40, providing for freedom to organize and to strike,
respectively. Since no enabling legislation has
yet been enacted for the implementation of said provisions, their coordination with preexisting laws
is required, many of which date back to the fascist
era and are therefore inspired by labor relations

concepts diametrically opposed to those acceptable
today.

This coexistence of norms that reflect con-
trasting ideologies has been and still is the cause
of conflicts that are frequently brought before the
Constitutional Court. This court has on various
occasions declared unlawful, in whole or in part,
certain laws inconsistent with Articles 39 and 40
of the constitution. Inasmuch as some of these decisions will be referred to further on, it could be
useful to underscore the radical differences existing between the fascist union system and that
brought into being by the new constitution.

The "corporative union system," created during
the fascist era, was based principally on Law 563
of April 3, 1926, and on the Carta del Lavoro
(Labor Charter) of April 21, 1927.[5] These authorities provided only formal recognition of the freedom to organize by allowing the de facto establishment of nonrecognized unions. But, in substance,
the power to engage in any union activity was reserved exclusively to the so-called recognized
unions. Only one such union existed for each category, and all were tightly controlled by the government and by the one political party in power.

The recognized unions had the power to enter
into collective bargaining agreements that were
binding on each individual of the category concerned,
including nonmembers of the union. Such agreements
could not be waived by individual employment contracts, unless the latter incorporated conditions
more favorable to the worker. Collective disputes
were to be brought before the labor courts in case
of failure to agree, after a statutory attempt to
settle. In this system, which presupposed the settlement of all disputes, strikes and lockouts were
prohibited.

This system was abolished with the fall of
fascism.* It was replaced by diametrically opposed
principles contained in the constitution granting

----

*See Law Decree 369 of November 23, 1944,
which suppressed the fascist union organization.

freedom to organize unions and the right to strike.
Article 39 of the constitution provides as follows:

> Freedom to organize. No obligation
> can be imposed on unions other than
> registration with local or central
> offices, as provided by law.
> A prerequisite to registration
> is that union bylaws provide for in-
> ternal organization along democratic
> lines.
> Registered unions have legal per-
> sonality. By representation propor-
> tional to their membership, the unions
> are entitled to enter into collective
> bargaining agreements binding on <u>all</u>
> the employees within the categories
> covered by the agreements.

Although the first paragraph of Article 39,
setting forth freedom to organize, is fully effective to the extent that no limitation may be imposed on the freedom of workers and employees to
organize for the protection of their respective interests, the subsequent paragraphs will not become
applicable until a law setting forth the formalities and prerequisites to union registration is
enacted.

Numerous bills were put before Parliament to
this effect, but none was ever approved. Given the
passage of many years, it seems even less probable
that the second part of Article 39 will be enacted
into law, the unions being the first to oppose the
system of registered organization, because this system would allegedly limit their freedom of action.
Therefore, at present de facto (as opposed to registered) unions are operating. These unions can enter
into collective agreements binding only on the members of said unions where collective bargaining is
permissible.

The de facto unions are free to organize according to preference. Nevertheless, in practice,
the major organizations have assumed structures
along similar general lines. Normally, labor unions

are organized on different levels. First, there
are unions that usually represent workers in a given
sector on a national scale. Second, these unions
then organize into federations of member unions.
The federations cover a larger economic area and
coordinate union policy within their sphere of influence. Finally, there are confederations compris-
ing federations and unions that are not members of
a federation.

The top union confederations are the Italian
General Labor Confederation (Confederazione Generale
Italiana del Lavoro, CGIL), Italian Labor Union Confederation (Confederazione Italiana Sindacati Lavoratori, CISL), Italian Labor Union (Unione Italiana
del Lavoro, UIL), National Confederation of National
Workers Unions (Confederazione Nazionale dei Sindacati Nazionali dei Lavoratori, CISNAL), and Italian
Confederation of Independent Workers Unions (Confederazione Italiana Sindacati Autonomi Lavoratori,
CISAL).

An example of confederate organization is fur-
nished by CISL, which groups the following federations and unions from the field of public employment:

> Italian Federation of Local Government
> Entities (Federazione Italiana Dipen-
> denti Enti Locali, FIDEL)

> Italian Federation of Hospital Workers
> (Federazione Italiana Sindacati
> Ospedalieri, FISO)

> National Federation of Employees of
> Public Entities (Federazione Nazionale
> Dipendenti Enti Parastatali e di
> Diritto Pubblico, FEDERPUBBLICI)

> Italian Federation of State Employees
> (Federazione Italiana Lavoratori
> Statali, FILS)

> National Elementary School Union (Sin-
> dacato Nazionale Scuola Elementare,
> SINASCEL)

National High School Union (Sindacato
Nazionale Scuola Media, SISM)

Italian Independent United Railroad
Workers Union (Sindacato Autonomo
Unificato Ferrovieri Italiani, SAUFI)

National Postelegraphic Workers Union
(Sindacato Nazionale Lavoratori Post-
elegrafonici, SILP)

Italian Postelegraphic Local Offices
and Agency Workers Union (Sindacato
Italiano Lavoratori Uffici Locali ed
Agenzie Postelegrafoniche, SILULAP)

Italian State Telephone Workers Union
(Sindacato Italiano Lavoratori Tele-
fonici di Stato, SILTS)

National State Monopoly Workers Union
(Sindacato Nazionale Lavoratori
Monopoli di Stato)

As noted, four federations and seven unions
are affiliated with CISL. In turn, numerous unions
belong to each federation; for example, FILS claims
the membership of 31 unions, among which are the
National Firemen's Union (Sindacato Nazionale Vigili
del Fuoco), Treasury-Ministry Employees National
Union (Sindacato Nazionale Dipendenti Ministero del
Tesoro), National Sheriff's Union (Sindacato Nazionale Ufficiali Giudiziari), and so forth.

The above-described union structure is also referred to as vertical, inasmuch as it groups its
members according to crafts or economic categories.
There is also a so-called horizontal structure,
which groups the various categories of workers in
local ambits. Thus, the major confederations have
a regional, provincial, or communal organization to
which the various local unions belong.

The ties between the unions and the federations affiliated with the same confederation are
rather close. Category unions are eligible to join

confederations if they share the same orientation
and have constitutions consistent with those of the
confederation. Furthermore, in most cases the confederation has control over the activities of member unions and federations.

        In particular, the constitution of the major
Italian confederation, CGIL, provides that matters
concerning collective bargaining be dealt with by
member unions under the general direction of the
confederation (art. 13), whereas union action, such
as strikes that concern various categories of essential public services or are considered of particular importance, must be authorized by the confederation, either locally or nationally (art. 14).

        Despite this, there are cases where the federa-
tions follow an independent policy, in conflict with
that of the confederations. This is more likely to
occur in the more important federations, which have
considerable influence within the governing offices
of the confederations.

        Management unions have a simpler structure,
but one that is similar in substance to that of the
worker unions. Further detail on this topic seems
superfluous, inasmuch as the major and most complex
of the management unions, the General Confederation
of Italian Industry (Confederazione dell' Industria
Italiana, Confindustria), organizes only private
business firms.

Principal Union Confederations

        The principal union confederations are the
following:

        1. CGIL. This is the most important confed-
        eration in Italy. It was the only labor union in
        existence from 1944 to 1949, at which time cer-
        tain factions broke away to form CISL and UIL.
        CGIL is closely tied to the Communist Party and
        to extreme-left socialists, notwithstanding an
        affirmation of political independence contained
        in Article 6 of its constitution. It is affili-
        ated with the World Federation of Trade Unions,
        of communist leaning.

2. CISL. Established in 1950 by noncommunist
groups that broke away from CGIL, it is linked
with leftist factions of the Christian Democratic
Party. This confederation, pursuant to Article 2
of its constitution, claims "complete independence
of any outside influence and absolute autonomy
vis-à-vis the State, the Government and political
parties." It is affiliated with the International
Confederation of Free Unions.
3. UIL. This association, too, was established by a schism of CGIL. Although officially
independent of political parties, it leans toward
the moderate democratic socialists. Like CISL,
UIL is affiliated with the International Confederation of Free Unions.
4. CISNAL. This is a confederation founded
on the principles of national syndicalism and
affiliated with the Italian Social Movement (MSI),
a neofascist-oriented party.
5. CISAL. This confederation comprises various autonomous workers' unions--that is, unions
independent of political parties. Although not
very important on the global level, it has great
influence upon some sectors of civil service.

The most important confederations are the first
three; their numerical composition, according to a
noteworthy authority, amounts to 4 or 5 million members, as indicated by the following breakdown:
CGIL, 2.75-3 million; CISL, 1.75-1.8 million; and
UIL, 0.25-0.35 million.[6] These statistics, difficult to verify, do not correspond to the claims of
the various unions, which indicate the following
memberships: CGIL, 3.4 million; CISL, 2.6 million,
and UIL, 1.5 million.[7]
The difference between data supplied by the
unions and those from other sources is basically
explained by the interest of the unions in inflat-
ing the numerical composition of their members for
many reasons. For one thing, it is a matter of
prestige; each of the three major confederations,
having come into being as the result of the schism
within one single organization and often competing
among themselves, is interested in appearing to be

more important than it actually is. Moreover, the
numerical importance of a union can be relevant
from the standpoint of the right to share the functions of certain public entities where the law
calls for the representation of the workers through
the most "representative" unions.

In principle, the number fixed at 4 or 5 million seems more credible. Such a number--in relation to the number of workers employed in the various sectors of agriculture (approximately 15 million[8])--would amount to a membership of from 25 percent to 37 percent of Italy's public employees.
The 25 percent figure would correspond to the unofficial data provided by the Ministry of Labor.

The three principal labor confederations (CGIL,
CISL, and UIL) have acquired, thanks to their numerical force, a certain monopolistic position in labor
union negotiations that has often been criticized by
minor associations. As a matter of fact, negotiations are normally conducted with the three confederations mentioned above, and the collective agreements are stipulated with them, whereas other unions
adhere to the contract later, without having had any
role in the determination of its content.

It is still more difficult to obtain even ap-
proximate figures regarding membership in the other
confederations. Thus, for example, CISNAL claims
about 900,000 members, but it is normally estimated
at about 100,000. As far as CISAL is concerned, a
study conducted by CISL, which, being a competitor,
would tend to underestimate rather than overestimate
the membership figure, estimates the number of workers belonging to independent affiliates at 100,000-
250,000.[9]

Principal Employers' Association Confederations

The organization of employers' associations is
much more homogenous than is that of labor unions.
In a given field there is normally only one employers' association, as opposed to the numerous labor
unions of differing political orientation frequently in competition with one another.

The most important employers' association confederation is Confindustria. This is practically the only organization of private industrialists, apart from the Italian Confederation of Small Industries (Confederazione Italiana delle Piccole Industrie, CONFAPI), which is of little importance. Besides Confindustria, there is Intersind, the union for enterprises in which the government holds a controlling interest. These enterprises are normally joint-stock corporations, private in nature, with the government as the major shareholder.

Formerly these government-controlled corporations belonged to Confindustria, along with private enterprises. Their separation from Confindustria was decided by Law 1589 of December 22, 1956, which established the Ministry of State Participation, consequently centralizing the policy of government-controlled corporations. According to Article 3 of this law, within a statutory period, "the government-controlled firms shall cease to be members of employer associations to which the others (private firms) belong."

This law has caused many arguments among the scholars and the courts. It was considered as conflicting with Article 39 of the constitution, imposing upon government-controlled corporations the obligation of belonging to a given union, thereby limiting the freedom to join unions. On January 26, 1960, the Supreme Court ruled that the law was not unconstitutional.

The foregoing applies to private corporations, whether or not they are state controlled. The situation in the field of public entities is more complex, where, at least in principle, state or public entity membership in unions is not possible. This principle and its exceptions will be analyzed subsequently.

Political Affiliations of Unions

As has been previously noted, four labor union confederations have a more or less clear-cut political orientation: CGIL tends toward the extreme-left

parties; UIL is tied to the moderate socialist factions; CISL is linked with the left-wing Christian
Democrats; and, finally, CISNAL is affiliated with
the neo-fascist MSI. In principle, therefore, the
most important labor unions are not independent of
political parties and bear the consequences of
their political affiliations. There is presently a
tendency to politicize the unions--a tendency that
manifests itself under various aspects.

The incompatibility of holding a political office and a union office is beginning to be felt.
For example, Article 7 of the CGIL constitution
lists as ineligible to hold a union office members
of Parliament, regional councils or assemblies, provincial or city councils, offices in a party's secretariat, and other political departments thereof.
Analogous provisions are contained in Article 24 of
the CISL constitution. This certainly affects relations between unions and parties, which are no
longer as close as they once were.

Furthermore, concerted efforts have been made
to achieve reunification of the three major confed-
erations--CGIL, CISL, and UIL. It is too soon to
tell if such efforts will be successful. These
three confederations are collaborating more closely
than in the past and often issue joint statements
on major union problems. With particular reference
to public employment, recent negotiations with the
government have been conducted jointly by the three
confederations.

In substance, therefore, the major confederations maintain their political affiliations, even
though it seems probable that these ties may be
broken in the future. The minor associations, such
as CISAL, to which independent unions belong, usually have no political affiliations. Nonetheless,
they have little weight except in particular fields.

Of special interest are recent developments in
the joint efforts of the three major confederations
to obtain from the government and Parliament reforms
in taxation (preferential treatment for income
earned through labor), health and welfare (general
free medical care), and housing (construction of
low-income houses and a ceiling on rents). Such

requests, pursued by means of strikes, highlight
the political nature of union activity. Although
the unions seem to be breaking away from political
parties, they are extending their field of action
from economic advancement to political claims for
structural reform.

UNIONS FOR PUBLIC EMPLOYEES

The right of public employees to organize for
the protection of their interests had already been
questioned by the government in prefascist days.
In fact, unionism in public employment was regarded
less favorably than was that in private enterprise.
Despite this attitude, numerous unions for public
employees existed in prefascist Italy.[10] The law
only limited the right to strike, imposing disciplinary sanctions on strikers.

During the fascist period, even the right to
organize was forbidden in the field of public employment. In fact, Article 11 of Law 563 of April
3, 1926, made the statute granting recognition to
unions inapplicable to public employees. In this
manner, public employees were precluded from belonging to recognized unions, the only ones qualified
to function as such, although these were under government control.*

Instead, government employees could unite in
de facto associations, subject to government authorization. These associations, however, were directly
answerable to the Fascist Party, and their function
was not to engage in union activities but to ensure
loyalty to the official ideology. Furthermore,
even this limited form of association was not permitted in particular categories--for example, servicemen, judges, teachers, and the like.

After the fall of fascism and the consequent
repeal of the corporative system, unions reorganized
freely in the liberated territories in the field of

---

*See the discussion, above, under "General
Principles and Structure."

both private and public employment. The previous
union system having been abolished, no restrictions
were now placed on the freedom to organize. Only
the military and civil police were, by Law Decree
205 of April 24, 1945, forbidden to belong to
unions, even of a nonpolitical nature.

Public Employees and Freedom to Organize

As has been seen, Article 39 of the 1948 constitution has expressly recognized the freedom to
organize unions. In the opinion of the scholars
this provision is applicable to private as well as
public employees.[11] In fact, although collective
bargaining is not allowed in public employment (except in particular cases, which will be treated
later) because the employment relationship is subject to acts of the government, the existence or
usefulness of unions is not therefore to be excluded.

To the contrary, because of the restrictions
placed on public employment, unionization, which
can exercise some form of pressure on the government without resorting to force, is considered desirable. Therefore, unions of public employees exist and are recognized by the government, which
consults with them at times of collective strife or
when measures that concern them are being prepared.

Whether or not unions for public employees
will be able to be registered pursuant to Article
39, Paragraph 2, of the constitution in the event
enabling legislation is passed is another question.
In fact, the entire system of registration aims at
making effective collective bargaining agreements,
applicable to all, even to nonunion members. This
would be of no interest to unions of public employees, inasmuch as collective bargaining is not permissible in this field.

Opinions differ on this point.[12] One of the
numerous bills put before Parliament (the Rubinacci
Bill of 1951) provided in Article 10 for the registration of unions for employees of the government
and other public entities. The problem at the
moment remains academic, because the possibility of
enabling legislation for Article 39 is very slim.

Restrictions on Freedom to Organize

The recognition, in principle, of the right of public employees to organize unions for the protection of their interests does not exclude restrictions being placed on certain categories of public employees whose jobs are of particular importance.

The problem has already been settled with respect to civil and military police. Law Decree 205 of April 24, 1945, expressly prohibits civil and military police from joining political parties and/or unions, even if not politically affiliated. In fact, in proceedings before the State Council (the supreme administrative court) the constitutionality of the prohibition to organize was challenged. The State Council in a decision handed down on February 4, 1966, ruled the claim prima facie groundless* and refused to refer the matter to the Constitutional Court.[13]

According to the State Council, in order to evaluate the compatibility of the prohibition for civil and military police to organize, the fact that unions have become political instruments must be taken into account. Under these circumstances, the express provision, in the bylaws or elsewhere, that the union has no political affiliation does not suffice to guarantee total independence. The very existence of other politically oriented unions makes it impossible for the independent union to avoid taking a political stand.

Consequently, the State Council concludes that membership in a union implies a political choice, thus bringing the question under the purview of Article 98, Paragraph 3, of the constitution, which authorized the legislature to restrict the right of certain categories of public employees--such as

---

*In the Italian legal system, when the question of constitutionality is raised during a proceeding, the judge must examine its merits. Only in cases where it is not prima facie groundless will he stay the proceedings and refer the case to the Constitutional Court.

judges, military personnel, diplomatic and consular
representatives abroad, and also officials of the
police department and <u>policemen</u>--to belong to political parties.

This decision of the State Council raised considerable criticism.[14] The objection was that Article 98 expressly mentions political parties but not
unions and that the prohibition to join political
parties could not be extended to cover unions.[15]
Furthermore, even if the prohibition contained in
Article 98 of the constitution were extended to
cover politically oriented unions, the conclusion
drawn by the State Council that every union must at
this moment necessarily be considered political
seems excessive.

In fact, the inaccuracy of this presumption is
demonstrated by the existence of two judges' associations (not technically unions but performing the
function of unions) of diverse orientation--one conservative and the other progressive--that nonetheless are tied neither to political parties nor to
politically oriented unions. In any case, the question of the constitutionality of Law Decree 205 cannot for the time being be considered settled because
it has not yet been brought before the only court
competent to decide the issue--the Constitutional
Court.

The question of the restrictions placed on
other categories of public employees by Article 98,
Paragraph 3, of the constitution--that is, on judges,
military personnel, and diplomatic and consular representatives abroad--is somewhat different. There
not being at present any law restricting their right
to join unions, it remains to be seen if in the future such a law can be passed without violating the
constitution. Opinions tend to favor restrictions
with respect to politically oriented unions, without depriving the categories in question of the
right to organize for the protection of their rights.

De Facto Status

At present Italian law seems to allow public
employees the freedom to organize, with restrictions

on certain categories having functions of particular
importance or discretion. This conclusion is amply
supported by facts. In the field of public employment there are numerous unions with which the competent government administrations discuss disputes regarding the treatment of public employees and to
which the law attributes certain powers within the
administration itself.

A good number of public employment unions belong to the confederations that concurrently operate
in the field of private enterprise--CGIL, CISL, UIL,
CISNAL, and CISAL, which are treated above. Besides
these there are other associations organized exclusively for public employment.

One of the most important of these is DIRSTAT,
an independent union federation representing state
executive personnel, which operates only in the
field of public employment. Its membership numbers
36 unions that cover the various branches of state
administration--for example, the Association of Ministry of Foreign Affairs Executive Personnel (Associazione Funzionari Dirigenti Ministero Affari Esteri),
the State Railroad Executive Personnel Union (Sindacato Dirigenti Ferrovie Stato), and the like.

DIRSTAT has features of considerable autonomy
with respect to other unions. This is to be expected,
though, since it represents a very particular category of public employees--the highest ranking, whose
interests do not necessarily correspond to those of
the majority of public employees.

The judges' associations are in a unique position, in that they do not have the technical features
of a union, although their purpose is to protect all
interests, economic included, of their membership.
There are two associations presently existing: the
Union of Italian Judges (Unione dei Magistrati
Italiani) and the National Association of Judges
(Associazione Nazionale dei Magistrati). The first
is composed of many of the Supreme Court of Cassation judges and is the more conservative. The second has a more numerous membership and is progressive. Although these two associations take different stands on the problems concerning judges' positions, which imply (in a broad sense) ideological

preferences, they are nonetheless completely independent of political parties and unions.

Union Representation in
Public Employment

The relative strength of the various unions, outlined above, is reproduced only in part in the field of public employment. As mentioned, many unions in this field are affiliated with the three major confederations--CGIL, CISL, and UIL--but along with these are numerous heterogeneous independent unions, which are of particular importance, at least in certain areas.

Reliable percentage figures on union membership in the field of public employment are not available. Research conducted among the unions indicated that 50 percent of public employees were organized, whereas the Ministry of Labor indicates only 10 percent, a figure clearly below the average normally agreed upon for workers of all categories.

In any case, the average percentage figures of union members in the field of public employment do not give a complete picture of the situation, as they vary considerably from category to category. It seems certain that union membership among the employees of independent government agencies--such as railroads and post office and telecommunications-- exceeds the average. Here the unions claim 80 percent membership. This is probably an inflated figure, but it is nonetheless an indication of union strength in these areas. This is understandable, since these agencies perform services similar to those in private enterprise, although their respective employees fall into the category of state employees.

The figures representative of union influence in the administrations are still more questionable. According to the unions, the penetration of CGIL, CISL, and UIL in independent government agencies (railroads, post office and telecommunications, the state telephone system, state monopolies, and so forth) is significant. It seems that CGIL has control of the railroad workers, whereas CISL is particularly strong among workers in the post office and telecommunications. In the remaining independent government agencies these two major union confederations have equal strength.

CISNAL claims to be in a position of strength among the central administrations, the ministries in particular. In certain ministries various independent unions seem to be strong. According to the CISL bulletin previously cited, which should not contain inflated figures (CISL being a competitive union), the members of independent unions number 6,000 out of 12,000 employees of the Ministry of Public Works and 550 out of 3,000 employees of the Ministry of Labor.[16]

Independent unions also have considerable weight in the field of education. The National Independent Grammar Schools Union (Sindacato Nazionale Autonomo Scuole Elementari, SNASE) has 25,000 members and has represented 34 percent of the vote at the elections of representatives to the Superior Council of Public Education. Another independent union has a membership of 40,000 among high school employees.

Another area in which unions are particularly strong is that of government agencies. In the principal health and welfare agencies, the CISL study indicates the following breakdown: in INPS 6,000 out of 20,300 employees are members of CISAL; in INAIL 3,500 out of 11,000 employees are members of CISAL, whereas 700 belong to independent unions; and in INAM 300 out of 20,000 employees are members of CISAL, whereas 3,000 belong to independent unions.[17]

Of extreme importance in its sphere of influence is DIRSTAT, which represents state executive personnel. It claims to represent 20,000 out of 35,000 officials. These figures must obviously be taken with a grain of salt; however, DIRSTAT no doubt carries considerable weight in its area.

The membership of judges to their associations is particularly high. According to reliable figures, 4,700 out of 6,800 judges belonging to the courts of ordinary jurisdiction are members of the National

Association of Judges and about 1,000 are members
of the Union of Italian Judges. This would mean
that 80 percent of judges belonging to the courts
of ordinary jurisdiction are organized.

Representative Associations
of Public Employers

As a rule, public employees cannot belong to
unions. There are, however, some exceptions with
respect to certain public entities where union membership and the entering into collective agreements
is allowed. These are government (profit-making)
corporations and some municipal agencies.

Government corporations, as mentioned above,
are entities that engage in profit-making activities on an equal and competitive level with private
enterprises of a similar nature. The right for
such entities to organize into unions is provided
by Royal Decree No. 1303 of June 16, 1938. Even
though this decree dates back to the fascist era
and therefore was promulgated with reference to the
corporative union system, the prevailing jurisprudence and doctrinal development consider it valid
to equate these entities with private enterprise
with respect to their right to organize.

The situation of municipal agencies--that is,
city agencies that manage public utilities (for example, transportation, gas, and electricity)--is
similar. The right of these agencies to organize
and to enter into collective bargaining agreements
also dates back to the fascist period. Such agencies are at present members of the Municipal Confederation (Confederazione della Municipalizzazione).

The above-cited cases are exceptions that are
explained by taking into account the particular
work relationship between public entities and municipal agencies on the one hand and their employees
on the other. Such relationships are normally considered of a private nature, even though the employer is a public entity. With reference, however, to
the state and public entities other than the ones
indicated above, union membership is not authorized.

This means that union relations will take place between the associations of public employees and the
individual public entities or the state.

As far as the relationship with the state is
concerned, it will be particularly difficult to determine in various cases which office is to carry
out collective bargaining with the unions. The law
is silent on this point. It has become customary to
discuss common problems of state employees with the
Ministry for Bureaucratic Reform, the only state
agency in a position to have a complete picture of
the problems relative to the employment status of
all state employees. Problems relating to certain
categories can be discussed, instead, with the competent offices of the relative ministries.

Position of Unions Within
Various Administrations

The question of free exercise of union rights
within the state administrations and public entities
is significant. Apropos of this, the restrictions
placed on the activities of public employees and
their unions and the power of the unions within the
administrations must be examined. This query can
be answered only in part because the internal regulations of the various public entities differ considerably from one another and, therefore, cannot
be covered in this chapter, which is of a general
nature.

With regard to civil servants, the problems
under discussion, which come under Presidential Decree No. 3 of January 10, 1957, are now governed by
Law 249 of March 18, 1968, which delegates to the
government the power to reorganize public administrations and also contains provisions for the partial revision of that presidential decree.*

Specifically, Article 146 of Presidential Decree No. 3, revised by Law 249, provides that

---

*See the discussion of state employees, above,
p. 210.

one-third of the administrative councils established
for each ministry or central administration be composed of representatives of the personnel. The representatives are designated by the national unions
having the greatest representation and nominated by
the minister, who makes his selection from the union
designees.

Furthermore, pursuant to Article 45 of Law 249,
civil servants in the various state administrations
who hold offices in the national unions having the
greatest representation can, upon request of the
union concerned, be temporarily suspended because
of a conflict of interest. These employees continue
to receive their usual salary, with the exclusion of
overtime or other allowances due with respect to
functions of a special nature when actually performed. The law also provides that employees holding union office who have not been suspended for
reasons of conflict of interest be allowed time off
to attend union meetings or to engage in normal
union activities.

The last innovation introduced by Law 249 is
the provision regarding the payment of union dues
within the state administration. Pursuant to Article 50 of Law 249, civil servants can delegate their
unions to withdraw part of their monthly salaries in
payment of union dues. This system has considerably
facilitated the collection of union dues. Once authorized by the employee, the administration automatically pays the amount withheld directly to the
union, until the authorization is revoked by the
employee himself.

COLLECTIVE BARGAINING IN PUBLIC EMPLOYMENT

Only in certain cases can the public employment relationship be regulated by a collective
agreement. This occurs in the field of profit-
making government corporations and municipal agencies. As mentioned previously, union membership in
this field has been accepted for some time; corre-
spondingly, the typical means of regulating contro-
versies between opposing unions, the collective

agreement, is also allowed. This is confirmed by
Article 2093 of the civil code, pursuant to which
the provisions regarding labor in Book V of the
civil code are applicable to public entities whose
employees are organized in "professional associations."

In effect, these are very particular situations.
The entities in question are certainly public, but
the employment relationships are governed according
to mainly private criteria. Besides being subject
to collective agreements, these relationships differ
from those of typical public employment in that con-
troversies are submitted to the jurisdiction of the
courts and not to special administrative judiciary
bodies.

In any case, although the question is disputed,
the prevailing opinion is that such relationships
must be considered of a private nature, notwithstanding the public nature of one of the parties to
the controversy. In substance, these are questions
of secondary importance with respect to the purpose
of this chapter. The legislation with respect to
strictly public employment--such as teachers, ministerial employees, judges, the military, and the
like--is completely different.

Pursuant to Article 2068 of the civil code,
"employment relationships which are governed by law
cannot be subject to collective agreements." This
provision primarily concerns "private employment relationships" that sometimes come under the purview
of the state--for example, concessionaires of public
services.

Nevertheless, it determines the absolute exclusion of collective agreements in the field of public
employment governed by law. It stands to reason
that, if an employment relationship is determined
by law, any revision of such relationship must be
effected by law. Therefore, there is no leeway for
collective agreements between public employees and
the state or minor public entities.

The exclusion of collective agreements, however, does not preclude the possibility of discussions between unions and the state or public entities. In practice, the legislation enacted in favor

of public employees is due largely to union pressures in negotiations conducted by associations of public employees.

The practical difference with respect to collective bargaining is that the agreement reached with the unions is not operative per se but requires enabling legislation. This system presents certain inconveniences. Foremost among these is the government's inability to guarantee the enactment of the legislation necessary to implement the agreements reached with the desired alacrity.

This situation can change radically in the near future. In fact, in the course of passing the law that extends the powers delegated to the government by Law 249 of March 18, 1968, to readjust advancements and salaries, the Chamber of Deputies introduced a provision granting the government power to implement by law decree the agreements regarding compensation of employees and workers of state administrations reached as a result of union negotiations.

If this provision is approved by the Senate, a considerable structural change in public employment collective bargaining will result. In such a case, once the government no longer needed enabling legislation to implement the agreements reached with the unions, the net result would be no different from that achieved in the private sector, although a collective agreement between the government and the unions would not exist in the strict sense of the term.

Union Negotiations in Public Employment

To understand better the manner in which union negotiations are conducted in public employment, it might be of interest to glance at the evolution of the negotiations conducted during recent years between the government and associations of state employees, which is the most important category of public employees.

From 1966, after an agreement had been reached between the government and the unions to combine the extra "bonus" checks with the regular paychecks (from this agreement stemmed Law 749 of June 5, 1965, which fixed the salaries currently in effect), the unions requested the government to readjust advancements and compensation of state personnel.*

In June 1966 CGIL, CISL, and UIL presented the government with a joint proposal, and, following the latter's counterproposal, a general agreement was signed on March 20, 1967. This agreement set up the framework for future negotiations. One of the points agreed to in this phase of the discussions regarded compensation. The government assumed the obligation of hiking salaries and expenses 2.4 percent each year, appropriating L 25 billion for 1967, L 75 billion for 1968, L 210 billion for 1969, L 345 billion for 1970, and L 480 billion for 1971.

In order to bring into effect the agreements reached, three commissions were formed, for the respective purposes of solving the problems of structural reform, readjusting job qualifications and compensation, and determining the rights and freedoms of unions. As a result of the work of the commissions, the government prepared a bill covering the reform of public administrations, which was put before Parliament in February 1968 and passed on March 18 of the same year (Law 249).

This law delegated to the government the power to issue law decrees for the reorganization of state administrations, for the decentralization of administrative functions, and for the readjustment of advancements and compensation of public employees. It also contained immediately operative provisions governing union rights of public employees. The law further provided for the payment to personnel of an extra "bonus" check equal to 3 percent of their respective salaries, in an amount that varies from Lit. 3,000 to Lit. 8,000.

With regard to other problems, Law 249 set forth only general principles for the government to follow in promulgating the relative law decrees. This led to further difficult negotiations with the unions. There were also general strikes of public

*See the discussion, below, pp. 240ff.

employees in November 1968 and January 1969, which
culminated in the agreement of May 1969, whereby
the government accepted the pay scales demanded by
the unions. This required an appropriation of
L 180 billion.

Nevertheless, this agreement was brought into
question by the unions after the government had improved the positions of teachers and executive personnel as a result of pressures brought to bear by
the independent unions. CGIL, CISL, and UIL took
the position that the preferential treatment of
those categories was unfair to the others and in
conflict with the principle of readjustment of ad-
vances and compensation based on equal treatment
for all categories.

There followed disturbances that led to a de-
finitive agreement in June 1969. The results
achieved by this agreement, together with the previous one, were as follows: an increase of salaries
starting July 1, 1970, at which time they were to be
calculated according to a scale determined by the
unions; an increase of the extra "bonus" check from
3 percent to 8 percent starting January 1, 1969
(this had already been provided for by the enactment of Law 464 of August 1, 1969); and a reduction
of the minimum time requirement of certain grades
with consequent acceleration of advancement.

But in the meantime the terms for governmental
readjustment of advancements and salaries pursuant
to Law 249 expired. It therefore became necessary
to amend the law in question in order to extend the
term of the powers delegated to the government. In
this manner problems that had appeared to be solved
once again came to the surface: for example, the
question of compensation of officials, who demanded
preferential treatment, was strongly opposed by the
other categories. This led to new strikes of both
executive personnel and other state employees in
the spring and summer of 1970.

At present the situation has been normalized
as a result of the approval by the Chamber of Deputies of the amendment to Law 249. Nonetheless, a
resurgence of problems can be expected when the
government has to act as a result of its delegated

powers after the Senate passes the bill. Similar
negotiations have been conducted and are still being
conducted with respect to various problems concerning employees of public entities.

COMPARISON OF WORKING CONDITIONS

This section will deal with the economic and
juridical structure of public employment and comparative conditions within the various branches of
the public administration and private enterprise.
A comparative study in this field must be limited
to general observations because of its complexity

In the field of public employment there are
considerable differences in the various sectors;
such differences are apparent not only within the
vast category of state employees (for example, the
differences existing between judges, military personnel, ministerial employees, and the like) but
also between these and the employees of public entities. Furthermore, for the latter the gap is
even greater because disparity in compensation paid
by the different entities renders a systematic
classification impossible.

Similar difficulties of classification exist
in the field of private employment because of the
great number of collective bargaining agreements in
existence and because the compensation called for
there constitutes a minimum wage subject only to
increase. In view of the foregoing this survey
shall be limited, with certain exceptions, to state
employees and particularly to those subject to
Presidential Decree No. 3 of January 10, 1957, containing the bylaws applicable to civil servants.

With regard to _private_ employees, reference
will be made to two collective agreements (one concerning the metal-machine industry of December 12,
1966, and the other concerning the rubber, electric
cable, and related products industry of February
13, 1968, hereafter referred to as "metal-machinists'
collective agreement" and "rubber-workers' collective agreement," respectively) and to the laws applicable to the cases in question. Only the

compensation of the employees will be considered.
In the field of public employment laborers are
numerically insignificant (approximately 50,000 are
employed by the state), and a comparison with the
private sector would, therefore, have little relevance.

Compensation

State Employees

At present, because of the compensation differential in the various categories of public employees
(particularly with reference to the employees of
public entities, which are not governed by uniform
legislation), it is not possible to furnish a complete picture of the career pattern and the relative
compensation in the entire public employment system.
Therefore, the situation relative to civil servants only will be discussed. The economic compensation of this category of public employees is determined primarily by Presidential Decree No. 749
of June 5, 1965, which incorporated, in the base
salary, various allowances previously paid separately. It should be noted, however, that the data
below are not complete, because there still are al-
lowances--sometimes variable from sector to sector--
that have not been taken into account.
State personnel are classified in the following categories: executive personnel, administrative
personnel, clerical personnel, and auxiliary personnel. Qualification for each category is determined
by public competitive examinations. Respective positions and gross annual salaries are noted below.[18]
1. Executive Personnel. A university degree
is necessary to qualify for this category. Responsibilities include the application of laws,
coordination and supervision, technical and scientific organization of the offices, and so forth.
Respective positions and gross annual salaries of
this category are as follows:

        Director general   Lit. 4,458,000
        Inspector general   Lit. 3,318,100

Divisional director	Lit. 2,248,700
Sectional director	Lit. 1,191,600
1st-class counsellor	Lit. 1,159,400
2d-class counsellor	Lit. 1,137,500
3d-class counsellor	Lit. 1,145,800

2. Administrative Personnel. Employees of this category perform administrative, accounting, and technical assignments. Respective positions and gross annual salaries are as follows:

Chief secretary	Lit. 2,478,700
Principal secretary	Lit. 1,991,600
First secretary	Lit. 1,599,400
Secretary	Lit. 1,397,500
Assistant secretary	Lit. 1,145,800
Deputy secretary	Lit. 1,032,600

3. Clerical Personnel. This category performs such tasks as filing, maintaining records, bookkeeping, and office routine. Respective positions and gross annual salaries are as follows:

Chief archivist	Lit. 1,397,500
First archivist	Lit. 1,145,800
Archivist	Lit. 1,032,600
Clerk	Lit. 890,400
Adjunct clerk	Lit. 800,200

4. Auxiliary Personnel. Personnel in this category maintain the offices to which they are assigned and perform services of ushers and other tasks of a material nature inherent to their jobs. Respective positions and gross annual salaries are as follows:

Chief attendant	Lit. 890,400
Attendant	Lit. 862,900
Chief usher	Lit. 808,000
Usher	Lit. 750,300
Steward	Lit. 715,800

The above concerns primarily ministerial employees--that is, employees of the central bureaucracy. Other categories of state employees that shall be examined have somewhat different career positions and compensations. With reference to

employees of independent state corporations (railroads, post office and telecommunications, and
state monopolies) the subdivision is more complex
in view of the peculiarities of the various entities.[19]

To cite a few examples, the salaries of executive personnel vary from a yearly minimum of Lit.
1,191,900 (3d-class counsellor in the Post Office
and Telecommunications Administration) to a maximum
of Lit. 4,807,200 (director general of the National
Railroad Authority and director general of the
State Monopoly Administration).

In the administrative personnel category the
spectrum extends from Lit. 1,070,300 on an annual
basis (deputy secretary in the Post Office and Telecommunications Administration) to Lit. 2,178,200
for the highest position (for example, chief secretary in the Post Office and Telecommunications Administration).

In the clerical personnel category the yearly
income in the lowest position (for example, adjunct
clerk in the State Monopoly Administration) amounts
to Lit. 800,200, whereas in the highest position
(for example, office manager in the Post Office and
Telecommunications Administration) the yearly income amounts to Lit. 1,769,000.

In the auxiliary personnel category the following salaries correspond, respectively, to the lowest
position (for example, steward in the State Monopoly
Administration) and the highest position (for example, head technical agent in the Post Office and
Telecommunications Administration), Lit. 741,300
and Lit. 1,183,500. A different wage scale is applicable to the personnel of the National Railroad
Authority, which takes into account the different
technical functions.

Another category that follows a different system regarding positions and salaries is that of the
judges. Without becoming involved in details, it
is sufficient to state that the gross annual salary
in the lowest position (judicial auditor) amounts
to Lit. 1,714,100; that of the highest position
(chief justice of the Supreme Court) amounts to
Lit. 9,199,100.[20] To cite another example, in the
sector of public education the minimum starting salary for an elementary school teacher is fixed at

Lit. 1,108,100 on a gross annual basis; the maximum
paid to a university professor is Lit. 5,149,300.[21]

Private and Public Comparison

The figures indicated below with respect to private employment represent minimum contractual wages.
Moreover, the data (except for managers) are limited
to one sector, chosen as an example. According to
the national agreement of July 29, 1970, starting
minimum contractual salaries for managers amount to
Lit. 465,000 on a monthly basis, equal to Lit.
6,045,000 annually, reduced to Lit. 425,000 monthly
for concerns with less than 100 employees. Actually,
salaries can be considerably higher.

The figures for employees' salaries are taken
from the wage scales of the metal-machinists' collective agreement of January 8, 1970, which can be
considered sufficiently indicative of the situation
in the more important industrial sectors. These
too are minimum and do not include extra allowances.

The following are the minimum rounded-off wages
for different grades of employees called for by the
metal-machinists' collective agreement for the area
in which salaries are highest* and for employees
above twenty-one years of age:

	Monthly Salary	Annual Salary (13 months)
Senior 1st grade	Lit. 166,000	2,158,000
1st grade	Lit. 165,000	2,145,000
2d grade	Lit. 126,000	1,638,000
3d grade	Lit. 97,000	1,261,000
4th grade	Lit. 88,000	1,144,000

In a comparison between the public and private
sectors, limited on one side to the ordinary career
pattern of the state employees and on the other to
the executives in the industrial field and to the

---

*Milan and Turin (Zone 0). In Zone IV, where
compensation is at its lowest, the monthly salary
for the highest category drops to approximately
Lit. 159,000.

employees in the metal-machine sector, it will be possible to gather merely indicative data that might not reflect the average situation. It should be borne in mind, moreover, that it was not possible to take into account extra allowances, which vary extensively in both the public and the private sectors. The resulting annual wage scale, on the basis of approximately equal functions, is as follows:

State Employees   Private Employees

Executive Personnel
Director general -
   Lit. 4,458,000   Executives -
Sectional director -   Lit. 6,045,000
   Lit. 1,991,600

1st-class counsellor -
   Lit. 1,159,400
3d-class counsellor -   Employees ranging from
   Lit. 1,145,300   senior 1st grade -
                                      Lit. 2,138,000
Administrative Personnel   to 3d grade -
Chief secretary -   Lit. 1,261,000
   Lit. 2,478,000
Deputy secretary -
   Lit. 1,032,600

Clerical Personnel
Chief archivist -   Employees belonging to
   Lit. 1,397,500   the 4th grade -
Adjunct clerk -   Lit. 1,144,000
   Lit. 800,200

It would appear from the above that, whereas executives' salaries are much higher in the private sector, the differential in the salaries of employees is smaller, although those in the private sector are, on the whole, better paid.

Such comparisons are, however, very difficult, especially since situations change rapidly. In the case at hand, for example, salaries of the private sector (as determined by a very recent collective bargaining agreement) have been compared with the

salaries of state employees, which have not been
subject to change since 1963. Obviously, the differential could be reduced or even disappear when
the government sets up a new pay scale for state
employees.

Working Hours and Overtime

The working hours of civil servants are still
determined by Article 106, Paragraph 1, of Royal
Decree No. 1960 of December 30, 1923 (the legislative text that preceded Presidential Decree No. 3
of January 10, 1957, which presently governs the
bylaws of state employees). Article 106, which is
the only article of Royal Decree No. 1960, calls
for a 42-hour week, spread over six working days
(seven hours daily).

It was amended during World War II by a decree
of the chief of state that fixed the working week
to 40 hours, spread over seven days--six hours on
weekdays and four hours on Sunday. These rules
were not rigorously observed, however, with the result that the work schedule presently observed
amounts to 36 hours a week--six continuous hours
(from 8 a.m. to 2 p.m.) every day, except Sunday.

The present situation has many disadvantages,
especially from the standpoint of job performance.[22]
As a matter of fact, Article 28 of Law 249 of March
18, 1968, establishes that changes in working hours
for state employees will be brought about by a later
law. The same work schedule is maintained by the
employees of local entities (communes, provinces,
and regions). As far as the employees of independent government agencies (the National Railroad
Authority, Post Office and Telecommunications Administration, and State Monopoly Administration)
are concerned, the work week varies from 40 to 46
hours.

In the field of public education the work
schedule is rather short--for example, 18 to 24
hours a week for high school teachers. For university professors a rigid schedule is not applied.
They must dedicate to their subject as many hours a

week as required by the nature and extent of the
subject, and they must hold at least three lessons
per week (Law 311 of March 18, 1958, art. 6). Another category to which virtually no schedule is
applied is that of judges, whose work schedule is
determined by the necessities of the service performed.

In the private sector the law limits itself to
fixing maximum working hours (which can be departed
from in those cases cited in the law itself) at
eight hours daily and 48 hours weekly (Royal Decree
No. 692 of March 15, 1923). The actual work schedule is normally shorter and comes close to 40-42
hours. Various firms have adopted the five-day
week.

It is not possible to furnish more precise
data in view of the differences in the various collective bargaining agreements and policies of various firms. Generally speaking, working hours are
longer in the private sector than in the public
sector, even if the opposite is true in certain
cases.

Overtime

Overtime, to be compensated for in addition to
the normal salary, is provided for by law in both
the private and the public sectors. In the public
sector Article 14, Paragraph 2, of Presidential Decree No. 3 of January 10, 1957, states that the employee must work overtime when required by the administration and has a right to compensation therefor.

It is difficult to determine the actual compensation for overtime because of the numerous regulations that relate to it. To cite an example, in the
state railroads overtime hours are compensated for
on the basis of the hourly rate taken from the initial salary for the position filled and increased
15 percent under ordinary conditions and by a greater percentage if overtime is performed at night or
on holidays (Law 685 of July 31, 1957).

One fact seems certain, however; the tendency
is to calculate overtime pay on minimum base pay

exclusive of allowances, thus computing a rather
low compensation for overtime. In the private sector the law authorizes work in excess of eight hours
daily and 48 hours weekly, in which case overtime
hours must be compensated for with an increase of
not less than 10 percent (Royal Decree No. 692,
amended by Law 1079 of October 30, 1955).

In general, collective bargaining agreements
provide for percentage increases higher than the
minimum prescribed by law. For example, the metal-
machinists' collective agreement calls for an increase of 25 percent; the rubber-workers' collective agreement calls for an increase of 25 percent
for the first hour and 35 percent for additional
hours. Such percentages are further increased when
overtime is performed at night or on holidays.

According to the above-mentioned collective
agreements, hourly compensation for overtime is calculated by dividing the monthly salary by 180
(metal-machinists' collective agreement) or by 175
(rubber-workers' collective agreement) and then increased by the above percentages. The monthly salary used for the computation of overtime is closer
to the real one, inasmuch as some of the allowances
are included.

In case collective agreements fix a work schedule of less than 48 hours, overtime is still paid
but at lower rates. All told, it seems, overtime
is better paid by private industry than by the public sector, with respect to both the amount of the
additional pay and the computation of the hourly
compensation.

"Weekly Rest" and Holidays

The right to "weekly rest" is granted by the
Italian legal system to both private and public employees, as provided by Article 36, Paragraph 2, of
the constitution. The right to weekly rest from
work finds further confirmation with reference to
private employees in Article 2109 of the civil code
and in Law 40 of February 22, 1934, regarding Sunday
and weekly rest. This law governs those cases in

which weekly rest may be granted on a day other than Sunday or, because of exceptional circumstances, may be suspended for brief periods of time.

This 1934 law, a very detailed regulation, is not applicable to the public sector (Law 40, art. 1, no. 11). A uniform regulation is, therefore, lacking for all categories of public employees. In any case, as far as one of the most important sectors of public employment is concerned, that of civil servants, Article 36 of Presidential Decree No. 3 of January 10, 1957, confirms the general principle of weekly rest, for it states that in those cases when the necessities of the administration require that the employee work on Sunday, a corresponding day of rest shall be granted.

The right to be off from work during festivities falling during the course of the week is granted to all employees, both public and private, by Law 260 of May 27, 1949, as amended by Law 90 of March 31, 1954. The law allows work on holidays, however, as long as it is paid for separately at a higher rate. In any case, there are no substantial differences between public and private employment on this point, except for the additional pay for work performed on holidays as determined in the private sector by the collective bargaining agreements and in the public sector by the provisions that govern the relationship of the various categories of employees.

Vacations and Leaves

Article 36, Paragraph 3, of the constitution guarantees the right to an annual paid vacation, without, however, determining its length. Pursuant to Presidential Decree No. 2 of January 10, 1957, civil servants are entitled to an annual paid vacation of one month to be taken during a continuous period if compatible with service requirements.

The situation is somewhat different for other categories of public employees. For example, state railroad employees receive vacation based on length of service--21 working days if it is under ten years and 26 working days if it is ten years or

over (Law 425 of March 26, 1958, art. 86).* The
vacation allowance for teachers, with the exception
of short tours of duty for remedial examinations,
corresponds to the period during which schools are
closed and is, therefore, much longer than one
month.

In the private sector paid vacations are provided for through collective bargaining agreements.
Both the metal-machinists' and rubber-workers'
agreements provide for 15 working days during the
first two years of service, 20 working days after
three years, 25 after eleven years, and 30 after
nineteen years.

Royal Decree No. 1334 of June 1937 provides
for a 15-day marriage leave for all employees of
both private and public sectors.

Article 37 of Presidential Decree No. 2 of
January 10, 1957, provides for emergency leave, not
to exceed two months in the course of a year, to be
granted to civil servants for serious reasons.
Article 38 of the same decree fixes payment for
emergency leave as follows: normal compensation
for the first month and one-fifth thereof for the
second.

This payment system is not applicable to all
public employees. State railroad workers, for instance, are governed by special legislation. Article 88 of Law 425 of March 26, 1958, provides for
the possibility of granting railroad employees a
maximum emergency leave of two months, but payment
is not automatic and, when authorized, is limited
to the first month. These provisions regarding
emergency leave have no counterpart in the field of
private employment.

According to Article 69 of Presidential Decree
No. 3 of January 10, 1957, civil servants may request a leave of absence for family reasons for a
period not to exceed one year. During such period
the employee receives no pay and acquires no

---

*Working days are those other than Sundays and
holidays. The vacation period is, therefore, length-
ened by including Sundays and holidays, if any.

seniority or benefits (advancements, salary increases, and so on). In the private sector there
are no general provisions governing leaves of absence. The aforementioned rubber-workers' collective agreement provides for leaves of absence not
to exceed three months, after a minimum of five
years of service.

Hiring and Trial Period

Hiring for state employment normally takes
place through public competitive examinations.
This is specifically determined by Article 5 of
Presidential Decree No. 3 of January 10, 1957, regarding the bylaws of civil servants. Those who
pass the competitive examination are hired on a
six-month trial period. An administrative council
then decides on the eligibility of the employees,
purportedly based on performance (art. 10). If the
decision is favorable, the employee is considered
permanent. If an unfavorable judgment is not expressed within three months from the termination of
the trial period, it is considered as having been
successfully completed.

The procedure is much simpler in the field of
private employment, where the employment relationship is established on the basis of an agreement between the parties. Even in this case a trial period
is provided for by Article 2096 of the civil code.
During this period each party has the right to withdraw from the contract without advance notice or
penalty. The law requires, however, that hiring on
a trial basis be indicated in writing, otherwise
the employment relationship shall be considered as
final in every respect.

As far as the duration of the trial period is
concerned, collective bargaining agreements (for example, in the metal-machinists' and rubber-workers'
collective agreements) normally call for a maximum
of six months for employees of the first grade and
three months for the other grades.

Seniority, Promotions, and Job Security

It must be pointed out that raises are fixed
for each particular job in both private and public
employment. For example, the metal-machinists' and
rubber-workers' collective agreements provide for
biannual raises of 5 percent. Even in the field of
public employment periodic raises are fixed.

It is very difficult to make a comparison between promotions in private and public employment.
In private employment promotions depend exclusively
upon the employer, with one restriction. If an employee is assigned to do a job of a higher classification for a certain period of time, he is automatically promoted to the classification covering
such job (according to Article 14 of the metal-
machinists' collective agreement and Article 6 of
the rubber-workers' collective agreement). In general, merit would seem to be the prime reason for
promotion in private employment, within the limits
of the employer's recognition of such when promotions are made.

In public employment the situation is more complex, being influenced by two opposing exigencies--
that of guaranteeing seniority advancement to all
employees and that of giving recognition to quality
performance by means of merit raises. In general,
the system is characterized by automatic promotions
matured within fixed time periods. These time requirements will be further reduced pursuant to recent agreements reached with the unions in 1969,
with the possibility of more rapid advancement for
those who qualify as a result of having passed
tests or competitive examinations designed for such
purposes.

This generally brings about a leveling in state
careers, limiting the possibilities of advancement
of the more capable employees as compared to private
enterprise (where the discretionary powers of the
employers are practically unlimited), whereas the
least gifted can in any case count on at least mini-
mal advancement, a situation that normally has no
parallel in private employment.

Until 1966 there was considerable job security
disparity between public and private employment.
Although a public employee could not be dismissed
or suspended from work except in the cases and with
the formalities provided for by law, the private employee could be fired at will as long as sufficient
advance notice was given.

Today the situation in private enterprise has
changed considerably. With the promulgation of Law
604 of July 15, 1966, dismissal is possible only
for just cause or justifiable reason. If a court
should find absence of just cause or justifiable
reason, the employer must rehire the worker and pay
him damages in an amount not less than five months'
salary.

In substance, therefore, the principle of just
cause or justifiable reason is applicable to public
as well as to private employment. Notwithstanding
the foregoing, there is still greater job security
in public employment, primarily because of a more
lax application of the rules that permit the dismissal of troublesome or inefficient employees.

STRIKES OF PUBLIC EMPLOYEES

It has already been noted that during the
fascist era the principle governing union organization consisted of the peaceful solution of labor
disputes. The implementation of this principle resulted in the unlawfulness of union struggle instruments, such as the strike and the lockout. The prohibition against strikes was introduced by Article
18 of Law 563 of April 3, 1926, and was reiterated
by the penal code of 1931, which classifies and
subjects to criminal sanction the following types
of strikes: strikes for contractual purposes (art.
502); political strikes (art. 503); strikes to
coerce state authorities (art. 504); and solidarity
or protest strikes (art. 505).

Moreover, Article 330 of the penal code classifies as crimes collective abandonment of public
functions, employment, services, or works, which
aims primarily at restraining strikes conducted by

public employees and public service employees. The
penal code of 1931 is still in effect; however, the
articles relative to the right to strike must be coordinated with Article 40 of the constitution, which
states that "the right to strike is exercised within
the purview of the laws which regulate it."

Through such norms the right to strike is guaranteed, although its exercise is subject to legal
limitations. The original intent was to have a subsequent law regulate the strike in conformity with
constitutional principles; however, the law in question has not as yet been enacted, nor does it seem
probable that it will come into existence within
the next few years. A situation of extreme uncertainty has consequently ensued, alleviated only in
part by court decisions that have upon occasion
faced the problems relative to the right to strike.

Arguments For and Against Strikes

Most unclear is the situation regarding strikes
in the field of public employment. Court decisions
that deal with the problem directly are very few,
whereas doctrinal pronouncements for and against
strikes on the part of public employees are very
numerous and contradictory. It is advisable to examine at the outset the argumentation offered by
the scholars.

The problem relative to the admissibility of
strikes regards essentially public employees in a
strict sense and not employees of state corporations
("public economic entities"). The employment relationship of the latter is, in fact, generally considered of a private nature, and the very presence
of collective bargaining, noted above, leads to the
almost unanimous consensus of opinion that the
right to strike is not subject to greater limitations in this field than in private enterprise.[23]
The admissibility of strikes by public employees in
a strict sense is, however, greatly argued about.
The following are some of the arguments more frequently adduced in this connection.

1. An initial argument against the admissibility of strikes in public employment is drawn from the type of relationship that binds the public employee to the state and to the public entity. It has been said that the above is an organizational relationship and not an employment relationship. According to this interpretation, Section III of the constitution, which sets forth the principles governing economic relations, including the right to strike guaranteed by Article 40, would be applicable only to workers in subordinate capacities and not to public employees.[24]

Such a theory has often been objected to on the following grounds: (a) even public employees are workers in subordinate capacities, being subordinate to the state, from which they receive compensation; and (b) constitutional principles, such as Article 36, which makes adequate compensation mandatory, have been established for the protection of the workers, public employees included, and presuppose the right to strike.[25]

2. A similar argument is that based upon the noncontractual character of the public employment relationship and upon the position of supremacy of the public employer with respect to the employee. According to certain authors strikes should have the function of reestablishing economic equality between the parties to the employment relationship and would presuppose, therefore, a legal equality, which is to be found only in relations governed by contracts.[26]

It is certain that a position of equality does not exist between the state and public employees; however, this does not infer that the object of strikes must necessarily be that of bringing about a position of actual equality. Strikes also serve the purpose of achieving greater social justice. From this standpoint there is no difference between public and private employees.[27]

3. The necessary connection between the right to strike and private enterprise has also been argued from another standpoint. The objective of the private entrepreneur is to achieve maximum profit by limiting the cost of production (salaries

included), thus placing the private employee in a
position of conflict with his employer. The former would consequently succumb, were it not for a
collective remedy, such as the strike, which can
reestablish economic equilibrium.

Such a situation would not occur in the employment relationship with the state, since the latter
does not aim at financial gain but at the general
interest of the entire community. According to
this theory, the public employment relationship
would not, therefore, bring about a conflict between two private interests but a contrast between
private and public interest, the latter of which
would have to prevail.[28]

Others have pointed out that lack of financial
gain pursuits on the part of the state does not
necessarily have any bearing in this matter. In
fact, it is well known that the state as an employer has a tendency to remunerate as little as
possible and to get as much as possible out of the
worker's performance.[29] Moreover, although it is
true that the public interest must be protected,
this does not mean that such protection should be
granted to the extent of paralyzing the right to
strike, which is explicitly granted by the constitution.[30]

4. It has also been held that the right to
strike is, on account of its nature, connected
with collective bargaining. Consequently, it
would have no significance in the field of public
employment, where the employment relationship is
governed by law.[31] It is possible to object, however, that, although the strike is traditionally
connected to collective bargaining, this does not
mean that recourse to this weapon should be excluded in all sectors where collective bargaining
is not authorized.[32]

5. Always on the premise that the employment
relationship is generally governed by law, it has
been stated that every form of abstention from
work directed at the modification of a relationship governed by law consists of a strike aimed
at coercing the legislative power to concede to
the demands of those on strike. As a result,

strikes by public employees would amount to political strikes, interfering with the exercise of
legislative power.[33]

As opposed to what occurs in the private sector, where strikes are directed against an individual who can grant the requests of the strikers,
such an individual is not to be found in the public sector. It could not be the government, since
a law is required to modify economic remuneration
of public employees; nor could it be Parliament,
because it cannot be the object of coercion.[34]

It has been noted that the arguments referred
to above are fallacious inasmuch as they posit the
government, Parliament, or any other individual organ of the state as the employer. As a matter of
fact, if demands are made by employees of public
entities, it will not be necessary for the government or Parliament to intervene in order to satisfy
said requests. In the case of demands by state employees, however, the employer must be considered
the state in its unity and not the individual organ
that represents only one sphere of competence.[35]

It cannot be said, therefore, that strikes by
public employees are political in nature only because they are directed against the state (which is,
after all, the employer) or because they are also
directed against Parliament. In any case, even
judicial pronouncements distinguish between economic
and political strikes of public employees, depending
on whether the goals in question are inherent or not
to the protection of the professional interest of
the strikers, thus implicitly excluding the notion
that strikes by public employees are political in
nature.[36]

Even the Constitutional Court has decreed that
Article 504 of the penal code (coercion of public
authority through strikes) is not applicable to
strikes conducted for economic purposes, whereby
strikers' demands are directed at the public author-
ity--which becomes a party to the employment rela-
tionship--in order to bring about the modification
of the employment relationship in their favor.[37]

As previously noted, arguments for and against strikes by public employees are not of such magnitude to sustain either position decisively. In view of this, it seems more realistic to examine the concrete attitude of the executive and judicial branches of the government toward public employees who resort to this form of union struggle.

The judicial branch has rarely expressed itself explicitly for or against strikes by public employees. Implicitly, however, judges seem to act on the premise that such strikes are lawful. As a matter of fact, in the course of several decisions the State Council has considered political strikes by public employees unlawful, thus implying that strikes aiming at the protection of their economic needs are legitimate.[38]

Other decisions of the State Council have affirmed the principle according to which compensation must be held from strikers' salaries for the hours of abstention from work on the grounds that striking brings about the suspension of the two fundamental duties inherent to the employment relationship-- performance of the work and payment of the compensation.[39] Such holdings appear to be hardly consistent with the alleged unlawfulness of striking by public employees, notwithstanding a more recent decision of the State Council whereby suspended compensation does not preempt the question of whether striking by public employees is lawful.[40]

Particularly clear is the position held by the State Council in its opinion of June 16, 1966, in which it stated the following:

> Public employees have equal right to strike as private employees without incurring the disciplinary penalty of suspension from their jobs because of interruption or upsetting of the rhythm of service or because of voluntary abandonment of service notwithstanding the singularity of the relationship, and the sensitivity and relevance of their function with reference to the fundamental interests of the community.[41]

This decision touches particularly on the basic
problem of determining whether present legislation
affords the possibility of imposing disciplinary
penalties upon state employees who abstain from
work because of motives connected with a strike.

Article 43 of Royal Decree No. 1960 of December
30, 1923--the legislative text that governed the
status of civil servants prior to the enactment of
Presidential Decree No. 3 of January 10, 1957--de-
clared that "employees who voluntarily abandon their
office or give personal assistance in interrupting
or upsetting the rhythm of service are considered
together with their instigators as having resigned,
still being subject to penal action." Such a norm
implicitly prohibited strikes of public employees
and called for penalties.

No regulation corresponding to Article 43 is
to be found in Presidential Decree No. 3. As a matter of fact, Article 81 of Presidential Decree No.
3, which calls for the suspension from the grade
(that is, temporary removal from service and the
withholding of salary), takes into consideration
abandonment of work but recognizes union rights by
referring to Article 4 of Law 1181 of December 20,
1954, which in turn remands to a future law insofar
as the means of protecting the collective and individual interests of employees are concerned. All
this means essentially that Article 81 may not be
applied to abstentions from work in relation to
union activity--that is, the strike--until an appropriate law regulates the exercise thereof.

Moreover, even the attitude of the public authorities toward strikes in the field of public employment appears to be based on the premise that
strikes are lawful. In fact, as noted above, the
state not only refrains from taking measures against
strikers but also grants economic and legal improvements as a result of union struggles conducted by
them.

In conclusion, apart from the validity of the
opinions of scholars denying the right to strike on
the part of public employees, the fact does remain
that public employees make use of this means of
struggle without encountering any opposition. This

certainly constitutes a firm point in the present union status.

Restrictions on Right to Strike

Although in the present legal and factual situation it can be said that the status of public employees does not of itself preclude the right to strike, limitations may take place with reference to certain categories of public employees because of the type of functions carried out by them. As a matter of fact, nearly all the authors who generally consider the right to strike admissible in public employment exclude from this right certain categories, such as judges, the police, and the like.[42]

Upon occasion, the opposite thesis has been proposed, which bases itself upon a literal interpretation of Article 40 of the constitution, whose dicta lay out a general recognition of the right to strike, delegating the legislature to regulate its exercise. From the foregoing it has been deduced that limitations may be imposed only with reference to the exercise of the strike and not with reference to the parties possessing the right to strike.[43] Such a thesis has been turned down by the Constitutional Court, which has stated the following:

> The regulatory power which the Constitution entrusts to the legislator has as its object the general right to strike and therefore appears applicable to each of the elements which it comprises, including the parties who can exercise the right.[44]

Although it is true that the right of certain categories of public employees to strike can be restricted, the problem of determining which categories remains unsolved in the absence of a governing law. The existing laws that govern strikes by public employees are of dubious applicability, having been enacted prior to the constitution, during the period in which the freedom to strike was denied to

everyone and in all cases. Nonetheless, on the
basis of the interpretation given to these norms by
the Constitutional Court, it is possible to set
forth some criteria for determining the limitations
presently in existence regarding strikes by public
employees.

The most important norm to be taken into consideration from this standpoint is Article 330 of
the penal code, which states the following:

> Public officials, personnel in charge
> of a public service in the status of
> employees, private citizens who oper-
> ate public services or services of
> public need, not organized as an eco-
> nomic concern, and employees of pub-
> lic services or public need concerns
> who, in the number of three or more
> collectively abandon their office, or
> who carry out their functions in such
> a manner as to disrupt its continuity
> or regularity, are subject to a maxi-
> mum penalty of two years imprisonment.

The prohibition contained here is applicable not
only to public employees but also to private employees who carry out public services.

In decision No. 123 of December 28, 1962, the
Constitutional Court decreed that, with reference
to Article 330, the raising of a question of constitutionality is unfounded as long as such norm is interpreted according to the criteria indicated by
the court itself. According to the court, the norm
in question cannot be applied when abandonment of
public offices, services, and the like constitutes
a legitimate strike as provided for in Article 40.
The problem, therefore, becomes a matter of interpretation of the concept of strikes.

According to the court, strikes must have as
their object the protection of economic interests
of the strikers and must not violate general interests that are directly protected by the constitution.[45] This means essentially that the judge can
apply Article 330 only to political strikes and to

strikes that undermine interests protected by the
constitution.

The court, however, has not clearly determined
which of these interests prevail over the right to
strike. It has merely observed that public services,
such as the one in question (the case brought before
the court dealt with a strike by employees of a
municipal streetcar company), do not represent a
sufficient degree of importance to jeopardize constitutionally protected interests.

The Constitutional Court, by the above-
mentioned decision, has kept Article 330 in effect
as long as it is interpreted according to the dicta
of the court. In a more recent decision the court
has departed from its original opinion, decreeing
that this norm is in part unconstitutional.[46] In
this decision the Constitutional Court ruled Paragraphs 1 and 2 of Article 330 of the penal code unconstitutional as applied to economic strikes that
do not jeopardize essential public functions or services of foremost general interest as indicated by
the constitution.

The above-mentioned decisions indicate that the
factor determining the lawfulness of strikes is to
be found in the functions performed rather than in
the employment relationship. Article 330 is applicable, in fact, to both public and private employees.
It follows, therefore, that, if the functions performed are not of preeminent public interest, the
strikes are legitimate, even if undertaken by public
employees.

Determination of Essential Services

Determining which are the "services of preeminent public interest according to the constitution"
remains essentially an open question, as does, consequently, the classification of public employees
who are not authorized to resort to strikes. The
Constitutional Court, in its last decision on the
matter, stated explicitly that it can set forth
only general criteria and that the judge of the subject matter is competent to apply such criteria on

the basis of the evaluation of all elements that in
individual cases have bearing on the membership to
categories for which recognition of the right to
collective abstention from work might compromise
functions or services considered essential.[47]

Doctrinal construction enumerates, among the
goods and interests constitutionally protected, public health and safety, human liberty and dignity,
the right to work, equal treatment, and justice as
the ultimate end of the judicial branch, thus reaching the conclusion that the right to strike should
be denied to the police, to wardens, to the military, to medical personnel, to judges, and the
like.[48]

Up to now, the judicial branch has had little
opportunity to apply these principles to concrete
cases. For example, the Supreme Court has decided
that strikes by employees of the state railroads,
as long as they are directed toward economic goals
and are put into effect with due security measures,
are legal because the railroad service does not
satisfy primary interests.[49]

One of the concrete cases more frequently examined during recent years is that of strikes by municipal police. This is a rather sensitive question,
since the municipal police (which are subordinate to
the communes) carry out various functions, including
police functions. Court decisions regarding the incompatibility existing between the right to strike
and police functions are almost unanimous.[50] Police
forces are not authorized to strike because they
represent the instrument used by the state to attain
the essential end of maintaining internal law and
order.

In the majority of the decisions referred to
above, however, municipal policemen have been ac-
quitted either because--in consideration of the
present situation of uncertainty in this matter--
the court held that they acted under the assumption
that they were exercising a right[51] or because the
court has held as being essential only those police
functions that the municipal policemen were willing
to carry out.[52]

Conversely, in the case of the military, judges, national police force, and the like, their exclusion from the right to strike seems in principle quite certain; however, since there have been no strikes in these sensitive sectors of public employment, there are no judicial pronouncements on them.

Within the judicial branch certain groups have discussed the possibility of resorting to strikes as the final means of obtaining their economic requests. Yet in 1967, during a speech delivered in his capacity as president of the Superior Council of the Judicial Branch, the chief of state reiterated the principle according to which the right to strike cannot be authorized within the judicial branch on account of the essential nature of the functions carried out.[53]

6

SWEDEN
Steven D. Anderman

The large-scale labor dispute in the public sector in Sweden in early 1971 came as something of a surprise to many people. It had not been commonly known that Swedish public officials were highly organized, enjoyed the right to strike, and engaged in collective salary negotiations with the government, let alone that labor relations in the public sector were more "strike-prone" than were those in the private sector.

This lack of knowledge is easy to understand. After all, most research efforts have concentrated on the system of collective bargaining for blue- and white-collar workers in the private sector.[1] Moreover, collective bargaining in the public sector is a very recent development. Although Swedish public employees have enjoyed a formal right to join trade unions for several decades, it was only in 1966, with the enactment of the State Officials Act and related legislation, that they were given the right to bargain collectively and to strike to support their negotiating claims.[2]

Accompanying the new legislation were two other related developments. First, the government signed a basic agreement* with the major trade

---

*The agreement in the public sector is known popularly as <u>Slottsbacksautalet</u> and was signed on December 29, 1965.

union confederations in the public sector providing
for general negotiations and grievance procedures,
an extensive "peace obligation" while procedures
were being exhausted, and a special procedure to
deal with conflicts threatening essential public
services.   Second, the government established a
National Collective Bargaining Office (NCBO) to
negotiate with the major trade unions in the public
sector.

Although the 1965 legislation considerably improved the existing legal position of public officials, the legal reforms stopped short of giving
public officials complete equality with private employees in two important respects. Special legal
restrictions were placed on the content and scope
of negotiation and collective agreements in the
public sector and on the right of public officials
to strike. Yet the overall effect of the 1965 reforms was to promote a system of collective bargaining in the public sector that is comparable in
many respects to that in the private sector--that
is, highly centralized in its structure and fairly
comprehensive in its coverage.

That this new system of collective bargaining
should evolve into one more highly prone to direct
action than that in the private sector is an issue
requiring a more extensive explanation. The purpose of this chapter is to examine the nature and
certain effects of the 1966 legal reforms in Sweden
in some detail and to indicate the characteristics
of the new system of collective bargaining that
they have fostered in the public sector. This can
best be done by first describing the types of employees in public employment in Sweden and the
trade union organizations that represent them.

EMPLOYMENT IN PUBLIC SECTOR

Public employment in Sweden is divided into
three broad sectors--national government service,
municipal government service, and the public corporations responsible for wholly nationalized industries. The national government service includes

TABLE 10

Salaried Employees in Government Service and in State-Subsidized Activities, Sweden, 1969

Authorities	Number of Employees		
	Males	Females	Total
General Civil Service and Defense Organizations			
Ministry of Justice	20,040	7,340	27,380
Ministry for Foreign Affairs	1,030	712	1,742
Ministry of Defense	33,171	8,988	42,154
Ministry for Social Affairs	3,470	6,572	10,042
Ministry of Communications	6,282	1,606	7,888
Ministry of Finance	5,445	2,997	8,442
Ministry of Education	13,874	10,154	24,028
Ministry of Agriculture	3,112	1,935	5,047
Ministry of Commerce	629	652	1,281
Ministry of Industry	673	288	961
Ministry of the Interior	3,324	3,244	6,568
Ministry of Civil Service Affairs	6,396	11,065	17,461
Riksdag (parliament), with Bank of Sweden and National Debt Office	537	586	1,123
Total	97,983	56,139	154,122
State Business Enterprises			
Post Office Administration	23,289	20,128	43,417
National Telecommunications Administration	13,691	13,857	27,548
Swedish State Railways	36,378	2,020	38,358
National Power Administration	3,888	771	4,659
Swedish Forest Service	1,199	401	1,600
National Defense Factories Organization	2,144	705	2,849
National Civil Aviation Administration	719	232	951
Total	81,308	38,114	119,422
All central government employees	179,291	94,253	273,544

Public primary education	23,922	44,965	68,887
School directors	119	3	122
General secondary schools and continuation schools	7,522	4,357	11,879
Other municipal schools	162	154	316
Vocational schools	5,041	3,377	8,418
People's colleges	850	579	1,429
Schools of agriculture	203	237	440
Schools for handicapped children	337	1,281	1,618
Retraining courses	1,000	244	1,244
Clergymen	2,487	37	2,524
Church organists	372	121	493
Museums	71	72	143
Research institutes	17	15	32
Public insurance offices			
Inebriates' institutions	264	181	445
Institutions for handicapped people	81	424	505
Art institutes	17	27	44
County forestry boards	1,187	380	1,567
Total	43,652	56,454	100,106
Grand total	222,943	150,707	373,650

Source: <u>Statistical Reports 1970</u>, National Central Bureau of Statistics.

all the main government departments, Parliament,
the Bank of Sweden, and the National Debt Office.
The public corporations include the post office,
telecommunications, Swedish railways, and the power
and forestry services.* Municipal government service includes not only the ordinary municipal administrative departments but also many important
social services--such as social welfare, secondary
and primary school education, child care, and public health--that are wholly financed by the national
government. (See Table 10.)

Any estimate of the total number of employees
in the public sector is bound to be very crude between national census years. Labor force surveys
carried out in the interim period suggest that employees in the public service may number more than
900,000 and constitute over 25 percent of the
Swedish labor force. They also suggest that the
public sector has been a growing proportion of the
labor force.[3] (See Table 11.)

If total employment in the public sector is
difficult to measure, there is one category of public employee for whom much more precise information
can be obtained--the Swedish state official. In
Sweden all public employees are divided by legal
and administrative measures into two groups: state
officials and ordinary public employees.

The latter are treated as if they were ordinary private employees for the purposes of collective bargaining and labor legislation. The former
hold special "positions of responsibility" and enjoy a highly favorable security of tenure. They
are regulated by separate statutes relating only to
officials and are covered by special collective
bargaining machinery in which the government nego-
tiates directly with the trade unions representing
them.

_____

*Those industries that are only partly nation-
alized are excluded from the public sector, even
though particular firms may be predominantly or
wholly state-owned.

TABLE 11

Employed Persons by Labor Market Sector,
Sweden, 1960 and 1969

Sector	1960 Number (thousands)	1960 Percent	1969 Number (thousands)	1969 Percent
Public Employment	597	18.0	951	25.4
White collar	385			
Blue collar	212			
Central government	313			
Municipal government	284			
Private Employment	2,195	68.0	2,423	64.9
White collar	748			
Blue collar	1,447			
Self-employed	450	14.0	365	9.7
Total	3,242	100.0	3,738	100.0

Sources: Data for 1960 from national census and
for 1969 from Labour Force Surveys, National Central
Bureau of Statistics, Statistical Reports.

This category cuts across all three sectors of
public employment. Thus, of the more than 373,000
state officials, approximately 154,000 are in the
national government service, 119,000 in the public
corporations in the nationalized industries, and
100,000 in state-subsidized activities at the
municipal level. (See Table 10.) It is this former

group of public employees--state officials--with
which this chapter will be principally concerned.*

Although the legal position and terms and conditions of employment can vary quite drastically
depending on whether or not a public employee is
classified as a public official, the criteria for
classification have never been clearly specified.
The 1966 reforms avoided tackling the definitional
problems, thus leaving a pattern of classification
consisting of an accretion of principles that, although covering certain obvious groups, occasionally
appear arbitrary and unsystematic in their application.

The first principle of selection, drawn from
criminal law, holds that those persons holding positions of public responsibility and, therefore,
subject to the penal code for misconduct in service
are state officials. The application of this principle has resulted in the exclusion of most manual
workers and many employees in very subordinate
grades of employment--for example, caretakers in
schools or assistant nurses.[4]

In all government departments and agencies
discharging traditional functions of the state,
however, the subordinate status of the employee is
disregarded. Thus, in the court system and in central government departments and agencies nearly all
employees--including typists, telephonists, and
messengers, as well as the higher civil servants--
hold "positions of public responsibility" and are,
therefore, state officials.

The second broad principle of selection is a
highly pragmatic one; it defines public officials
as those persons listed as officials by their employing authority. This principle is particularly
applicable to the municipal sector and has resulted

----

*Municipal officials, other than those offi-
cials employed in state-subsidized activities, are
covered by separate legislation and negotiate separately, but in both respects the pattern is similar to that for state officials.

in some anomalies. Thus, although most employees in municipal government departments and the professional and supervisory grades in municipal services --such as road maintenance, sanitation, water, power, and transport--are fairly consistently listed as officials, other grades of employers-- such as bus drivers, bus conductors, and firemen-- find their status varying, depending on the particular municipality with which they find employment.[5]

Finally, there is one group of employees in municipal employment that are not only classified uniformly as public officials but also treated as state officials in the sense that their terms and conditions of employment are regulated as if they were formally employed by the state--namely, persons employed in the state-subsidized services provided by the municipalities, notably social welfare, education, child care, public health, land-planning, and the like.

TRADE UNIONS IN PUBLIC SECTOR

Although it was not until 1966 that public employees formally enjoyed the right to bargain collectively and to strike, their right to join trade unions was legally recognized as early as 1937. In the exercise of their legal freedom of association since 1937, Swedish public officials have not been noticeably restrained. Not only is the overall density of unionization quite high--that is, 75-80 percent--but the 315,000 public officials have also joined no fewer than 62 different trade unions, with widely varying and sometimes overlapping organizational structures.

Yet, if they have permitted themselves a wide latitude in membership grouping, they have also displayed a high degree of discipline in the central coordination of their negotiation efforts. All 62 trade unions in the public sector are affiliated with one of four central trade union confederations that are recognized as "principal organizations" for the purpose of negotiating directly

TABLE 12

Trade Union Membership, Sweden, 1969

Sector	LO			TCO			SACO			SR		
	Affiliated Unions	Membership Thousands	Per-cent	Affiliated Unions	Membership Thousands	Per-cent	Affiliated Unions	Membership Thousands	Per-cent	Affiliated Unions	Membership Thousands	Per-cent
Public employment												
Central government	(SF) 1*	147	8.9	(TCO-S) 13	159	30.0	30	44.5	55.0	36	19	100.0
Municipal government		200	12.3	(TCO-KO) 4	79	14.9						
Private employment												
Private employers		1,280	78.8		292	55.1		13.3	16.4			
Self-employed (professions)								7.9	9.8			
Total	29	1,627	100.0	25	530	100.0	30	80.9	100.0	36	19	100.0

*An amalgamation of eight unions, formerly in a confederation. Distribution of other unions within LO unavailable except for total.

272

with the government over terms and conditions of
public employment.*

The four central confederations differ widely
in their coverage. Only one organizes exclusively
in public employment. This is the rather tiny National Federation of Government Employees (SR),
which has 18,000 members in 34 affiliates, organizing the middle and higher ranks of civil servants.
Another confederation, the Swedish Confederation of
Professional Associations (SACO) is predominantly
a public employee grouping with almost 60,000, or
74 percent, of its members in 20 unions in public
service.

The two largest confederations, however, draw
a considerable proportion of their membership from
private as well as public employment and consequently
have had to create special organizational arrangements for employees in the public sector. Thus,
the Central Organization of Salaried Employees (TCO)
has a separate division for its 17 affiliated trade
unions and 159,000 members in national public employment (TCO-S), as well as one for its four member unions and 79,000 members in municipal employment (TCO-K). The Confederation of Swedish Trade
Unions (LO) with 1.6 million members and 29 affiliated unions, which organizes primarily among manual
workers, has recently established one large trade
union, the State Employees' Union (SF), for its
147,000 members in public employment.

The differences in coverage reflect important
differences in origin and have led to considerable
differences in organizational structure and orientation. Thus, the SF, the public officials' section of LO, is an amalgamation of unions of white-
collar workers in the lower grades of state and

---

*The central trade union confederations not
only negotiate but also represent their members on
government agencies--for example, the National Labor
Market Board--and in the legislative process when
the government elicits the formal reactions of the
organizations to legislative proposals on social and
economic issues.

local government and the nationalized industries and utilities--such as the railways, the post office, telecommunications, and so forth--that chose to join trade unions affiliated with LO before any separate unions for white-collar workers were formed.

Even when a separate white-collar confederation, TCO, began to organize salaried employees in the public service in 1937, these employees continued to favor their association with LO, forming the Federation of State Employee Unions (SK) within the LO organization. In June 1970 the eight unions in this federation amalgamated into one union, SF, organized along sectoral lines.[6] Until that point, however, the member unions were organized along industrywide lines, in keeping with LO's vertical organizational structure. Furthermore, these organizations have supported LO's highly egalitarian wage policies and have followed the political orientation of other LO members by affiliating with the Swedish Social Democratic Party.

The TCO-S was founded in 1937 by eight unions when the right of association was granted to public employees. It merged with the salaried employees' confederation in the private sector (DACO) in 1944 to form an association bridging the two sectors.[7] Its organization is extremely complex, for it contains affiliated unions that organize along vertical lines--such as the Swedish Union of Municipal Employees, the Federation of Civil Servants, and the Union of Civilian Employees--together with several organized along horizontal or occupational lines--notably, the Swedish Union of Specialist Teachers and the Swedish Nurses Association. In addition, owing to its position as a link between two sectors, the TCO frequently has to promote policies in the public sector that are compatible with its policies in the private sector. Unlike LO, it has no direct affiliation with a political party.

The two confederations of professional associations are more elitist in origin and orientation. Thus, the SR grew up to cater to those higher ranking civil servants who would not join the TCO, and its membership remains confined mainly to the

middle and higher grades of officialdom in the nationalized industries, particularly post office and
railways, in the customs office, and in the armed
forces. It too has no political affiliation.

SACO was founded in 1947 by a group of associations established by university graduates expe-
riencing difficulties in finding employment in the
early postwar period. The organizational structures of its member unions are horizontal, with
some affiliates organized along the fairly conventional concept of occupational unionism--for example, the Association of Secondary School Teachers
--whereas others are organized according to the
more unusual concept of educational unionism--that
is, with all graduates with the same university degree, notably graduate engineers, liberal arts
graduates, social science graduates, and the like.*
Because of its coverage, SACO's orientation and approach to economic and social policies in general
and wage and salary policy in particular are highly
sectional; it attempts to promote the interests of
its relatively small core of professional employees
at times quite openly at the expense of other employee groups. It has no political affiliation.

This pattern of trade union organization in
the public sector offers Swedish public officials a
wide choice of organizational representatives,
varying by type, size, and orientation. One result
of the organizational pattern is that differences
in interests find their expression in separate organizations and institutions rather than in factions of the same organizations and tend to create
rather more strongly entrenched differences in bargaining approach.

Another consequence of the mixture of trade
union organizational structures is the tendency for
the recruitment areas of different unions to overlap and for two or more unions to compete for membership within the same employee group. This is

_____

*SACO maintains that this is essentially only
a variant of occupational unionism.

true not only for different unions in different
confederations--as is the case, for example, with
the two teachers' unions in SACO and the TCO--but
also for two unions in the same confederation--for
example, the two university lecturer unions in
SACO. In the latter situation the problems can be
eased by double affiliation and amalgamation.* In
the former situation solutions have been less easy
to devise.

     Yet, although the competition between trade
unions in different confederations does occasionally cause complications and could conceivably be a
source of some difficulty in the future, the growth
of coordinated bargaining between the four confederations and the government has thus far tended to
promote cooperation at the central level, which
largely restrains the display of excessive competitive zeal at lower levels. This and other aspects
of collective bargaining machinery in the public
sector will be examined in greater detail below,
after a look at the legal framework within which it
operates.

LEGAL FRAMEWORK AND DEVELOPMENT

     Although the legal reform of 1965, which
granted public officials the right to bargain collectively and to strike, stopped short of giving
public employees complete parity of treatment with
private employees, it marked a clear advance on the
1936-37 legal position, which had been based on the
somewhat outdated concept of the public official as
the obedient and loyal civil servant.

----

     *There is evidence that the experience of col-
lective bargaining in the public sector has acted
as a spur to amalgamations within trade union confederations. This was a major factor in the LO
amalgamation, and it appears to be an important
consideration in SACO's proposals for amalgamation
as part of its planned reorganization.

In the 1936-37 period the legal position of public officials had been defined in the context of a
general labor law reform for employees in the private
sector. When the Collective Bargaining Act of 1936
gave to employees generally the right to join trade
unions, bargain collectively, and strike, it expressly excluded public employees in central and local
government who held positions of responsibility.[8]
Although the government recognized that it could no
longer regulate the terms and conditions of employment of public officials entirely on a unilateral
basis, it was unwilling to accept the notion that
public employees could bargain collectively through
representative organizations in a joint or bilateral
procedure along the lines suggested in the 1936 act.[9]

The government's unwillingness could be traced
to several factors, all reflecting the influence of
an excessively formalistic approach. Thus, the government was unwilling to give formal recognition to
the further erosion of its sovereignty in general and
that of its constituent departments or agencies vis-
à-vis employees. Similarly, it was reluctant to create a new legal position that might undermine the existing obligations of public officials holding positions of responsibility to perform their duties under
the penal code, for these obligations were regarded
as a guarantee that essential government functions
and services could be performed without interruptions.

Yet, in fact, public employees could and did
strike, and the penal code did not comprehensively
cover all crucial public employees. Finally, it was
felt that the security of tenure enjoyed by public
officials in order to give them the requisite degree
of independence of decision-making would act as a
limitation on the employer's right to use a lockout
in a conflict situation. Yet, of course, just as a
strike can be viewed simply as a suspension of the
employment relationship, it would have been possible
to regard a lockout in the same way.

Instead of authorizing collective negotiating
procedures and collective agreements for public officials, the government provided in a special decree in
1937 that government departments and agencies had a
duty to consult with and inform organizations of public officials. Moreover, before final decisions

could be made relating to new forms and conditions of employment, the organization or an individual had to be notified sufficiently early to allow negotiation and discussion on the issue to be proposed. The decree was quite explicit, however, that the employer had the exclusive right to make the eventual decisions as well as the right to discontinue negotiations at will.[10]

Yet, if the government's position on legal reform in the act of 1936 and the decree of 1937 was marked by an unwillingness to accept collective bargaining in the public service formally, its actions in succeeding years were characterized by an acceptance of collective negotiation by public officials in practice, for the philosophy and assumptions underlying the 1936-37 reforms were outdated shortly after they were given legislative effect. The 1936-37 reforms stimulated trade unionism in the public sector by implicitly authorizing the right of association. With the growth of civil service unionism and the expansion of activity in the public sector, a form of central negotiation developed between the trade union confederations and the Ministry of Civil Service Affairs. By the late 1950s these de facto negotiations had become highly developed.

T. L. Johnson described the position in 1961 as follows:

> The government, via the Ministry of Civil Service Affairs, is in effect collaborating in the development of a collective bargaining system for public activity, and is making no pretence of having an objective salary policy, based on justice or fair comparison. The economic model of the bargaining process in the public sector is now based on bilateral organization, which means that the freedom to negotiate must be permitted. The government has washed its hands of any attempt to follow the 1937 policy, of simply announcing its attentions and discontinuing discussions at its discretion. . . . To put the point another way, the government is not

> looking to the public sector to give
> a lead in wages policy by elaborating
> bargaining principles but simply ac-
> cepting a collective bargaining system
> based on organizational strength.[11]

It was largely in recognition of these developments that in 1965 in a series of legislative measures the Riksdag (Swedish parliament) formally
granted public officials the right to bargain collectively and to strike (and the government the right to
lock out) and authorized the establishment of the
NCBO to negotiate for the government. Yet the 1965
reform did not entail a shift to complete comparability between public and private employees. The government preferred to proceed with caution; the 1966
State Officials Act curtailed the new rights of public officials to negotiate and to strike in two essential respects.

First, certain subjects were excluded from negotiation in the public sector. Article 3 of the act
provided that no agreement could be made with respect
to the creation or abolition of a post, promotion,
the requirements and duties of a position, the organization of the public service, the supervision and distribution of work within a department, office hours,
the right to leave of absence, discipline, and, finally, the all-embracing category of "terms and conditions of employment or service which are regulated
by the State Officials Act or by other related legislation or which by law are the prerogative of the
government, Parliament [Riksdag] or specific government authorities."

Second, certain types of direct action were prohibited. Under Article 15 of the act state officials
could resort to a strike only when the dispute was a
"negotiable" one and the strike was officially authorized by the employees' union organization; wildcat or
unofficial strikes were illegal. Moreover, the statute did not allow public officials to engage in "partial strikes"--such as slowdowns, overtime bans, and
the like--although these were allowed in the private
sector. Public officials could either organize an
all-out strike or resort to a boycott or blockade designed to prevent the employer from hiring new employees. Finally, the act greatly restricted the

rights of public employees to strike in sympathy with other employees. Under Article 17 an official who is not himself involved in a labor dispute is bound to perform the ordinary duties of his office.

In addition to the special restrictions contained in the State Officials Act, public officials were made subject to the restraints on the right to strike contained in the general labor laws applicable to private employees--notably, the Collective Bargaining Act of 1936, the Collective Contracts Act of 1928, the Mediation Act of 1920, and the Labor Court Act of 1928.[12]

There are several restrictions on the right to strike in the Collective Contracts Act of 1936 and the Labor Court Act of 1928.* The most important of these, however, is the statutory restriction on issues covered by the contractual obligation. These issues are "justiciable" and must be settled by arbitration or appeal to the Labor Court but in any case without resort to industrial sanctions. Disputes of right are included in the justiciable category. Thus, where a dispute concerns the interpretation of a term of an existing collective agreement and where the parties exhaust voluntary procedures, they are obligated to take their dispute to the Labor Court.**

The concept of disputes of right has been further widened by the Labor Court interpretation that the very issue of whether a particular dispute is or is not justiciable is itself a justiciable issue. Thus, where either party asserts in good faith that the dispute relates to a matter regulated by the agreement, the other party may not take direct action until the Labor Court has decided whether or not the issue is justiciable.

Although direct action is limited in these aspects, it is condoned in two important areas. First,

_____

*These provisions prohibit strikes (a) to change existing contract terms during the period of the contract, (b) to invoke provisions that come into force after the contract has expired, and (c) to assist others where they are not entitled to resort to direct action.

**Justiciable disputes also include disputes about the application of an act.

the parties to collective agreements can use industrial sanctions even when bound by agreement, if they
are engaging in purely sympathetic action. Second,
where the dispute is one of interest, or nonjusticia-
ble--that is, a new claim--there is no prohibition
on direct action even during the contract term.

In the latter case, however, there is one further statutory limitation on direct action, contained
in the Mediation Act of 1920.[13] This act places on
the parties an obligation to give seven days' notice
of work stoppages, whether lockouts or strikes, to
the other party and to the mediators, together with
an obligation to attend a mediation procedure if required.* But the obligations under this act are
largely procedural, the parties being required only
to participate in the mediation process, not to
reach agreement. Once mediation proves to be unsuc-
cessful, the parties are free to resort to ad hoc
arbitration or industrial action.

The intended effect of this legal framework is,
thus, to limit and channel open conflict by public
officials. The only "strikeable" disputes are interest or nonjusticiable disputes over "negotiable" issues. The only acceptable forms of industrial action are union-authorized strikes after due notice
is given and the mediation process has failed.

BASIC AGREEMENT

Closely related to the legal reforms of 1966
was the basic agreement signed by the government and
the four central trade union confederations in the
public sector. The signing of the basic agreement
was in keeping with the tradition in the private
sectors of the Swedish labor market according to
which central agreements serve as a substitute for,
or complement to, legislative enactments. The tradition was started in the manual worker sector when
LO and the Swedish Employers' Federation (SAF) signed
the basic agreement of 1938 prescribing negotiating
and grievance procedures for each industry, regulating questions of layoffs and dismissals, and

----

*The sanction for failure to give notice is
only a fine not to exceed 300 Swedish krona.

placing certain limits on the use of economic sanctions.[14] It was extended into the salaried employee
sector in 1957, when a similar basic agreement was
signed between the two key white-collar confederations, SIF and SALF, and SAF.[15]

In 1965, as legislation was being prepared for
state officials, a similar basic agreement was
signed for the public sector. Following the pattern
of other basic agreements, the basic agreement in
the public sector provides for two types of procedures to regulate collective bargaining: a procedure for the negotiation of new claims and the processing of grievances--that is, disputes over the
interpretations of rights under existing agreements--
and a procedure for dealing with conflicts threatening essential public services.

Negotiation and Disputes Procedure

Under the basic agreement the negotiation and
disputes procedure has three distinct functions.
First, it recognizes the four central trade union
confederations as the bargaining agents for public
officials competent to conclude central collective
agreements or authorize sectoral agreements. Second, it sets out a two-stage disputes procedure,
with time limits, to process grievances and disputes arising while a collective agreement is in
force.* Thus, according to the basic agreement,
Article 12, in "any dispute between the parties to
a collective agreement, whether or not over the interpretation or application of the agreement, the
issue shall be referred in the first instance to
'local negotiation' within two weeks of request."

According to Articles 4-11 of the basic agreement, the local negotiations take place between the
public authority designated by the NCBO and the

---

*There are other time limits on the right to
process grievances. According to Article 12 of the
basic agreement, after six months the right to process a grievance is lost, as the right to call for
negotiations over any issue after two years.

trade union concerned. If there is failure to agree
at the local level, the issue can be referred to
"central negotiations," which must begin within
three weeks of the referral. The appeal from the
local to the central stage must be lodged within
two months. At the central level, if the dispute
concerns an existing agreement, the parties to the
procedure will be the parties to the agreement.
Otherwise, the parties at the central level will be
the parties relevant to the particular issue who
are competent to negotiate a collective agreement
on the issue.

The third function of the negotiation and disputes procedure is to enunciate and extend the
peace obligation, or "no-strike" promise. According to Article 14 of the basic agreement, no offensive action may be taken by either side until that
party has exhausted the required procedural steps
or has given the other party notice in writing
within three months of the termination of negotiations.

Procedure for Protecting Essential
Public Services

Under the procedure applicable to conflicts
that threaten the performance of essential public
services, when either party thinks that a dispute
may disturb important public services, that party
can request the other to negotiate with a view toward avoiding, limiting, or resolving the conflict
without harm to the public. If the other party refuses to negotiate or if such negotiations break
down, either party can refer the issue to the State
Employee Council to determine whether or not the
conflict threatens an essential public service.

The State Employee Council consists of eight
members, four appointed by the state and four representing the central trade union confederations.
The council elects a chairman and vice-chairman
from among its members and decides all issues by a
simple majority vote. All members must be present
before a vote can be taken. If the conflict is
thought to be dangerous to a public service, the

council can recommend measures to limit, avoid, or
resolve the conflict.

According to Articles 16-18 of the basic agreement, if a question is referred to the council, all
offensive actions must be postponed for two weeks
or until the council makes a decision, whichever
occurs first. If after two weeks the council has
not reported, the parties are still not free to
take industrial action if the council has informed
the parties that it needs more time to make the
decision. In that event the parties must abstain
from direct action either until the council reports
its decision or until three weeks have elapsed from
the time the issue was first referred to the council.

It is important to note that both the peace
obligation in the negotiation and disputes procedure
and the reference to the State Employee Council in
the basic agreement augment the limitation on the
right of public officials to strike contained in
the 1965 State Officials Act, for Article 15 of
that act provides that strikes or lockouts are unlawful if forbidden by collective agreements.

STRIKES IN PUBLIC SECTOR

Although the incidence of strikes in the public
sector has been higher than has that in the private
sector, the legal framework has been largely successful in achieving its objectives. This is so
mainly because of the limited ambitions of the web
of legislative and contractual limitations on the
right to strike, for the peace obligations are designed not to prevent strikes in support of collective bargaining demands at the end of contract
terms but, rather, essentially to prevent conflict
while a contract is in operation.* That there have
been end-of-contract work stoppages is more a reflection of the failure of the negotiation processes
than the legal framework.

----

*The six-week strike prohibition passed in
March 1971 was considered to be only an ad hoc measure.

Examination of the Swedish experience since 1966 suggests that the legally enforceable peace obligations have had the effect of "channeling" conflict by discouraging strikes during the terms of collective agreements. Since the acquisition of the formal right to strike in 1966, all direct action has taken place in connection with the negotiation of new collective agreements.

The 1966 round of negotiations resulted in a four-week dispute in the educational sector. The four-week teachers' strike in 1966 started with a spot strike by 1,200 SACO members in universities and secondary schools. After about a week the NCBO responded by locking out all SACO members in the categories affected by the spot strike. SACO retaliated by calling out 7,500 public officials in ministry and central and local government administrations for a three-day strike. At its height the dispute involved almost 30,000 officials. The issue involved was one of salary allowances. The results were mixed. The strikers did not get retroactive pay.[16]

In the 1969 round of negotiations there were four strikes in different government administrative departments: roadworks, navigation, the state railways, and the prison administration. The strike affecting the roadworks board lasted 22 weeks and affected foremen in five of the 24 road administration regions. The strikers in the prison administration were 80 foremen in four institutions. The navigation board suffered a strike of 300 of its 460 pilots for five weeks. On the Swedish railways 800 out of 5,000 engine drivers and their assistants called a 48-hour strike. The NCBO countered with a lockout of the two unions for the same period. In 1971 the dispute extended to the railways, civil service departments, and secondary and higher education. Yet of all three rounds of disputes not one involved a violation of the peace obligation or the statutory limitation on particular types of strikes; all were authorized by trade unions and took the form of overt work stoppages.

The success of the peace obligation in helping to channel and reduce conflict in the public sector

during 1966-71 can be attributed to several factors.
One is the habit of accepting the peace obligation
in the private sector. Another, possibly, is the
particular willingness of public officials to accept procedures and avoid open conflict. The most
important factor, however, is the point that the
legislative and contractual peace obligations attempt only to channel conflict, not to prohibit it
entirely.* Public officials and their unions know
that at the end of the contract term they are free
to negotiate the agreement and challenge the existing rule, for the legislative structure leaves much
scope for negotiations on the right to strike in
support of the negotiation claim.**

COLLECTIVE BARGAINING IN PUBLIC SECTOR

In introducing collective bargaining to public
officials the reforms of 1966 placed certain restraints on its scope. Not only were special restrictions placed on the right of public officials
to strike, but, as noted above, certain subjects
were also excluded from collective negotiations by
the operation of the State Officials Act. Moreover,

---

*It is true, however, that the unions have
seriously criticized both the breadth of the legislative peace obligation and the limits on particular types of strikes.

**Although there were some reservations ex-
pressed by the government in 1966 that the right to
back up negotiation by strikes would severely alter
the balance of power between the state and its employees, it is now accepted that the right to lock
out employees allows the state to maintain a satisfactory balance. Both the NCBO and the trade union
confederations are building up war chests for future conflict.

certain high public posts were excluded from negotiations by agreement.*

Yet despite these restrictions, the overall
effect of the reforms was the establishment of a
new system of collective bargaining for public officials. The most distinctive feature of this system is its high degree of centralization of negotiations. Not only do the central parties lay down
the general increase in salaries and fringe benefits
from year to year, as is done in the private sectors, but the central negotiations for public officials also go further and determine the composition
and development of the salary structure.

That a highly centralized system of collective
bargaining should evolve in the public sector in
Sweden was not particularly surprising, for it was
to be expected that the public officials would tend
to emulate the pattern in the private sector. That
the degree of centralization of negotiations in the
public sector should exceed that in the private
sector can be explained only by the government's
need to pursue a bargaining policy that is consistent in its application throughout the various government departments and agencies.

Government's Negotiating Machinery

To the government a highly important element
of the 1965 reforms was the reorganization of its
machinery for collective bargaining with public officials. Before 1965 the government had dealt with
trade unions in the public sector through one of

---

*Thus, even before the introduction of the
system of joint negotiation, the Ministry of Civil
Service Affairs had agreed with the principal trade
union organizations to omit certain high civil service positions--notably, Supreme Court justices,
the public prosecutor and ombudsman, the higher
grades in the ministries (and in the NCBO), and the
chief official of the administrative agencies.

its departments, the Ministry of Civil Service Affairs. After 1965 the task of negotiating with the
central trade union confederations was entrusted to
a new public agency, the NCBO.

The reorganization after the 1965 reforms at-
tempted to balance several, not altogether harmonious, objectives. To achieve a consistent and acceptable bargaining policy on the government side,
the central bargaining agency had to be able to
reconcile the widely differing interests and coordinate the varying activities of the many different
government departments and agencies. In addition
to this need for horizontal coordination, there was
a need to coordinate vertically between the negotiating body and the other levels of the government
hierarchy, the government itself--that is, the executive branch--and the Riksdag. Yet here the need
for the negotiating body to have an adequate degree
of autonomy in direct negotiations with the central
trade union confederations had to be balanced with
the need to ensure that the bargaining results fit
in with the government's and the Riksdag's budgetary
decisions and policies.

The influence of these factors can be discerned
both in the organization of the NCBO and in the
actual negotiating procedures. In the organization
of the NCBO an attempt is made to ensure adequate
coordination by a form of integration. The 11-
member governing board contains a majority of representatives from its client departments: the director generals of the National Accounting Bureau, the
Central Bureau of Statistics, the National Telecommunications Administration, the Post Office Administration, and the Swedish State Railways; the
chancellor of the universities; and the head of personnel and welfare in the defense staffs.

In addition, there are two officials from the
Ministry of Finance: one an undersecretary in
charge of the ministry's unit for salaries, pensions, and general staff questions; the other a
representative of the ministry's budget department.
Finally, there are two officials from the NCBO itself, the head of the legal department and the director general of the NCBO, who is chairman of the

governing board and who also has overall responsibility for conducting negotiations. The board is
supported by a large secretariat.

The design of the negotiation procedure, in
contrast, contends with the problems of coordination not by attempting integration but, rather, by
separation of negotiation into two stages. The
first stage consists of direct <u>negotiations</u> between
the NCBO and the central trade union confederations.
The second stage, once agreement is reached in negotiation, consists of a process of <u>ratification</u> by
the government and the Wage and Salary Delegation
of the Riksdag.

In the first stage, direct negotiation, the
negotiating round formally begins three months before an existing agreement terminates, usually after
the principal organizations have given their notice
of termination and have presented their claims for
salary increases and changes in other terms of employment. Technically, all contracts end on January 1, but Swedish public officials have not adopted
a "no-contract, no work" policy. They have on occasion agreed to, and have probably established a
precedent for, a prolongation of negotiations with
the results to be applied retroactively.

In the NCBO draft plans are prepared for the
round of negotiations and are submitted for approval
first to the governing board and then to the government, primarily through the minister in charge of
the unit for salaries and personnel questions. The
government gives the NCBO certain guidelines for the
negotiations concerning the total amount and the
form of the increase, in line with budget forecasts.
In the course of the actual negotiation direct contact is maintained by the NCBO with the various departments, since issues related to these departments
arise in negotiation. When the negotiating parties
reach agreement, the NCBO signs only conditionally--
subject to the approval and ratification of the
Council of State, which in turn presupposes ratification by the Wage and Salary Delegation.

The ratification process is short, usually no
more than two weeks. It consists of two meetings
of the Council of State and an intervening meeting

of the Wage and Salary Delegation. This delegation
has 16 members--eight for each chamber--and is responsible not only for ratifying collective agreements for public officials but also for following
the negotiations throughout their course. The head
of the finance department of the NCBO acts as a
link man between the NCBO and the government and
parliamentary delegation, informing both groups of
developments in negotiations and passing along governmental and parliamentary reactions to these developments.

It has been subjected to severe criticism by
the central trade unions in the public sector. The
unions maintain that under the present arrangement
they negotiate with the weakest level of the government hierarchy and that negotiations are made
undesirably complicated by the lack of decision-
making authority on the part of the NCBO. The
unions give two examples of this: first, the inci-
dent with the "Night Agreement" in the 1966 teachers' strike, when a preliminary agreement hammered
out by the NCBO and the unions was found unaccept-
able by the government, although the unions thought
that the agreement had in fact been approved; and,
second, the tendency of the NCBO at certain critical
stages in the mediation process to refuse to agree
to a change without referring back to the relevant
department.

It has been suggested by at least one union,
SACO, that the government should attempt to inte-
grate its negotiation machinery by creating an independent wage and salary negotiating delegation to
represent the entire employer side--that is, the
Riksdag, the government, and the various departments.
From the preliminary reports of the Commission of
Inquiry appointed to examine this question, however,
it appears likely that the reforms will be largely
concerned with an internal reorganization of the
NCBO to improve horizontal and vertical coordination
rather than any change in the two-tiered process of
negotiation and ratification.[17]

Central Wage and Salary Negotiations

As has been seen, the government's need to pursue a consistent bargaining policy throughout the public sector has provided the impetus for the high degree of centralization of wage and salary negotiations for public officials. The four central trade union confederations and the NCBO determine in central agreements not only the general increase in salaries and fringe benefits from year to year but also the composition and development of salary structures.

Until the 1971 salary round, centralized negotiations appeared to be functioning fairly successfully, in the sense that they provided a uniform policy for public officials regarding salary level and structure that was generally accepted by the parties covered by the agreements. Yet the breakdown of the 1971 negotiations was a symptom of the growing feeling among the central unions in the public sector that both the high degree of centralization and the coordinated salary policy have become less acceptable.

Since 1966 there have been two sets of central agreements, or "package deals," for public officials: one for the 1966-68 period and the other for 1969-70. The 1966-68 agreements established the initial salary structure by adopting the existing salary schemes that had been worked out by the Ministry of Civil Service Affairs and the central trade union confederations in 1957 and set out criteria for the allocation of posts to particular salary schemes and grades.*

---

*The "package deal" consists of three agreements--the General Pay Agreement for State Officials (Allmänt avlöningsavtal for statliga och vissa andra tjansteman), the General Agreement on the Allocation of Posts to Salary Grades (Allmänt tjänste-förteckningsavtal), and the Agreement on the Allocation of Posts to Salary Grades in the Educational

The 1966-68 agreements also provided for a progressive increase of salaries throughout the three-year period. For 1966, the first year, the central agreement stipulated not only the general increase but also the way in which the increase would be distributed to different groups of public officials. In the second and third years, however, the central agreement stipulated a general salary increase, which provided a cost framework or salary kitty for each sector, and set out guidelines for the distribution of the increase in each sector.

Consequently, the central negotiations had to be complemented by a second round of negotiations, at departmental and agency level, to allocate the total cost increase among the different grades within the sector. This second round of negotiations—called distribution negotiations—was carried

---

Sector (_Tjansteforteckningsavtal for tjanster inom undervisningsomradet_).

These agreements provide for four main salary schemes—A, B, C, and U. Scheme A comprises 33 grades and almost all lower and middle grades of government service. Scheme B applies to the lower echelons of the higher civil servants—for example, division heads in central administration and heads of regional agencies. Scheme C applies to the highest-paid civil servants, heads of departments, and so forth. Scheme U is a special scheme applying only to the educational sector, particularly university jobs.

Each salary grade in Scheme A and the first 22 salary grades in Scheme U contain four salary steps, each applicable at three-year intervals. The lowest step in each salary grade is the same number as the grade itself—for example, in A17 the four steps for the grade would be A17, A18, A19, and A20 —and most grades overlap. Moreover, there is some differentiation by cost-of-living zone. In Schemes B and U26-31, however, there is only one step to each grade and no provision for cost-of-living zones.

out under a contractual peace obligation--that is,
the parties were not able to resort to direct action to support their claims.

In the 1969-70 agreement, however, the decen-
tralized methods of distribution negotiations were
abandoned. The two-year agreement laid down a general percentage increase of 1.5 percent in 1969 and
an across-the-board flat-rate increase of 40 Swedish
krona in 1970, as well as special increases designed
to alter the salary structure. In particular, all
employees in the lower grades of the structure--
Grades A and U1-23--received a supplementary increase.

Even under the highly centralized agreements
of the 1969-70 period there has been some flexibility in the system. Thus, when a department is
"substantially reorganized," there is room for new
group negotiations--called AB negotiations during
the contract term. A second source of salary increases during the contract term are individual attempts to have jobs regraded or the creation of new
posts by public authorities. These methods constitute a source of salary drift in the public sector,
accounting for an average annual increase of 1 percent of the total salary bill. There are, in addition, certain negotiations in which the NCBO has
delegated its authority to particular departments
and agencies, although these are fairly marginal in
scope.

In some ways the results of centralized negotiation have been quite favorable. The total salary
increase of 55.5 percent during the 1963-69 period
compares favorably with an increase of 46.5 percent
for salaried employees in industry but falls short
of the wage increase of 60.8 percent for manual
workers during the same period. But, when the
costs of fringe benefits are taken into account,
the state officials appear to move more closely in
line with manual workers. (See Tables 13 and 14.)
Moreover, central negotiation has produced a distinct upward shift in the distribution of posts in
the salary structure. (See Table 15.)

The fringe benefits derived from collective
agreements have, in addition, placed public officials

TABLE 13

Salary Increases for State Officials,
Sweden, 1963-69
(Percent)

Year	Annual Increase	Salary Drift*
1963-64	5.1	1.0
1964-65	5.5	1.0
1965-66	7.9	1.0
1966-67	10.5	1.0
1967-68	9.9	0.8
1968-69	7.0	1.3
1963-69	7.0	1.3

*Figures for salary drift for 1963-65 are approximations.

Sources: Tjansteman inom statliga och stats-understodd verksamhet, National Central Bureau of Statistics (Stockholm, 1965); and SAV lonestatistik (1969), Statens Avtalsverk.

TABLE 14

Labor Cost Increases in Three Sectors,
Sweden, 1963-69
(Percent)

Sector	Wage or Salary Increases	Other Labor Costs*	Total Increases
Manual workers in industry	60.8	10.0	70.8
Salaried employees in industries	46.5	7.0	53.5
State officials	55.5	12.0	67.5

*Include pension, sick pay insurance, industrial accident insurance, life insurance, severance pay, and holiday pay. Figure for state officials is a crude estimate.

Source: National Central Bureau of Statistics.

TABLE 15

Distribution of Jobs in Salary Grades,
Sweden, 1963 and 1969
(Percent)

Salary Grades	1963	1969
A1–A8	27	7
A9–A12, U1–U4	27	28
A13–A19, U5–U11	35	38
A20–A30, U12–U22	10	25
All grades above A30, including those in schemes B, C, and U	1	2

Sources: Tjansteman inom statliga och stats-
understodd verksamhet, National Central Bureau of
Statistics (Stockholm, 1965); and SAV lonestatistik
(1969), Statens Avtalsverk.

in a favorable position vis-à-vis other groups.
Thus, although the standard workweek of 40 hours is
comparable to that for white-collar workers in the
private sector, public officials, through collective agreements, enjoy somewhat longer holidays,
higher pensions, and more favorable sick pay and
maternity benefits.*

---

*According to legislation, workers are entitled
to a vacation with pay of at least 24 days or, including the intervening Sundays, just under four
weeks a year. In the private sector a collective
agreement varies the annual vacation only with the
salary level, whereas for public officials the annual vacation varies with salary grade and age in
the following way:

Salary Grade	Age −29	Age 30–39	Age 40+
A1–9	24	27	30
A10–20	27	30	33
A21 or higher	33	36	40

Yet, despite these favorable results, there is
some question whether the tight degree of control

Most public officials receive an annual vacation of
more than four weeks.

According to the government's service pension
regulations, the retirement age varies depending on
the position, but the usual upper, middle, and
lower limits for retirement are 60-63, 63-65, and
65-66 years of age. A full pension--that is, after
30 years of service--generally amounts to 65 percent
of the official's salary, with other benefits also
salary related. The level of pensions is not adjusted by a cost-of-living index but, rather, is
raised regularly by collective negotiation. As a
general rule, the pension increases by approximately
the same percentage as does the salary. The pension, in fact, consists of three components: the
national basic old age pension and the national supplementary pension, which all employees get, and an
additional supplementary pension especially for public officials.

Sickness benefits and allowances of various
kinds in connection with illness or injury (for
example, reimbursement of costs for treatment,
traveling expenses, and so forth) are regulated by
collective agreement and constitute additions to
benefits available under the ordinary rules to the
general public. According to legislation, the employing authority pays out comprehensive benefits
to the official, generally in the form of a full or
slightly reduced salary (reductions of 8-11 percent)
but takes over the official's claim against the
national insurance authorities.

Maternity benefits are payable as a lump sum
under the national insurance scheme. In addition,
sickness benefits are payable for the time, not ex-
ceeding 180 days, that the mother is away from work.
But, where the mother is a public official, she is
paid her normal salary with a slight reduction
(8-11 percent), with the public employer taking
over the mother's claim against the national insurance authorities.

at the central level can be maintained. One source
of strain is the developing reaction to the monopoly on negotiation rights enjoyed by the four principal trade union confederations. Already there
are signs of employees wishing to be represented in
negotiations by unions other than those in the "big
four." A common characteristic of the four strikes
in the 1969 negotiations was that they were initiated by unions that had broken away from the
principal confederations and wished to conclude
their own agreements with the NCBO.

Other pressures for decentralization appear to
be emanating from the central union confederations
themselves. Both the TCO and SACO have recently
committed themselves to a return to a two-stage negotiation procedure, along the lines of that followed in 1965-7, with a central agreement setting
out the general increase in the cost framework,
followed by local negotiations to distribute the
salary kitty for each sector. But the primary
source of centrifugal pressure is the growing di-
vergencies in salary policy between the four central trade union confederations.

Even during the first five years of collective
bargaining (1965-70) in the public sector, the four
confederations could not always agree on the general
policy that the increase in the salaries of public
officials should follow the pay trend in the private sectors of the economy. That the negotiations
for public officials would take as a guideline the
negotiated increase in wages for blue-collar workers, together with the estimated wage drift, as the
starting point for increases in the public sector
was only grudgingly accepted, particularly by SACO.

From the start SACO was unhappy with the so-
called follow-John mode of negotiating salaries in
the public sector. In recent years and particularly
in the 1971 salary round SACO's concern with the
basis for negotiations has been augmented by its
discontent with the effects on its more highly paid
members of the generally accepted egalitarian wage
and salary policy pursued by LO, the TCO, and SAF
in the private sector. In the 1971 round SACO
found an ally in the SR, which also represents the
higher-paid civil servants.

The prime mover of the policy of wage and salary solidarity has been LO. Originally its policy was based on narrowing differentials created by market forces and bargaining power within each industry. By 1951 this policy had widened its focus to interindustry differentials and had taken on an element of differentiation. All "work of a similar kind" was to be "equally expansive for all employers," and the weighting of pay between different types of work was to "be done with reference only to the difficulty of the job and the requirements placed on the employees" regarding training, demanding conditions of work, risk of accidents, and seasonal unemployment.[18]

More recently, however, the emphasis has once again shifted. Now the focus is on the low-paid worker, and the policy consists of systematically narrowing existing pay differentials. Thus, it is suggested that special pay increases should be given automatically every year to employees receiving less than 96 percent of the average wage and salary earnings. In addition, the new LO union in the public sector, SF, supports the policy of adjusting the salary structure in the public sector systematically in favor of the lower-paid public officials.

In its salary structure policy for public officials, the TCO also appears to be influenced by the policies formulated for TCO members in the private sector. The TCO places great emphasis, however, on the need for equitable differentiation of salaries. Its policy stresses the need to retain differentials based on job evaluation and merit evaluation rather than market forces.[19] Its aim is for equal pay for equal work and differentiation based on the degree of difficulty of the job and the effort and skill of the individual employees in the job. Yet it endorses the need for a gradual reduction of differentials by special increases to the lower-paid officials, although it would not go along completely with LO's policy.

Conversely, SACO has become acutely disturbed about the effects of wage and salary equalization policies in negotiations in the private and public

sectors. It maintains that these policies have resulted in a steady deterioration of the real salary
levels of the middle- and higher-grade public offi-
cials--that is, its membership. To counteract this
development it has suggested that negotiations over
salary increases should take into account not only
the effects of prices on nominal salary earnings
but also the effects of direct taxation on gross
salary earnings.

The only meaningful trends to compare, it ar-
gues, are the trends in "net real earnings." It
maintains that its duty to its members is to ensure
not only that net real earnings do not decline but
also that they increase slightly, allowing SACO
members to share in the growing standard of living.
Its only concession to the more widely supported
goal of greater pay equality is its pronouncement
that net real earnings for its members should rise
at a lower rate of increase than does the average
for all employees.

The difficulty with SACO's argument is that a
"net real" increase in the earnings of the higher-
paid public officials, even if well under the average for all employees. requires a gross pay increase
of no small magnitude. Thus it was that SACO opened
up the 1971 round of negotiations with a pay demand
of almost 25 percent for its highly paid members.
And thus it was that SACO was willing to isolate
itself from the TCO and LO sections representing
public officials.

**SUMMARY
OF COMPARATIVE
PUBLIC POLICIES
AND PROCEDURES**
Seymour P. Kaye

Although the labor turmoil and tumult plaguing
the public sector may be time-capsuled for posterity,
the problem of impact and control is here and now.
Whether it be postmen or policemen in London, Berlin,
Milan, Brussels, Stockholm, or New York, the public
scene is "where the action is."

Concentrated attention has focused on moon
landings, tracking planetary wastelands, and chart-
ing expansive seas rather than on man-created
threats to the survival of fragile cities. Admit-
tedly, the world seems strangely homogeneous, with
the world awakening to orbit and environment, and
impressively universal in global concern with space
and waste.

Even on this terra firma of threshold conflict,
space semantics have become the mother tongue to
describe earthly problems of collective labor disputes and urban crisis. "In these days, when you
can reach for the moon," observed one spokesman for
public employees, "how can union leadership settle
for less?"[1] And there has been said to be two
great flights of Americans in the 1960s--"away from
crumbling cities and to the beckoning stars."[2]

Ever present, between ocean depths and solar
heights, are the rugged realities confronting and
forming the terrain of this book. Rather than won-
dering and theorizing, the international commentators here have explored the inner workings and
outer limits of public bargaining in the United

States, Belgium, Great Britain, the Federal Republic of Germany, Italy, and Sweden. The route was
programmed to view the right to associate or organize, the structure of employee organizations, the
framework of consultation and negotiation procedures,
and methods of impasse settlement.

Within these topical boundaries one encounters
common and uncommon links formed by the bridge of
common elements and the gap of dissimilar characteristics. Transcending geographical borders are
the prevailing patterns of the burgeoning growth
of public employment, the spiraling increase in
union membership, the trend of representation by
employee organizations, the competitive quest for
equality between the public and private sectors,
and the varying governmental resistance to full-
fledged collective bargaining between coequals,
justified by rules of sovereignty, maintenance of
the public interest, continuity of services, protection of the public good, and conservation of
fiscal resources.

The character and highly visible nature of
public bargaining generates heated conflict, fired
by press and partisans, that too frequently ex-
plodes settlements. The bargaining dialogue becomes, in the public eye, a civic plot played by a
cast of victims and villains, with the resigned
role of the public portrayed as a numbed citizenry
that, under the bludgeoning of strikes and slowdowns, comes to take a certain pride in surviving
the fates.

A comparison of the United States with Europe
reveals a fundamental disparity in the focus and
cohesion of decision-making with budget-making.
Centralized European settlements, fused into national or regional agreements, contrast with the
broad-scale U.S. situs of public labor relations,
diffused into federal, state, county, and municipal
areas.

The locus of U.S. bargaining is at the local
level, and the urban boiling point of New York City
has propelled its mayor into flight, as he takes
to helicopters to survey multiple civic caldrons.
In beleaguered New York City, the civic transfer

from sovereignty to sufferance has been challenged
for creating a crisis-ridden metropolis challenged
to govern the ungovernable.

Chaotic competition and confusion spring from
a melee of leapfrogging and one-upmanship played on
federal, state, and local fields of contest between
U.S. unions vying for bigger and better settlements.
Local contests are waged with municipal rivalry between police, fire, and sanitation forces contending for priorities and premiums allied to their respective hazards and hardships.

Three-tiered interplay may find a pension
claim aimed at the state legislature, fired at the
city bargaining table, and lodged with the federal
government for revenue support. This cross fire
can wreck the truces and pile up contract casual-
ties. Such fragmentation makes for short-term im-
prints rather than long-term patterns.

In contrast, broad-scale but controlled European negotiations seem to promote the necessary per-
spective for concluding long-term agreements and
for diminishing border labor skirmishes that cul-
minate in open-end amnesties. On the Belgian public front, for instance, the government may passion-
ately condemn strike coalitions of unions as a combined assault upon the entire nation; but, nevertheless, the very nature of concentrated combat by a
centralized command allows for easier armistices.

Battling for money is also less of a European
struggle due to the cohesiveness between budget-
making and contract decision-making. In contrast,
the typical U.S. city suffers the common urban
malady of mounting costs supported by an overbur-
dened tax base and ailing with bargaining table decisions that are circumscribed by predetermined
budgets and threatened by state legislative disapproval.

Unlike the facile European parliamentary implementation of cabinet and ministerial decisions, the
U.S. public scene lends itself to rivalry and contests between legislatures and executives of different political creeds and breeds described in the
capitol voyage of New York City Mayor John V. Lindsay
as follows: "When I prepare for the Albany journey,

I think of Henry Hudson who began his journey as captain of the stately Half-Moon and ended it in a rowboat somewhere off the coast of Canada."[3]

In funding agreements, as in other labor relations facets, however, the unworkable is made to work. More flexible and viable practice presents a different everyday countenance to rigid statutory appearances once the legislative veil is stripped from the real operative look. Therefore, comparative readings require depth soundings to deflect ritual from reality truly and to reflect transition from tradition. The fact of practiced de facto collective negotiation makes a comparative fiction of prescribed de jure advisory consultation. Thus, the "pleasure of the crown" may really operate like the public will, exemplified in private law-making between associations and government; and employment status changes its origins from allegiance to agreement.

Practical necessities explain the erosion of sovereignty and the shoring up of bilateral settlement. The currents of change are caused by the need to recruit and maintain qualified employees, compensate for the leveled or lost privileges of public employment, and deal effectively with strong employee associations. There still remains, however, a gulf separating the public and private sectors. Resisting substantial drift toward parity are the impediments of guaranteeing continuity of essential public services, securing compatible coexistence between collective bargaining and merit systems, and providing skilled, sophisticated management bargainers. Perhaps the strongest deterrent is the becalming effect of budgetary restraints on bargaining.

ILO PROFILE ON PUBLIC SERVICE

Just as labor relations in the private sector were nursed from turbulent infancy to pacific maturity, so the emerging public sector has been cradled in unrest. But, with the growth of dialogue, displacing the restraint of authority, the public

sector is coming of age, as witnessed by the following ILO comment:

> The restricting of the right to organize,
> the limitation of consultation and col-
> lective bargaining procedures, and un-
> satisfactory methods of settling dis-
> putes concerning terms and conditions
> of employment are tending to disappear.
> There is an increasing disposition to
> seek ways of reconciling the sover-
> eignty of the State with the accepted
> practice of good employers. The growth
> of trade unionism among civil servants
> . . . and the extent to which civil
> servants in many countries increasingly
> claim and assert the same rights as
> enjoyed by workers in the private sec-
> tor, are important factors in this
> situation.[4]

ILO conventions are multifaceted, dealing with
three fundamental labor relations freedoms: the
right to associate, to represent, and to strike.
But, contrasted with the private sector, public employees are specially viewed with discrimination,
mirrored in the two following resolutions. Convention No. 87, ratified by 78 countries, provides
that "workers and employers, without distinction
. . . shall have the right . . . to join organizations of their own choosing" (art. 2) whose exercise "shall respect the law of the land" (art. 8.1)
and whose "guarantees for the armed forces and the
police shall be determined by national laws and
regulations" (art. 8.2).* Convention No. 98, implementing the right to organize and bargain collectively, qualifies the position of public servants
by excluding them from its scope without "prejudicing their rights or status in any way" (art. 6).**

---

*See Appendix A, below.

**See Appendix B, below.

To correct this appearance of a double standard, a committee of ILO experts have noted and/or recommended the following:

1. The action and performance of local government officials and those working in public services of a commercial or industrial nature resemble practice in the private sector.

2. There was substantial ratification of the right of public, as well as private, employees to organize subject to the consistent law of the land and limitations on members of the armed forces and police.

3. Countries should encourage public servants to be members of organizations of their own choosing.

4. The "law of the land" should not impair guarantees.

5. Appeal procedures should be established to review refusal or withdrawal of recognition of representatives.

6. Implementation of minimum protections should include expeditious hearings by authorized employer representatives, organization entrée and access to workplace premises consistent with safety and security, facilities for posting information, reasonable use of premises for holding meetings, dues collection during working hours, defense of members before judicial or statutory bodies, regular information to representatives on subject matter of hearings, assistance to organizations in training officers and representatives, travel allowances and transport facilities to employer and employee representatives in their joint collaborative efforts, and granting of special full- or part-time leave without loss of seniority, promotion, or pension rights.

7. Exclusions and restrictions exist that affect special categories of public servants like the police and armed forces (except for qualified military rights in the Federal Republic of Germany, Norway, Sweden, and the United Kingdom; and qualified police rights in Belgium, the Federal Republic of Germany, Norway, Sweden, and the United Kingdom).

8. There is equality of status for low-echelon salaried and manual workers, and employees of state-industrial corporations with the private sector (in Belgium, the United Kingdom, and the Federal Republic of Germany).

9. Collaboration should be encouraged between the state and its staff on matters of common interest through either consultation, legislative hearings, or collective bargaining.

10. Collective bargaining or consultation should be utilized on such problems as conditions of employment, safety and health, recruitment, promotion, and training.

11. Governmental executives should be authorized to make decisions on wage matters.

12. Dispute settlement procedures should be established within the framework of law, customs, and practices.*

There is no common mold to shape a uniform, formfitting right to organize that is adaptable to all countries. Patterns, varied in form and fit, recognize freedom to associate through the following:

1. Legal recognition accorded through general legislation applicable to public and private employees--as in the Federal Republic of Germany, the Netherlands, and Sweden

2. Legal protection accorded as a basic civil liberty under common, customary, or constitutional law--as in Norway, the United Kingdom, the Federal Republic of Germany, and Italy

3. Legal sanction extended by public service or special statutes--as in Belgium and the United States.

There is less diversity and much more of a common denominator in the national exercise of association. This overall similarity is explained by the hard core of European power that resides with a few unions speaking for many employees

---

*See Appendix C, below.

before one or several ministries or agencies. This
centralized European cast contrasts with the splin-
tered cut of the fragmented U.S. system.

Concentrated European representation lies with
three unions in the Federal Republic of Germany
speaking for nearly 1.5 million manual workers,
salaried employees, and civil servants; three Swedish unions speaking for over 0.5 million public employees; two Belgian unions welded into a "common
front" to match the national locus of decision-
making by one employer; and the National Whitley
Council in Great Britain that coalesces 50 public
service organizations with over 3 million members.

Across the sea, much of the U.S. "labor cool"
has been "blown" in the heat of labor competition
fired by fractionalized craft and horizontal lines
that spills over municipal, county, state, and federal boundaries. The European experience offers,
for the United States, the promise of increased opportunity to plan policies and procedures, as well
as greater release from pressures of deadlines and
deadlocks.

REPRESENTATION PROCEDURES

Translating policies on association into procedures for participation involves a choice of informal or formal consultation, de facto or de jure
collective bargaining, or joint negotiations. Skeletal organizations' rights are fleshed alternatively
into different forms by way of being styled by law,
sized by custom, or shaped by necessity.

For instance, Italy, an emerging nation among
labor relations sophisticates, diversely guarantees
freedom of association by its constitution, officially disallows public collective bargaining except for employees of state corporations, continues
reviewing implementation, and engages in informal
consultation that concludes agreements operative
per se or enabled through legislation. The legal
format of employee participation for the Federal
Republic of Germany, Belgium, and Great Britain
runs the following gamut of more formal, structured
consultation:

In the Federal Republic of Germany civil servant organizations submit their views, comments, and recommendations on proposed legislative drafts. Work councils, which are personnel committees of employees rather than union bodies, participate in limited decision-making on such matters as hours of work and scheduling of vacations. Actual collective bargaining by associations of manual and salaried (white-collar) workers is theoretically subject to superior government approval.

In Belgium there is de jure consultation by and with civil servants in the shadow of collective bargaining. Legally prescribed joint advisory committees at national, departmental, and local levels have given way to de facto centralized bargaining on national "social programming" agreements covering wages, hours, and benefits; and these unenforceable agreements receive pro forma parliamentary or royal implementation. Manual employees and employees of state corporations enjoy labor relations comparable with those of the private sector.

In Great Britain there is bilateral, but not binding, negotiation and grievance determination by joint Whitley councils. Agreements are generally implemented without cabinet clearance and parliamentary approval. The processing of impasses to arbitration is based upon agreed minutes of relevant material arguments. Great Britain and Sweden merit special analysis--the former for its success with democratic consensus through joint consultation and the latter for its innovation with full-fledged, comprehensive bargaining.

The proponents of Whitleyism in Great Britain credit the effectiveness of joint consultation to centralization of administrative authority; standardization of practice; power support from the two-party political system; the relative demise of sovereignty; the flexibility of British law, recognizing resilient custom over rigid legal enforceability; and the "esprit" of the public corps, making a myth of Parkinson's law.

There are other unique traits of this agreement by consensus, such as the virtually unlimited scope of the powers delegated to the National

Whitley Council and the unanimity of decision by agreement between the two sides so that a deadlock cannot be resolved by a mere majority vote. Either the system or the British "stiff upper lip" deserves credit for surviving the onslaught of garbage from dustmen strikes and the drought of mail from postal stoppages.

The British system extends to other countries politically related to the United Kingdom in the present or the past. But in its own theater of action British verdicts are mixed, from objective audiences with "rave" reviews for responsive agreement to computerization, geographical transfer and relocation of personnel, and economic controls to critical notices for hampering productivity, inhibiting experimentation, and restricting innovation.

In balance, Whitleyism merits its applause and plaudits for its past performance of agreement and arbitration to harmonize partisan claims with the public interest. Whether the system continues to be a "good show" awaits future evaluation and judgment. Coexisting with joint councils are direct negotiations, with recourse to arbitration, for over 2,000 urban and rural, municipal and provincial, services employing workers of all professions and crafts.

There are, finally, countries that have evolved, in whole or in part, to legally authorized collective bargaining between near coequals. Public employees, with few exceptions, have the right to engage in collective negotiations and to exercise collective sanctions in both Sweden and Norway. This private lawmaking through agreement substantially resembles the private sector--that is, total identity between the sectors is broken by special public features and exceptions limiting, to some degree, public employees. But even in proscribed areas of limitation state employees significantly influence all relevant matters of interest.

For its innovative bargaining look and as a precursor of the future labor relations vogue the Swedish structure deserves close scrutiny. Closing the gap between private and public sectors, the law provides the following:

1. Established civil servants shall be included with other workers under a 1963 law on the right of association and of collective negotiation.

2. Such civil servants' organizations shall be equal partners with the employing authorities in negotiations of salaries and conditions of employment.

3. Agreement shall be reached in the form of collective agreements.

4. The interpretation of the meaning of collective agreements and their implementation shall, in the final instance, be decided by the Labor Courts, which operate for other categories of workers and on which both sides of industry are represented by the competent parties (that is, the employers' federation, SAF; the public employing authorities; and the two trade union centers, LO and the TCO).

5. Lockouts and strikes are permitted as coercive measures in a labor dispute about conditions of engagement or conditions of work for which collective agreements may be concluded.

6. The right to take coercive action applies to all those in the employ of the state, regardless of the way in which their working conditions and other such things are decided. This right is to be enjoyed by both permanent and temporary civil servants, manual and nonmanual, in the employ of the state.

7. In a separate law applicable to civil servants the basic duties and rights of state civil servants are laid down, as is the scope of the agreements to be concluded.

8. An agreement has been concluded between the state and the main civil servants' organizations (the civil service sectors of the four Swedish national centers) regarding negotiating methods and the treatment of disputes that may be injurious to the community.

Legislation is so worded that agreement can be reached on all conditions of employment except those specifically exempted in the state civil servants' law or in other legislation. Some of the exceptions

reserved for unilateral decision are the establishment, organization, and discontinuance of a service;
and the work of a department or service, the management or distribution of work, and the fixing of
working hours and leaves other than annual holidays.

This means that all other salary and working
conditions can be settled by collective or individual agreements, such as the salary system and salary
amounts, special allowances additional to salary--
that is, compensatory payments, grading of jobs in
the salary system, level of pensions and pensionable
age, length of working hours, per diem allowances
and travel allowances, deductions of various kinds
for time not worked, length of holidays, length of
notice of termination of employment, and so forth.

Neighboring Norwegian public employees cen-
trally negotiate wages and working conditions
through three main federations of civil servant
unions. Together with their bargaining partner,
the Ministry for Prices and Income, bilateral wage
agreements are jointly presented for parliamentary
approval. There is a comparative U.S. match for
the Scandinavian way in the "mod" statutory look of
Pennsylvania and Hawaii. But for the rest of the
United States mixed labor relations are traditionally attired in either sovereignty, limitation, or
qualification.

Uniquely, perhaps, the United States lends
much to comparative experience and experiment in
its prolific use of comprehensive statutory enactment; regularized administrative machinery, enforcing both policy and procedure; and adaptable impasse settlement procedures. Unlike the compact
European scene, the U.S. scene is balkanized with
fragmented negotiations conducted federally, statewide, countywide, municipally, or by school district and diverse representation in the form of permissive bargaining, mandatory bargaining, meet-and-
confer consultation, or full-fledged bargaining.

Such diversity and decentralization permit new
problems to overtake current policies and to outrun
existing procedures. Thus, runaway disputes have
blanketed many U.S. cities over "bread and butter"
issues of pay, hours, and benefits. These urban

tempests backtrack on progress and revive basic
questions such as the following:

1. Whether administrative authority over employment conditions, traditionally exercised by
public officials, should now be shared with public employees
2. Whether the allocation of public funds,
much of it for labor costs, should be heavily influenced through collective negotiations
3. What degree of freedom public employee
labor organizations should have in pressing their
demands.

STRIKE ISSUE IN PUBLIC SERVICE

The public scene has been targeted by the
burst of militant strikes, stoppages, slowdowns,
picketing, demonstrations, and other protests disabling community services. The presence of "pickets at City Hall" generates the kind of inflamed
conflict that makes people choose sides rather than
seek solutions. What would be a mishap in the private sector becomes, by community passion or public
impact, a disaster.

In Great Britain, for instance, the $72 million
postal strike of 1971 ruffled enough political
feathers to change "angry silence" into "voice of
doom," as a cabinet minister intoned, "We're like a
destroyer heading at full steam towards the shore.
. . . There's only so much sea room and it's running out fast."[5] Equanimity of Swedish "solidarity"
broke with the lockout of 3,000 army officers, augmenting the ranks of striking teachers, railwaymen,
and other public workers to a strike swell of
50,000 disputants. Far off in New York City draw-
bridges were raised and locked, police and fire coverage faltered, garbage piled up, and schools closed.

Although most actions aimed at pay and benefit
increases, Italy's top civil servants struck to
streamline and speed up alleged elephantine administrative machinery. Protesting their roles as
"bureausaurs"--a word combination of "bureaucrats"

and dinosaurs"--chiefs of government departments, treasury inspectors, and certain foreign ministry officials took refuge from desks, phones, and documents.[6] Such action may be politically sheltered, based on noneconomic motives, or socially keyed to the expanding union role played in housing, education, and consumer protection.

The right to strike is internationally observed in the breach. Nowhere in the international public sector is there an absolute right to strike. Unlike the private sector, freedom to strike is restrained by reins that check or control stoppages. Patterns, ranging from outright prohibition to partial limitation, are as follows:

1. Statutory bans: U.S. strikes by federal and most state employees are prohibited.

2. De facto prohibition: The tacit intent of silent law in the Federal Republic of Germany, Belgium, and Great Britain is interpreted to prohibit strikes by civil servants.

3. Qualified strike rights: Sweden, Norway, and certain U.S. states, like Pennsylvania and Hawaii, grant freedom to strike in interest disputes, subject to exhaustion of peace machinery and exclusion of certain classes of essential employees.

4. Equality with the private sector: Constitutionally, Italian public employees enjoy parity with private employees but within the limits of regulatory laws. Ambiguously, applicable penal law would prohibit strikes by public servants; governing constitutional decision would permit such strikes for economic and nonpolitical reasons.

Law and practice within most of the countries blends strike rights for a few, qualified rights for some, and no rights for most. Thus, European nations generally equate manual, lower-echelon salaried, and state industrial employees with the private sector. The United States, without much logic and reason, generally prohibits strikes by public hospital employees but usually permits action affecting private hospitals.

Militancy is urged and condemned on both sides
of the Atlantic Ocean for the same reasons. Those
opposed to strikes in the public sector cite the
loyal obedience of the faithful public employee to
the sovereign prince and nation; the pledged commitment to the public interest served by continuity of
essential services; coercion of the law-making process; and the special, privileged status and treatment accorded public employees.

Those supporting the right to strike give the
following reasons: the rationale of equality for
private and public sectors; the noncoercive and nonessential character of most strikes, which inform
and rally public opinion; the accepted rule of contract over allegiance as contemporary criteria of
legal obligation; shadowy or blurred distinctions
between nonessential and essential services; the
diminution of special status and privileges of public employees; and the failure of unworkable sanctions to deter job actions.

The U.S. controversy rages over whether legislated morality breeds sin, whether strike prohibitions tempt strikes, and whether stoppages are
symptomatic of the prevailing protest syndrome.
The following case for true public bargaining, with
strike rights, is advanced by Theodore W. Kheel:

> There is no workable substitute for
> collective bargaining--even in govern-
> ment--and . . . our best chance to pre-
> vent strikes against the public inter-
> est lies in improving the practice of
> bargaining. In an environment conducive
> to real bargaining, strikes will be
> fewer and shorter than in a system
> where employees are in effect invited
> to defy the law in order to make real
> the promise of joint determination.
> In a real bargaining environment, the
> employee representatives, I am con-
> vinced, can more effectively meet their
> dual responsibility to negotiate and to
> lead. Only if leaders do both can
> there be constructive labor relationships

in place of the chaos resulting when
agreements reached in negotiations
are rejected by an angry rank and
file or defied by subterfuge forms of
strikes such as working to the rule.
    My suggestions are not put forth
with a guaranty that they will bring
a complete end to public employee
strikes. They will not. Rather I
suggest that reliance on legal prohibitions, penalties, and elaborate
third-party recommendations has not
worked, and that before we turn in
desperation to compulsory third-party
determination, which cannot serve as
a steady diet, we should give bargaining in the public sector the same opportunity it has received, with bene-
ficial results, in the private sector.
The most effective technique to produce acceptable terms, to resolve disputes in voluntary agreement of the
parties, and the best system we have
for producing agreements between groups
is collective bargaining--even though
it involves conflict and the possibility of a work disruption. There is no
alternative.[7]

But, with qualification, Theodore Kheel advocates
"cooling off" strikes, based upon injunction and
impasse settlement, to temper the heat of action,
which might jeopardize public health or safety.
    There is universal agreement on the need to
mate strike prohibition with impasse settlement in
order to yield a progeny of peaceful labor agreements and to wed strike rights with conciliation,
arbitration, and other dispute procedures in order
to propagate the several species of essential services. "Sane" impasse settlement is necessary, for
the barren specter of public strikes casts gloom
upon most public services and spells doom for some
essential operations.

IMPASSE SETTLEMENT

No single labor peace formula enjoys a halo of absolute virtue for every country or blessed solution for every dispute. Law and custom influence the choice of procedure; the character of the dispute sways the selection of method. Historically, law-makers have been loath to sanctify impasse settlement. First, there was the conviction that third-party intervention improperly trespassed on sovereignty and invaded authority. Second, dispute procedures were thought to delay and prolong decision-making. Thus, although tradition fought change, necessity forced innovation. This agonized appraisal was caused by despair, as high strike fever, epidemic of protest, and contagion of unrest compelled remedy and solution.

Once the dispute can be identified as to cause, diagnosed as to its course, and prognosticated as to its impact, it becomes possible to prescribe either conciliation, mediation, fact-finding, or arbitration. Thus, the formality of third-party intervention corresponds frequently to the demands of systematized bargaining.

The range of ad hoc or established dispute procedures includes the following:

1. Referral for further review and negotiation to a higher administrative authority (as in Belgium and the Federal Republic of Germany)
2. Voluntary conciliation initiated ad hoc or formally established (In Norway, for instance, the parties are required to apply to a conciliation officer or to accept an offer of conciliation. The competent forum in certain countries is the labor court.)
3. Fact-finding akin to advisory arbitration
4. Mediation or voluntary arbitration
5. Compulsory arbitration
6. Boards or courts of inquiry.

For instance, the absence of statutory provision for settlement machinery leads to the Italian practice of ad hoc consultation. In Belgium a 1969

national agreement established a joint committee
for the adjudication of local disputes covering all
public employees. Although the Federal Republic of
Germany provides no official mediation and arbitration machinery to settle interest disputes, the parties may agree to a mediation procedure exemplified
by the national collective agreement for municipal
councils and undertakings.

Joint Swedish committees may be established to
deal only with certain types of disputes. For instance, the Public Service Council is empowered to
handle refusals to bargain and threatened disrup-
tions of essential services. In addition, formal
machinery may be fixed by legislation, collective
agreements, or a combination of the two. Under
Swedish law parties may request independent arbitration, or the government may appoint an arbitration
commission.

In Great Britain Whitley and other class disputes can be channeled to settlement through conciliation, inquiry, and arbitration. Arbitration
for most of public employment is involuntary or compulsory, since the government must accede to arbi-
trable claims other than those that challenge major
policy and usually agrees to be bound by awards,
subject to the overriding but rarely invoked authority of Parliament.

By comparison with the prolific use of impasse
settlement in the United States, Europe offers little
in the way of formalized policy and procedure governing new, renewed, or modified agreements. But
there is extensive adjudication for individual
claims and for group claims relating to breaches of
existing agreements. The United States offers
broad experience, by way of precedent and practice,
in impasse settlement, maturing considerably in approach from prohibitions and penalties to rights
and remedies.

On both the federal and the local scene the
United States employs structured impasse settlement
to heal contract bruises, repair dispute damages,
and immunize against potential breakdown. In fact,
several states and cities have come to accept compulsory arbitration as a means of cooling labor

passion. Thus, New York City has chosen this route
as the road to labor peace governing new and modified agreements involving several hundreds of thousands of employees.

Compulsory arbitration, viewed as a perilous
avenue by conservative travelers, offers the promise of coupling neutral determination of the fair-
ness of adversary claims with a mutual pledge by
both sides to comply with any determination. Despite ritualized objections, there is labor recognition of the important role played by compulsory
arbitration in assuring equity without the coercive
pressure of walkout and the compelling stress of
member dissidence.

For a final fade-out, but with a lingering
view, this international roundup closes with the
following observations:

1. The changing public establishment tends
toward collective bargaining; de jure consultation is "flexed" to permit de facto negotiation;
and sovereign rule by decree is stretched to bilateral law-making through contract agreement.
2. The universal status of the collective
agreement, as a governing instrument for the establishment of public working conditions, is
still distant. In Norway and Sweden the collective agreement reigns over workers in the employ
of the state, public undertakings, and provincial
and local authorities. In a number of countries--
such as Denmark, Finland, Belgium, the Federal Republic of Germany, and Great Britain--public servants are divided into two groups, which come
under different legal provisions. For one group,
composed of unskilled workers, conditions are
fixed by collective agreement; for the other,
more professional group, composed of civil servants, conditions are fixed by statutory enactment. Elsewhere, as in Sweden, all public employees closely simulate the status of the private sector.
3. Reality indicates the need for formal, comprehensive recognition and use of bargaining techniques, since practice does not suffice for

provision and consultation does not equate with
collective bargaining. Consultative bodies--as
in Belgium and the Federal Republic of Germany--
mitigate rather than dissipate disagreement.

4. Comprehensive status, as employed by Sweden,
Norway, and a few of the U.S. states, provides the
advantages of methods for recognition, guidelines
for bargaining, procedures for impasse settlement,
and mechanics for implementation.

5. The scope of full-fledged bargaining generally embodies wages, hours, benefits, safety or
health, recruitment, transfer, promotion, and
training.

6. There is a prevailing right of public employees to form and join organizations. Thus,
trade union influence is assured through burgeoning membership.

7. There is worldwide consensus for the need
to prohibit or inhibit strikes, although "wildcat"
protest continues to frustrate community controls.
For Scandinavia and a few U.S. states or cities
the approach is to "cool" or delay disputes affecting essential services; for the greater part
of the globe the pattern is to prohibit all public
stoppages.

8. The impact of public disputes requires the
formal establishment, available use, and constant
refinement of impasse settlement to resolve conflict over "interests" as well as over "rights."

Enunciating an international role for public
unions, the Public Services International, a worldwide organization, observes the following:

> The providing of efficient public ser-
> vice is a primary duty of the public
> authorities. The efficient operation
> of that service is the primary duty
> of the public employee.
>
> Public servants are entitled to
> conditions of employment that corre-
> spond to modern precepts of social
> justice in matters of remuneration,
> stability of employment, social

security, assistance in acquiring
knowledge and skill for professional
advancement, justly regulated promotion on the basis of merit, and improvement of the conditions of life
pari passu with economic and technical progress.

Public servants should have the
guarantee of regulated and collectively agreed [upon] working conditions, the regulation to take, according to circumstances, the form of
a collective contract or Statute which
should be open to review in order to
adapt conditions of employment to economic, technical and social changes.

Public employees' trade unions
should contribute to the improvement
of public services. They should pay
particular attention to the good functioning of public services directly
affecting the life of the community,
such as education, public health,
water supply, light, transport, food
supply, etc.[8]

Equal in global scope is the necessary challenge and
response of those who speak for government:

With the increasing numbers of officials employed by the central and
local administration or other public
services and with the expanding payroll of publicly owned undertakings
or industries, the State has every-
where long been the largest employer
by a wide margin. It is universally
agreed that the role of the State in
the field of Labour-Management relations is therefore of vital importance. Conditions of employment in
private industry, of course, often
set the pattern in labour relations
and are subsequently more or less

observed by State undertakings. Nevertheless, as an employer, the State
can use its example to convince employers and trade unions outside its
own sphere as to what it considers to
be the best mode of behaviour or procedure.[9]

Meaningful interrelationship is keyed to
(a) identification of issues and interests; (b) comparison of practices, patterns, and programs; and
(c) realization of means and methods for achieving
harmony of interests and unity of understanding.
The search for roots hopefully has been a matter of
relevance rather than of rhetoric, a quest "far be-
neath the surface of . . . facile maneuver and easy
answer. . . . The roots mark values not evasions.
They trace firm beginnings, not forced endings.
And the purpose of their search is to learn, not to
hide."[10]

The General Conference of the International Labor Organization,

Having been convened at San Francisco by the Governing Body of the International Labor Office, and having met in its Thirty-first Session on June 17, 1948;

Having decided to adopt, in the form of a Convention, certain proposals concerning freedom of association and protection of the right to organize, which is the seventh item on the agenda of the session;

Considering that the Preamble to the Constitution of the International Labor Organization declares "recognition of the principle of freedom of association" to be a means of improving conditions of labor and of establishing peace;

Considering that the Declaration of Philadelphia reaffirms that "freedom of expression and of association are essential to sustained progress";

Considering that the International Labor Conference, at its Thirtieth Session, unanimously adopted the principles which should form the basis for international regulation;

Considering that the General Assembly of the United Nations, at its Second Session, endorsed these principles and requested the International Labor Organization to continue every effort in order that it may be possible to adopt one or several international Conventions;

adopts this ninth day of July of the year one thousand nine hundred and forty-eight the following Convention, which may be cited as the Freedom of Association and Protection of the Right to Organize Convention, 1948:

----

*Date of coming into force: July 4, 1950.

PART I: FREEDOM OF ASSOCIATION

Article 1

Each Member of the International Labor Organization for which this Convention is in force undertakes to give effect to the following provisions.

Article 2

Workers and employers, without distinction whatsoever, shall have the right to establish and, subject only to the rules of the organization concerned, to join organizations of their own choosing without previous authorization.

Article 3

1. Workers' and employers' organizations shall have the right to draw up their constitutions and rules, to elect their representatives in full freedom, to organize their administration and activities and to formulate their programs.
2. The public authorities shall refrain from any interference which would restrict this right or impede the lawful exercise thereof.

Article 4

Workers' and employers' organizations shall not be liable to be dissolved or suspended by administrative authority.

Article 5

Workers' and employers' organizations shall have the right to establish and join federations and confederations and any such organization, federation or confederation shall have the right to affiliate with international organizations of workers and employers.

Article 6

The provisions of Articles 2, 3 and 4 hereof apply to federations and confederations of workers' and employers' organizations.

Article 7

The acquisition of legal personality by workers' and employers' organizations, federations and confederations shall not be made subject to conditions of such a character as to restrict the application of the provisions of Articles 2, 3 and 4 hereof.

Article 8

1.   In exercising the rights provided for in this Convention workers and employers and their respective organizations, like other persons or organized collectivities, shall respect the law of the land.

2.   The law of the land shall not be such as to impair, nor shall it be so applied as to impair, the guarantees provided for in this Convention.

Article 9

1.   The extent to which the guarantees provided for in this Convention shall apply to the armed forces and the police shall be determined by national laws or regulations.

2.   In accordance with the principle set forth in Paragraph 8 of Article 19 of the Constitution of the International Labor Organization the ratification of this Convention by any Member shall not be deemed to affect any existing law, award, custom or agreement in virtue of which members of the armed forces or the police enjoy any right guaranteed by this Convention.

Article 10

In this Convention the term "organization" means any organization of workers or of employers for furthering and defending the interests of workers or employers.

PART II: PROTECTION OF THE RIGHT TO ORGANIZE

Article 11

Each Member of the International Labor Organization for which this Convention is in force undertakes to take all necessary and appropriate measures to ensure that workers and employers may exercise freely the right to organize.

PART III: MISCELLANEOUS PROVISIONS

Article 12

1. In respect of the territories referred to in Article 35 of the Constitution of the International Labor Organization as amended by the Constitution of the International Labor Organization Instrument of Amendment, 1946, other than the territories referred to in Paragraphs 4 and 5 of the said Article as so amended, each Member of the Organization which ratifies this Convention shall communicate to the Director-General of the International Labor Office with or as soon as possible after its ratification a declaration stating--

(a) the territories in respect of which it undertakes that the provisions of the Convention shall be applied without modification;

(b) the territories in respect of which it undertakes that the provisions of the Convention shall be applied subject to modifications, together with details of the said modifications;

(c) the territories in respect of which the Convention is inapplicable and in such cases the grounds on which it is inapplicable;

(d) the territories in respect of which it reserves its decision.

2.   The undertakings referred to in Subparagraphs (a) and (b) of Paragraph 1 of this Article
shall be deemed to be an integral part of the ratification and shall have the force of ratification.

3.   Any Member may at any time by a subsequent
declaration cancel in whole or in part any reservations made in its original declaration in virtue of
Subparagraph (b), (c) or (d) of Paragraph 1 of this
Article.

4.   Any Member may, at any time at which this
Convention is subject to denunciation in accordance
with the provisions of Article 16, communicate to
the Director-General a declaration modifying in any
other respect the terms of any former declaration
and stating the present position in respect of such
territories as it may specify.

Article 13

1.   Where the subject matter of this Convention is within the self-governing powers of any nonmetropolitan territory, the Member responsible for
the international relations of that territory may,
in agreement with the government of the territory,
communicate to the Director-General of the International Labor Office a declaration accepting on
behalf of the territory the obligations of this
Convention.

2.   A declaration accepting the obligations of
this Convention may be communicated to the Director-
General of the International Labor Office--
(a) by two or more Members of the Organization
in respect of any territory which is under their
joint authority; or
(b) by any international authority responsible
for the administration of any territory, in virtue of the Charter of the United Nations or otherwise, in respect of any such territory.

3.   Declarations communicated to the Director-
General of the International Labor Office in accordance with the preceding Paragraphs of this Article

shall indicate whether the provisions of the Convention will be applied in the territory concerned without modification or subject to modifications; when the declaration indicates that the provisions of the Convention will be applied subject to modifications it shall give details of the said modifications.

4.   The Member, Members or international authority concerned may at any time by a subsequent declaration renounce in whole or in part the right to have recourse to any modification indicated in any former declaration.

5.   The Member, Members or international authority concerned may, at any time at which this Convention is subject to denunciation in accordance with the provisions of Article 16, communicate to the Director-General of the International Labor Office a declaration modifying in any other respect the terms of any former declaration and stating the present position in respect of the application of this Convention.

PART IV: FINAL PROVISIONS

Article 14

The formal ratifications of this Convention shall be communicated to the Director-General of the International Labor Office for registration.

Article 15

1.   This Convention shall be binding only upon those Members of the International Labor Organization whose ratifications have been registered with the Director-General.

2.   It shall come into force twelve months after the date on which the ratifications of two Members have been registered with the Director-General.

3.   Thereafter, this Convention shall come into force for any Member twelve months after the date on which its ratification has been registered.

Article 16

1. A Member which has ratified this Convention may denounce it after the expiration of ten
years from the date on which the Convention first
comes into force, by an act communicated to the
Director-General of the International Labor Office
for registration. Such denunciation shall not take
effect until one year after the date on which it is
registered.
2. Each Member which has ratified this Convention and which does not, within the year following
the expiration of the period of ten years mentioned
in the preceding Paragraph, exercise the right of
denunciation provided for in this Article, will be
bound for another period of ten years and, thereafter, may denounce this Convention at the expiration of each period of ten years under the terms
provided for in this Article.

Article 17

1. The Director-General of the International
Labor Office shall notify all Members of the International Labor Organization of the registration of
all ratifications, declarations and denunciations
communicated to him by the Members of the Organization.
2. When notifying the Members of the Organization of the registration of the second ratification communicated to him, the Director-General
shall draw the attention of the Members of the Organization to the date upon which the Convention
will come into force.

Article 18

The Director-General of the International
Labor Office shall communicate to the Secretary-
General of the United Nations for registration in
accordance with Article 102 of the Charter of the
United Nations full particulars of all ratifications,

declarations and acts of denunciation registered by him in accordance with the provisions of the preceding Articles.

Article 19

At such times as it may consider necessary the Governing Body of the International Labor Office shall present to the General Conference a report on the working of this Convention and shall examine the desirability of placing on the agenda of the Conference the question of its revision in whole or in part.

Article 20

1. Should the Conference adopt a new Convention revising this Convention in whole or in part, then, unless the new Convention otherwise provides,
    (a) the ratification by a Member of the new revising Convention shall _ipso jure_ involve the immediate denunciation of this Convention, notwithstanding the provisions of Article 16 above, if and when the new revising Convention shall have come into force;
    (b) as from the date when the new revising Convention comes into force, this Convention shall cease to be open to ratification by the Members.
2. This Convention shall in any case remain in force in its actual form and content for those Members which have ratified it but have not ratified the revising Convention.

Article 21

The English and French versions of the text of this Convention are equally authoritative.

The General Conference of the International
Labor Organization,
Having been convened at Geneva by the Governing Body of the International Labor Office, and
having met in its Thirty-second Session on June 8,
1949, and
Having decided upon the adoption of certain
proposals concerning the application of the principles of the right to organize and to bargain collectively, which is the fourth item on the agenda
of the session, and
Having determined that these proposals shall
take the form of an international Convention,
adopts this first day of July of the year one
thousand nine hundred and forty-nine the following
Convention, which may be cited as the Right to Organize and Collective Bargaining Convention, 1949:

Article 1

1. Workers shall enjoy adequate protection
against acts of antiunion discrimination in respect
of their employment.
2. Such protection shall apply more particularly in respect of acts calculated to--
(a) make the employment of a worker subject to
the condition that he shall not join a union or
shall relinquish trade union membership;
(b) cause the dismissal of or otherwise preju-
dice a worker by reason of union membership or
because of participation in union activities outside working hours, or, with the consent of the
employer within working hours.

---

*Date of coming into force: July 18, 1951.

Article 2

1. Workers' and employers' organizations shall enjoy adequate protection against any acts of interference by each other's agents or members in their establishment, functioning or administration.

2. In particular, acts which are designed to promote the establishment of workers' organizations under the domination of employers' organizations, or to support workers' organizations by financial or other means, with the object of placing such organizations under the control of employers or employers' organizations, shall be deemed to constitute acts of interference within the meaning of this Article.

Article 3

Machinery appropriate to national conditions shall be established, where necessary, for the purpose of ensuring respect for the right to organize as defined in the preceding Articles.

Article 4

Measures appropriate to national conditions shall be taken, where necessary, to encourage and promote the full development and utilization of machinery for voluntary negotiation between employers or employers' organizations and workers' organizations, with a view to the regulation of terms and conditions of employment by means of collective agreements.

Article 5

1. The extent to which the guarantees provided for in this Convention shall apply to the armed forces and the police shall be determined by national laws or regulations.

2. In accordance with the principle set forth in Paragraph 8 of Article 19 of the Constitution of the International Labor Organization the ratification of this Convention by any Member shall not be deemed to affect any existing law, award, custom or agreement in virtue of which members of the armed forces or the police enjoy any right guaranteed by this Convention.

Article 6

This Convention does not deal with the position of public servants engaged in the administration of the State, nor shall it be construed as prejudicing their rights or status in any way.

Article 7

The formal ratifications of this Convention shall be communicated to the Director-General of the International Labor Office for registration.

Article 8

1. This Convention shall be binding only upon those Members of the International Labor Organization whose ratifications have been registered with the Director-General.
2. It shall come into force twelve months after the date on which the ratifications of two Members have been registered with the Director-General.
3. Thereafter, this Convention shall come into force for any Member twelve months after the date on which its ratification has been registered.

Article 9

1. Declarations communicated to the Director-General of the International Labor Office in accordance with Paragraph 2 of Article 35 of the Constitution of the International Labor Organization shall indicate--

(a) the territories in respect of which the Member concerned undertakes that the provisions of the Convention shall be applied without modification;

(b) the territories in respect of which it undertakes that the provisions of the Convention shall be applied subject to modifications, together with details of the said modifications;

(c) the territories in respect of which the Convention is inapplicable and in such cases the grounds on which it is inapplicable;

(d) the territories in respect of which it reserves its decision pending further consideration of the position.

2. The undertakings referred to in Subparagraphs (a) and (b) of Paragraph 1 of this Article shall be deemed to be an integral part of the ratification and shall have the force of ratification.

3. Any Member may at any time by a subsequent declaration cancel in whole or in part any reservation made in its original declaration in virtue of Subparagraph (b), (c) or (d) of Paragraph 1 of this Article.

4. Any Member may, at any time at which the Convention is subject to denunciation in accordance with the provisions of Article 11, communicate to the Director-General a declaration modifying in any other respect the terms of any former declaration and stating the present position in respect of such territories as it may specify.

Article 10

1. Declarations communicated to the Director-General of the International Labor Office in accordance with Paragraph 4 or 5 of Article 35 of the Constitution of the International Labor Organization shall indicate whether the provisions of the Convention will be applied in the territory concerned without modifications or subject to modifications; when the declaration indicates that the provisions of the Convention will be applied subject to modifications, it shall give details of the said modifications.

2. The Member, Members or international authority concerned may at any time by a subsequent declaration renounce in whole or in part the right to have recourse to any modification indicated in any former declaration.

3. The Member, Members or international authority concerned may, at any time at which this Convention is subject to denunciation in accordance with the provisions of Article 11, communicate to the Director-General a declaration modifying in any other respect the terms of any former declaration and stating the present position in respect of the application of the Convention.

Article 11

1. A Member which has ratified this Convention may denounce it after the expiration of ten years from the date on which the Convention first comes into force by an act communicated to the Director-General of the International Labor Office for registration. Such denunciation shall not take effect until one year after the date on which it is registered.

2. Each Member which has ratified this Convention and which does not, within the year following the expiration of the period of ten years mentioned in the preceding Paragraph, exercise the right of denunciation provided for in this Article, will be bound for another period of ten years and, thereafter, may denounce this Convention at the expiration of each period of ten years under the terms provided for in this Article.

Article 12

1. The Director-General of the International Labor Office shall notify all Members of the International Labor Organization of the registration of all ratifications, declarations and denunciations communicated to him by the Members of the Organization.

2. When notifying the Members of the registration of the second ratification communicated to him, the Director-General shall draw the attention of the Members of the Organization to the date upon which the Convention will come into force.

Article 13

The Director-General of the International Labor Office shall communicate to the Secretary-General of the United Nations for registration in accordance with Article 102 of the Charter of the United Nations full particulars of all ratifications, declarations and acts of denunciation registered by him in accordance with the provisions of the preceding Articles.

Article 14

At such times as it may consider necessary the Governing Body of the International Labor Office shall present to the General Conference a report on the working of this Convention and shall examine the desirability of placing on the agenda of the Conference the question of its revision in whole or in part.

Article 15

1. Should the Conference adopt a new Convention revising this Convention in whole or in part, then, unless the new Convention otherwise provides,
    (a) the ratification by a Member of the new revising Convention shall _ipso jure_ involve the immediate denunciation of this Convention, notwithstanding the provisions of Article 11 above, if and when the new revising Convention shall have come into force;
    (b) as from the date when the new revising Convention comes into force, this Convention shall cease to be open to ratification by the Members.

2. This Convention shall in any case remain in force in its actual form and content for those Members which have ratified it but have not ratified the revising Convention.

Article 16

The English and French versions of the text of this Convention are equally authoritative.

The Meeting of Experts on conditions of work and service of public servants,

Having been convened by the Governing Body of the International Labor Office,

Having met in Geneva from November 25 to December 6, 1963, with the following agenda:

(a) methods of staff representation and consultation in public administrations;

(b) nonestablished staff, its conditions of work and service;

Adopts this sixth day of December 1963 the conclusions set out below,

Draws attention to the report containing its discussions which should be considered jointly with these conclusions, and

Invites the Governing Body of the ILO to communicate these conclusions and the report to the States Members of the Organization and to international and national organizations of public servants.

I. METHODS OF STAFF REPRESENTATION AND CONSULTATION IN PUBLIC ADMINISTRATIONS

A. Introduction

1. The public services are at a turning point in their development. The expansion of their role in economic and social life makes for continuing problems of adaptation and change in administrative structures in most States, particularly those which have recently become independent and which are in the course of development. In many countries the State and its personnel have established a working system of labor-management relations and, depending upon the particular objectives concerned, apply administrative practices, adopt rules, establish structures and institute bodies with a view to perfecting the internal operation of public administration,

increasing the interest on the part of the staff in
the objectives of the administration, improving the
services expected of the administration, and con-
tributing to the progress of the whole population
while ensuring that workers in the public service
share in the fruits of this progress.

2. The experts had to limit their consideration to staff of services, the administration of
which is the direct responsibility of the central
government. They were not in a position to include
in their examination local government officials and
those working in public services of a commercial or
industrial nature, whether autonomous or not, the
activities and the management of which closely resemble practices in the private sector. They consider that most of the conclusions herein are valid
for the entirety of public administrations and particularly lower-level public administrations such
as those at the regional or local level. Differences in the legal systems have not prevented the
experts from reaching agreement as follows.

B.   Freedom of Association and Protection
of the Right to Organize

3. Convention No. 87 Concerning Freedom of
Association and Protection of the Right to Organize,
1948, has been ratified by sixty-five States. These
States have undertaken to guarantee to workers,
without distinction whatsoever and without previous
authorization, the right to establish and join organizations of their own choosing. This Convention
applies without discrimination to all workers including those in the public service. Apart from
respecting the law of the land governing workers
and their organizations in the same manner as other
persons or organized groups, the only limitation
provided for in the Convention is that which national laws or regulations might make on the exercise of freedom of association in respect of members of the armed forces or the police.

4. The international instruments adopted by
various sessions of the International Labor

Conference which deal with labor-management relations constitute basic standards of civilization,
the practical application of which in an increasing
number of countries can only create a favorable
climate for the establishment of good relations between public administrations and their staff, freely
organized in organizations, the fundamental and permanent objective of which is the economic and social
progress of their members.

5.   The experts are not unaware of the technical and legal difficulties faced by certain countries in connection with the ratification of these
instruments and the application of all their provisions to workers in the public service. Nevertheless, they request that the Director-General of the
ILO avail himself of every occasion and set in motion every means which the Constitution allows the
Organization to obtain additional ratifications of
these Conventions, better application of the Recommendations and the improvement, both in letter and
spirit, of the measures of implementation which are
taken for these purposes in the public service.

6.   The experts noted that at its 43rd Session
(Geneva, 1959), the International Labor Conference
had before it the report of the Committee of Experts
on the Application on Conventions and Recommendations which, among other things, dealt with the application of a series of international instruments
mainly concerning freedom of association, collective
bargaining and collective agreements, and which was
based essentially on information that States Members
had been invited to submit under Articles 19 and 22
of the Constitution of the International Labor Organization.

7.   They consider that such overall examination
of the effect given to the mentioned instruments by
States Members of the Organization, whether these
States have or have not ratified the Conventions and
whether or not they apply the Recommendations concerned, would, if periodically carried out, allow
for an evaluation of the progress achieved in this
fundamental area.

8.   They express the opinion that on the occasion of such examination particular emphasis shall

be given, in appropriate cases to the application
of these standards to public servants. The results
of this examination should enable the Governing
Body to consider whether some of these instruments
should be revised.

9. They, therefore, request that the Director-
General of the International Labor Office propose to
the Governing Body that in the near future it call
for a new examination of this nature of: the Freedom of Association and Protection of the Right to
Organize Convention, 1948 (No. 87), the Right to
Organize and Collective Bargaining Convention, 1949
(No. 98), the Right of Association (Nonmetropolitan
Territories) Convention, 1947 (No. 84), the Collective Agreements Recommendation, 1951 (No. 91) and
the Voluntary Conciliation and Arbitration Recommendation, 1951 (No. 92).

10. The efforts to introduce these international standards into the law and administrative
practice of the various countries will depend on
the real willingness of governments to consult or
negotiate, as appropriate under national laws and
regulations, with trade unions or other representative bodies, on conditions of work and service, including social and economic conditions of the workers. The experts recommend that countries should
create a climate of opinion which would encourage
public servants to be members of organizations of
their own choosing.

C. Recognition of Organizations for
Purposes of Representation

11. Alongside a number of countries in which
no procedure exists for recognition of public servants' organizations for purposes of representation,
the experts noted that in other countries regulations required observance of certain formalities or
the fulfilling of certain conditions in order that
freely constituted organizations can either validly
represent the staff or participate in the system of
consultation or collective bargaining.

12. The experts are of the opinion that organizations which are freely established, i.e. without previous authorization, may be required to respect formalities provided for by law. However, while the law must be respected, Article 8, Paragraph 2, of the Freedom of Association and Protection of the Right to Organize Convention, 1948 (No. 87), provides that "the law of the land shall not be such as to impair, nor shall it be so applied as to impair, the guarantees provided for in this Convention." This would be the case if the formalities and conditions required were such as to make previous authorization for the existence or functioning of these organizations, or if they constituted such an obstacle to the free establishment and normal development of organizations that the practical effects amounted to their prohibition.

13. Various conditions may be imposed in accordance with particular national circumstances. Without wishing to comment on each of these conditions, the effects of which can only be evaluated by taking into account the particular situation of the countries which have adopted them, the experts consider that the only conditions which may be provided for are those which would permit an evaluation of the representative character, responsibility and durability of the organizations concerned. The measures taken with a view to assessing if these conditions are fulfilled should not permit investigation on matters such as the number of members and accounts of these organizations except within the framework of procedures agreed to by the parties.

14. Where the regulations in force allow for the refusal or withdrawal of recognition of an organization for purposes of representation, an appeals procedure accepted by both parties should be established.

D.   Staff Representation

15. In those countries which have instituted a permanent system of relations, staff representatives

are designated either by trade union organizations
or by way of election in which all members of the
staff can participate. In the former case the administration should not interfere in the designation
of representatives by these organizations in conformity with their rules. In the latter case, the
organizations should, at least, have the right to
present or support candidates.

16. The establishment of continuous and fruitful relations with the staff and its organizations
requires that, beyond the minimum protection assured
by Convention No. 87 Concerning Freedom of Association and Protection of the Right to Organize, a set
of rules for collaboration be adopted either by
regulations or by agreement. These rules may vary
according to the method of collaboration adopted.

17. The facilities accorded to staff representatives for the exercise of their functions,
which are often the same as those enjoyed by recognized staff organizations, should not be such as to
impede the normal course of relations between the
State as an employer and the representative, responsible and durable organizations.

18. The administration should take all measures compatible with the normal functioning of its
services in order to ensure that the representatives
of the organizations, at a minimum, can:

(a) be heard, without unjustified delay, upon
request, by the administrative or political authorities which have decision-making power;

(b) freely enter the workplace, subject only
to the requirements of state security and safety;

(c) post in accessible places information for
the staff, possibly within authorized limits;

(d) enjoy the free use, possibly under agreed
conditions, of premises for holding meetings;

(e) collect organization dues, possibly under
agreed conditions, during working hours, either
directly or by means of material facilities
placed at their disposal; and

(f) defend the members of their organizations
before judicial or statutory bodies.

19. The details of the application of the measures mentioned in the preceding Paragraph should,

where necessary, be the subject of agreement between administration heads and the officers of the organizations. None of these measures should permit any interference by the administration in the internal operation of the organizations.

20. It is in the interest of effective collaboration for the administration to ensure that it regularly informs representatives in connection with all problems on which they may be called upon to be heard. The means of information may vary and, according to national circumstances, range from meetings at the governmental level to informational meetings or joint studies. In return, the administration should be able to require that representatives act with discretion regarding the utilization of information of a confidential nature.

21. With a view to successful collaboration, the administration should do what it can to help the organizations in their training programs for officers and representatives.

22. Staff representatives, where designated by organizations or elected by the staff to take part in collaboration bodies, should, in the exercise of their mandate, enjoy analogous conditions to those enumerated above. In such cases, and in cases when they are convened by the administration, they should be granted travel allowances and enjoy the same transport facilities as those accorded by the administration to its own representatives.

23. Since such representatives are frequently public servants, it would be desirable to adopt, through regulation or by agreement, rules indicating the conditions in which they are to exercise their functions.

24. Public servants who are occupied full- or part-time by representative organizations should be granted special leave which would have no effect on the normal progress of their career, e.g. on the calculation of their seniority, or on promotion or pension rights. Their right to total or partial wages should be decided by agreement, taking into account the national situation of each country. Staff delegates or representatives of organizations taking part in collaboration bodies should enjoy a

reasonable amount of time off for such activities
without loss of remuneration.

25. Appropriate measures should be taken to
guarantee staff representatives adequate protection
against any discrimination based on their functions.

E.   Consultation and Collective
Bargaining Systems

26. While there is no question that the State
as an employer and its staff should avail themselves of all possible means to ensure their full
collaboration in dealing with matters of common interest, it seems difficult to recommend any detailed, universal method for national action.

27. The choice of methods depends on many circumstances and particularly on the stage of development of particular countries, the nature of their
political structure, the particular concept which
they have of the duties of the public servant, the
administrative means available and the degree to
which organizations of public servants are representative.

28. This method might consist of occasional
or periodic consultation of the organizations by
the administration; such consultation itself might
take the form, under varying circumstances, of an
exchange of correspondence or of official or unofficial conversations. It might take the form of hearing representatives of the organizations by the
legislature. It might take the form of collective
bargaining entered into at times judged appropriate
by the parties. In any case, the utmost must be
done to ensure a rapid solution of the problems
posed.

29. Special attention should be given to the
practice, in certain countries, of having permanent
machinery for consultation or collective bargaining.
This has the advantage of ensuring continuity in
the administration's policy of collaboration with
its personnel, and, because it is entered into in a
spirit of complete equality, of promoting continuous mutual comprehension and good faith. The

framework, functioning and scope of these systems
are naturally determined by the particular circumstances of each country. They are characterized by
the existence of permanent bodies which are established at all appropriate administrative levels and
within which workers are represented either by
spokesmen of representative organizations or by representatives they have directly elected. These representatives are in a position to gain a wide experience and an overall view of the needs of sound
administration which increases their competence to
deal with the questions before them. The importance
of these systems should not, however, a priori eliminate from consideration other means of collaboration which have proved successful in certain countries.

30. The examination of various national ex-
periences shows that it is difficult to establish a
clear distinction between consultation on the one
hand and collective bargaining on the other. The
generalization of formal collective bargaining can
be impeded by the diverse concepts which in the different countries have inspired the distribution of
power between the various organs of the State. In
certain countries the executive authority is not
authorized to engage in real negotiations in various
fields such as wages.

31. It appears, however, that real consultation by governments or administrations can in fact
take place, resulting in a situation during which
no effort is spared by either party to reach agreement or a compromise which is submitted to the authority competent to make a decision. Such procedures, through the climate of confidence required,
will facilitate acceptance by the parties of final
decisions taken on the basis of previous joint ac-
cord. It was noted that such results achieved
within the framework of official consultation procedure are more apt to be realized to the extent
that staff organizations are more representative.

32. In view of the foregoing, the experts consider that measures appropriate to national conditions should, where necessary, be taken to encourage
and promote the widest development and utilization

of collective bargaining and consultation procedures,
in respect of such problems as conditions of employment, safety and health, recruitment, promotion and
training.

    33. The functioning of such procedures will
be facilitated if the administration and the representative staff organizations understand the increasing necessity of preparation on the part of
their representatives through adequate training in
the field of labor-management relations and human
relations.

F. Direct Participation in Administration

    34. Collaboration between the administration
and its staff or their representatives has taken
the form in many countries of participation in the
management of social, cultural or similar services
in regard to which it seems appropriate to associate the staff in the management of schemes for their
benefit and in the building up of the funds to which
they may have contributed. The experts noted ex-
periences in regard to the management of social services and social security funds. The State as an
employer and the staff are represented in differing
proportions. The tendency is developing under
which the staff seeks exclusive responsibility for
the management of funds for social services.

    35. The presence of staff representatives on
bodies participating in the administration of personnel in such fields as promotion, training and
discipline seems now to be rather widespread and
not to give rise to any particular problems in those
countries where this takes place.

G. Collective Disputes and Their Settlement

    36. Although the administration and represen-
tative staff organizations in an increasing number
of countries have adopted a system of consultation
and collective bargaining, and every effort is made
to render such systems as effective as possible

with a view to avoiding collective disputes there
does not seem to be the same widespread adoption,
in law or in practice, of conciliation or arbitration procedures.

37. The experts noted that legal disputes
which might arise out of the interpretation or application of a statute or collective agreement, and
disputes relating to questions of competence, recognition or the representative character of a staff
organization, are generally decided on the basis of
existing regulations.

38. The reasons mentioned in Paragraph 30
which impede the extension of collective bargaining
systems in certain countries also render difficult
the establishment of conciliation and arbitration
procedures.

39. On the basis of their examination of
these questions the experts consider that voluntary
conciliation and arbitration procedures, as defined
in Recommendation No. 92 Concerning Voluntary Conciliation and Arbitration (1951) should be established at all appropriate administrative levels,
taking into account the national legal framework
and customs and practices in respect of collective
relations in the public service.

H. Future International Action

40. The experts were unanimous in the view
that the International Labor Organization should
pursue its action in the field of staff representation and consultation in public administration by:

(a) the increased dissemination of information
on national laws, regulations and practices, on
the work of trade union congresses, etc.;

(b) the publication of studies undertaken by
the ILO either independently or in cooperation
with research institutions;

(c) the organization of regional seminars;

(d) the carrying out of a specialized program
of technical assistance in coordination with that
already undertaken by the United Nations in the
general field of public administration.

II.   NONESTABLISHED STAFF, ITS
CONDITIONS OF WORK AND SERVICE

41. The problem of nonestablished staff in
the public service arises in all countries under
widely varying conditions. The experts noted the
need for fuller information for a comprehensive
study of this problem. Nevertheless, they consider
that certain principles can be decided on at this
stage and these are dealt with in Paragraph 5. In
particular, it appeared to the experts that statistical data is inadequate for evaluating the number
and to define the categories of staff concerned.
It would be desirable for the ILO to collect comparable data of this type.

42. The experts recognize that needs of administrative organization of States are such that the
employment of a certain number of nonestablished
staff in public administrations can scarcely be
avoided. This is the case, for example, when the
posts they occupy are themselves of a temporary
nature or require a degree of technical knowledge
such that only highly qualified specialists who are
not officials can fill them.

43. Nevertheless, the experts consider that
this situation cannot justify administrative practices likely to cause or encourage discrimination
in the exercise of trade union rights and in the
conditions of work and service of workers performing the same duties in the same public administrations. Moreover, they note that such discrimination raises a problem of far-reaching magnitude,
when, for instance, large numbers of temporary staff
are retained in permanent posts for many years and
there is too great a discrepancy between their legal
and social status and those of established staff.

44. Although the principle of according the
same conditions of work to all staff, whether established or not, involves practical difficulties,
the experts, nevertheless, stressed a certain number of principles with a view to solving the problem of nonestablished staff or preventing it from
arising. How they are applied, and their effectiveness, depend on the particular conditions of each
country.

45. The experts agreed on the following principles:

(a) as far as possible, staff who are required to perform permanent duties should be recruited on an established basis;

(b) temporary staff should have the opportunity to become established within a reasonable time;

(c) when temporary staff are established, the length of their temporary service should be taken into account, as far as possible, particularly for purposes of pension rights to which they and members of their families may be entitled;

(d) the difference in legal status between established and nonestablished staff should not constitute a reason for discrimination in respect of remuneration and conditions of service as a whole.

Since 1933, Norway has had a separate act respecting the right of negotiation for civil servants (Act of July 6, 1933). This act introduced the <u>right</u> of negotiation for the organizations of civil servants and the <u>duty</u> of negotiation for the state authorities in the matter of wages and working conditions of civil servants. Through their negotiators the civil servants were given an opportunity to discuss their claims with the state negotiators both by word of mouth and in writing, and by means of voting the individual civil servant was afforded an opportunity to adopt an attitude toward the result of the negotiation. The state authorities still had the right, however, to reach a final decision independently.

Through a newer act respecting public service disputes (Act of July 18, 1958), a further step was taken. In accordance with this act the wages and working conditions of civil servants would be established mainly by agreement between the parties on an equal footing for fixed periods, just as is the case in private employment. The agreement is binding on both parties during the period to which it refers, and the civil servants will thus obtain a stronger position than before through their organizations but will also simultaneously incur a greater responsibility.

The 1958 act also introduces more modern forms of procedure as far as the actual negotiations between the state and the civil servants' organizations are concerned. Furthermore, it contains exhaustive provisions with regard to the consideration of the disputes that may arise. This act is based primarily on the recommendations of a special committee--the Committee of Public Service Disputes of 1955--consisting of Henrik Lundh, chairman;

---

*Document submitted by government.

Magnus Bjerkolt, office manager for the National
Arbitrator; and Kai Knudsen, district stipendiary
magistrate.

The recommendations of the committee were submitted to the organizations of the civil servants
for their opinion; and, furthermore, several drafts
of a bill reflecting the recommendations were discussed verbally with them. Prior to introducing
the bill (Bill No. 20, 1958) in the Storting (the
Norwegian parliament), the opinion of Kristen Ander-
sen, a professor at the University of Oslo, was
also procured. In the course of the preparation of
the bill various opinions made themselves felt with
regard to the right of civil servants to negotiate;
however, this chapter will deal mainly with an account of the Ministry's bill and the motives governing its wording.

STATE EMPLOYEES COVERED BY LEGISLATION

The Act of July 6, 1933, on negotiation covers
civil servants only, but not teachers in the elementary and continuation schools or state workers covered by the Act of May 5, 1927, respecting labor
disputes. The 1958 act comprises all employees who
are engaged in the civil service and have a term of
notice of two months or more. Temporarily engaged
persons, reserve employees, and candidates for the
civil service are also included in this act, even
though they have a shorter term of notice than two
months. Other workers engaged purely by the state
are, however, still outside the scope of this act.

The King-in-Council (the government) is authorized to include in the 1958 act groups of employees
who are not civil servants but whose wage and working conditions are stipulated by collective agreement with the state or through decisions otherwise
reached by the state. Thus, teachers in the elementary and continuation schools and a number of other
groups of official employees engaged by the local
authorities and counties are also covered by this
act.

Employees engaged in activities carried on by
the state as proper juristic persons are not as a
rule considered to be engaged in the service of the
state and are consequently outside the scope of the
1958 act. The same applies to employees in public
corporations run by the state as joint-stock companies.

RIGHT OF NEGOTIATION

Prior to 1933 civil servants were at a disadvantage as far as negotiations with their employers
were concerned, but this changed with the passage
of the Act of July 6, 1933. This act was favorably
received by civil servants, and it operated very
satisfactorily for a long time. As mentioned above,
it conferred the "right of negotiation" on civil
servants; that is, they were given an opportunity
to discuss their wages and working conditions with
state representatives at great length.

Furthermore, the various bills presented by
the government in the Storting were accompanied by
the minutes of proceedings in the form of printed
supplements, thus affording the deciding state authority a complete survey of the demands of the
civil servants and the justification for the views
of the parties concerned.

The 1933 act was based on the principle that
the right of negotiation on the part of civil servants was attached to <u>the organizations of civil
servants and the affiliates of such organizations</u>.
On special occasions, however, the right of negotiation might be exercised by groups of nonorganized
employees numbering at least 50 persons.

The 1958 act respecting public service disputes
maintains the principle that the right of negotiation on the part of civil servants is attached to
organizations of civil servants and affiliates of
such organizations but omits the right of negotiation for groups of at least 50 nonorganized civil
servants.

There are currently approximately 160 organizations of varying sizes within the civil service.

Of these, no less than about 130 are attached to
three of the central federations of civil servants:
the Cartel of Civil Servants, the Federation of
Civil Servants, and the National Federation of Civil
Servants (public officials).

Even though the right of negotiation has been
made more stringent under the 1958 act, the majority of these 160 unions will still have the right
of negotiation. In order to obtain the right of
negotiation these organizations must have at least
50 members, and the number of members must simultaneously constitute no less than half the number
of civil servants in the relevant service or branch
of service in the country.

In the explanatory statement accompanying the
1958 bill, the Ministry noted that, in order to obtain the concentration and centralization of the
right of negotiation desirable from a social point
of view, the great number of minor organizations
and local organizations, which are liable to adopt
a narrow attitude toward their claims, ought not to
be admitted. The new system involving collective
agreements that was a presupposition of this bill
also, in the opinion of the Ministry, of necessity
required that the organizations with which the state
concluded agreements were truly representative of
the civil servants within the relevant service or
branch of service.

In the course of the discussion of the matter
in the Storting two minority groups argued that a
number of small alterations or modifications ought
to be made regarding this part of the bill. Thus,
one minority suggested that, in addition to organizations with at least 50 members that simultaneously
represented at least half the number of the civil
servants of the relevant service or branch of service in the country, organizations with no less
than 500 members should also be granted the right
of negotiation, provided the number of members simultaneously constituted at least one-quarter of
the civil servants of the relevant service or branch
of service in the country.

The majority of both the Odelsting and the
Lagting (the two chambers of the Storting) endorsed

the proposal of the Ministry. Under the 1958 act a
local union can therefore in general no longer be
granted an independent right of negotiation. It
may, however, achieve a "derivative" right of negotiation by joining a main union. Those local organizations that presently enjoy an independent
right of negotiation have been granted a transi-
tional period of two years in which to adapt themselves to the new state of affairs. The same terms
apply to minor organizations consisting of less than
50 members and other smaller organizations that do
not fulfill the requirements of the new act.

In addition to the purely civil service organizations already mentioned, there also exist occupational organizations that admit members from both
inside and outside the civil service--for example,
the Medical Association, the Association of Dentists,
the Association of Engineers, and the Norwegian Organization of Engineers and Technicians. Under the
1958 act the King-in-Council has the authority to
grant an independent right of negotiation to state
employees who constitute an independent part of an
occupational organization.

As mentioned above, there exist at present
three main unions enjoying the right of negotiation
in addition to individual organizations entitled to
negotiate. A main union is a combination of organizations of civil servants entitled to negotiate.
The three main unions represent the predominant part
of the actual civil servants; accordingly, they have
occupied a dominant position during wage negotiations, particularly when negotiations of a general
character are involved.

The 1958 act assumes that the arrangement with
regard to main unions of civil servants will be
maintained and, therefore, imposes certain conditions with which the main union must comply in order to be entitled to negotiate. The main union
must include civil servants of at least five services and have at least 7,000 members; further, at
least five of the affiliated organizations must fulfill the requirements for obtaining an independent
right of negotiation.

In addition, the 1958 act provides that claims
with respect to a general regulation of collective
agreements for civil servants of several ministries
may only be presented by a main union. Consequently,
the main unions will also retain their dominant position after this act has come into force.

COLLECTIVE AGREEMENTS

The negotiations between the state and the organizations of civil servants have, so far, not resulted in any reciprocal, legally binding agreements. The state authorities were still in a position to stipulate the rates of pay to be observed;
however, it would take much for the authority with
the right to appropriate money to oppose a result
reached through negotiation and agreed on by both
parties.

The 1958 act respecting public service disputes
introduces a legal arrangement with regard to collective agreements for civil servants and the remaining employees included in the act. There is apparently no major difference between the current
system and the new system of collective agreements
at the negotiation stage, at any rate. The essential difference lies in the mutual duty of peace--
that is, the obligation of the parties not to engage in conflicts over the wages and working conditions agreed on in the collective agreement during
the period to which it refers.

In the explanatory statement accompanying the
1958 bill the Ministry pointed out that the claim
regarding the transition to collective agreements
by the civil servants was based essentially on the
unreasonable and inexpedient state of affairs involved in the legal relationship between the civil
servants and their employer, which differs from the
relationship existing between private employees and
their employers. Civil servants' organizations
also argued that the duty of peace resulting from
the system of agreements would be conducive to
strengthening the responsible organs within their
organizations and facilitating their work.

The state particularly noted that the transition to the system of collective agreements--with the consequent duty of peace during the periods to which the collective agreements refer--would entail more undisturbed conditions within the civil service, since the wage claims of the various organizations of civil servants would be postponed to a collective discussion on expiration of the collective agreements. Furthermore, the Ministry pointed out that the arrangement of collective agreements had proved a significant element in advancing peaceful working conditions in Norway, the system having resulted in a reduction of open labor conflicts.

CONCILIATION

As mentioned previously, the 1958 act also introduces more modern forms of procedure regarding actual negotiations. Further, it provides that should the negotiations prove abortive, the National Conciliator shall be called upon to conciliate. Thus, a system similar to that enjoyed by employees in private economic life for over 40 years will be introduced for the benefit of civil servants.

When bringing forward the grounds adduced in support of the proposal, the Committee of Public Service Disputes stated inter alia that the purpose of the arrangement of conciliation was to imbue civil servants with a sense of security and a guarantee that adequate importance would be attached to their points of view. Simultaneously, the use of conciliation would more easily ensure the clearing up of possible misunderstandings between the parties concerned, and the authorities on their part might through impartial conciliation obtain a more comprehensive foundation on which to arrive at a final decision with regard to the claims of the civil servants.

STRIKES, LOCKOUTS, AND BOYCOTTS

Should conciliation prove abortive, a dispute (conflict of interests) might result in open conflict

in the same way as in private economic life; however, the civil servants might not automatically
resort to strike means if the parties should agree
to submit the conflict of interests to arbitration
(a voluntary wages committee) or if the Storting,
through a special act, should decide on establishing compulsory arbitration in the case of a specific
conflict of interests. This point will be discussed
further below.

There follows a brief account of the general
right to strike of civil servants, together with
the restrictions on this right and the right of the
state to resort to a possible compulsory stoppage
of work (a lockout).

There exist no legal provisions respecting the
right to strike of the higher civil servants (public officials); however, it is generally accepted
that the higher civil servants are not entitled to
strike by reason of the position enjoyed by them in
Norway according to the constitution. It is further assumed that people in the military service
are also not entitled to strike. In addition to
this, by the Act of June 19, 1959, a strike ban was
introduced with respect to civil servants on the
police force.

With regard to the remaining civil servants it
is noteworthy that the Act of February 15, 1918--
the Civil Servants Act--does not prohibit striking
among civil servants. Section 27 of this act,
which treats the right of civil servants to give
notice, makes no reservation with regard to collective notice. The means afforded the authorities
under the Civil Servants Act in cases of collective
notice is the right to impose upon the civil servants in question the obligation to remain in the
service for a period of up to three months beyond
the term of notice, provided this is dictated by
vital public interests.

The 1958 act respecting public service disputes
retains the indirect right to strike that the civil
servants can be said to have under Section 27 of
the Civil Servants Act. In order to grant society
a respite in the face of strike actions on the part
of civil servants, however, the 1958 act--like the

present act--entitles the authorities to prolong
the ordinary term of notice by three months. At
the same time, the corresponding provision in the
Civil Servants Act has been repealed.

RETENTION FACTORS

It should be noted, however, that the arrangement with collective agreements (and the attendant
duty of peace in the period of agreement) suggested
in the 1958 act will result in the right of management to determine the categories of work in which a
reduction in force must take place, if such should
become necessary. Once it is decided which jobs are
to be abolished, a more automatic procedure determines who stays and who goes. In general, the following factors must be considered, as they apply to
employees in the kind of work being discontinued:
(a) tenure of employment, (b) length of state service, and (c) performance rating.

Bumping

As stressed above, when a reduction in force
becomes necessary, management has full discretion
in deciding which jobs are to be abolished. This
does not mean, however, that the incumbents of these
abolished positions are always the ones who leave
the rolls, since the "bumping" process of higher-
tenure employees over lower-tenure employees often
causes chain reactions that result in the layoff of
employees in other positions.

Helping Laid-Off Employees

To ensure the maintenance of a true career system, the government must make every effort to find
other jobs for career employees who lose their jobs
through no fault of their own. The full cooperation
of state administrators is essential to the success
of such efforts. The Department of Wages and Prices

operates a program to ensure that separated employees are fully considered for other jobs in the civil
service. Such employees, when qualified, are referred for placement to any agency having vacant
positions.

SICKNESS INSURANCE

All employees and their families are automatically covered by the state's sickness insurance fund
for a very low rate. This sickness insurance covers
all hospital costs for the employees and their families.

ARBITRATION

The Committee of Public Service Disputes discussed this question exhaustively and came to the
conclusion that the constitution does not prevent
the Storting from entrusting the solution of a concrete conflict of interests to an independent ex-
traneous institution. Furthermore, the committee
was of the opinion that such an arrangement with regard to arbitration ought to be introduced and suggested establishing an independent arbitration organization for the civil service.

The Ministry agreed in principle with the Committee of Public Service Disputes but was of the
opinion that it would be more in keeping with the
main principles on which the 1958 act is otherwise
based if the general provisions of the Act of December 19, 1952, respecting the National Wages
Board in labor disputes were applied to public service disputes.

In the 1958 act this has been reflected in the
arrangement whereby the permanent arbitration committee (the National Wages Board), which deals with
conflicts of interests with regard to wages and working conditions in private economic life and in the
local districts, has also been charged with the consideration of general conflicts of interests in the
state sector.

The National Wages Board consists of a chairman and four other permanent neutral members who
are appointed for a period of three years by the
King-in-Council. The 1958 act provides that in conflicts of interests between the state and the organizations of civil servants, the composition of
the board shall be altered to the effect that one
member of the National Wages Board shall represent
the interests of the state and another the interests of the civil servants. In an individual dispute the board is supplemented in the usual way--
that is, each party nominates an additional member
of the board.

Under the 1958 act a conflict of interests may
be submitted to the National Wages Board only
through the joint action of the parties concerned.
Thus, this act does not entitle the state in its
capacity as employer to submit a case to the National Wages Board without the cooperation of the
relevant civil servants' organization.

This does not, however, prevent the Storting
from providing, through a special act, that a current dispute is to be settled by the National Wages
Board, provided such a procedure is prompted by the
welfare of the community. In this case the civil
servants will occupy precisely the same position as
do other employees. The decision of the National
Wages Board is substituted for a collective agreement and has the same effect.

Under the 1958 act only conflicts of interests
of a more general nature are supposed to be discussed by the National Wages Board. According to
this act, the National Wages Board shall not attempt to solve disputes of more concrete claims
regarding alterations in the scale of wages, disputes with regard to adjustments of positions from
lower to higher levels, and disputes with regard to
claims concerning special increments.

Instead of the National Wages Board, a special
arbitration committee, the State Wages Committee,
has been organized for the purpose of final settlement of conflicts of interests regarding more concrete questions. The State Wages Committee comes
into operation at the request of one of the parties.

Thus, the parties concerned need not agree on submitting such cases to arbitration.

The State Wages Committee consists of three
neutral members who are appointed by the National
Arbitrator. For the rest, the state and the civil
servants' organizations are represented. Thus, the
three main unions each have one representative on
the State Wages Committee, but the independent organizations may also enter into the picture when
they are parties to a dispute.

HEARING OF LEGAL DISPUTES

By the 1933 act a special tribunal, the Civil
Servants Court, was established for the purpose of
hearing legal disputes between the state and the organizations of civil servants--that is, disputes regarding the interpretation of an adopted scale of
wages or a concluded agreement.

The 1952 act on labor disputes refers legal
disputes concerning civil servants' wages and working conditions contained in collective agreements
to the same tribunal that passes judgment on such
matters in the private sector--namely, the Labor
Court. The reasons adduced in support of this are
inter alia that legal questions involving principles
concerning collective agreements should not be heard
by two separate tribunals, both of which are assumed
to be the court of last instance. In addition to
this, the Labor Court even now passes judgment in
cases between the local communities and their employees.

The 1958 act, however, provides that the Labor
Court shall be somewhat differently composed than
usual when hearing cases concerning civil servants.
The three legal judges shall not vacate their seats
on the bench; but, of the remaining four judges,
two shall represent the interests of the state and
two the interests of the civil servants. The latter two judges shall be appointed at the proposal
of the main unions entitled to negotiate.

Legal disputes concerning wages and working
conditions that are not regulated in collective

agreements are not to be heard by the Labor Court
but by the ordinary tribunals. In addition to this,
it should be noted that in all disputes of such
character as mentioned above the parties may agree
to private arbitration.

NATURE OF STATE REPRESENTATIVE

According to the usual constitutional rules,
the King-in-Council acts on behalf of the state in
negotiations and when disputes are being dealt with.
The King-in-Council is not, however, entitled to
reach decisions that involve the Exchequer in ex-
penditures without the consent of the Storting. In
the explanatory statement accompanying the 1958 act
respecting public service disputes the question was
discussed concerning whether the King-in-Council
ought to be authorized to commit the state through
the conclusion of collective agreements with the
civil servants regardless of the constitution.

Although practical considerations might dic-
tate such authority's being given to the King-in-
Council, the Ministry came to the conclusion that
it would not bring up for discussion any proposal
to this effect. The Storting endorsed the opinion
of the Ministry; and, consequently, the 1958 act
provides that it is the King-in-Council, with the
consent of the Storting, that enters into collective
agreements on behalf of the state.*

---

*Prior to adopting an attitude toward the pro-
posal of the Ministry, the Storting had procured
the opinions of Professor Frede Castberg and Professor Johs. Andenaes on the constitutional aspects
of the 1958 bill. In Document No. 11, 1958, the
opinions of the two professors are included in
their entirety. Both treat at great length the
question concerning the right to commit the state
by collective agreements, the question of leaving
the solution of general conflicts of interests to
an impartial instance, and the question regarding
alterations in the scale of wages and adjustments

The King-in-Council must also have the consent
of the Storting to put a conflict of interests before the National Wages Board. The consent of the
Storting is, however, not necessary before submitting a case to the State Wages Committee.

CONCLUSIONS

As indicated above, the 1933 act regarding
negotiations did not include any provisions concerning arbitration in the case of conflicts of interests that might arise during negotiations concerning the wages and working conditions of civil servants. Now that explicit rules have been introduced in this field, they should form the basis for
more extensive peace and stability in the matter of
wage negotiations within the state. A transition
to the system of collective agreements, with the resulting obligation of peace in the periods to which
the agreements refer, will have a similar effect.

In particular, great hope is held out in regard to the new organ of arbitration, the State
Wages Committee, which will be entrusted with the
settlement of disputes respecting the relatively
assigned places on the scale of wages of the various groups of civil servants within the state services. Indeed, it is particularly in this sphere
that the controversial issues have been prominent
in recent years.

In addition to the representatives of the parties, the State Wages Committee is composed of
three neutral members. It goes without saying that
the decisions of the committee will be greatly dependent on the views of the neutral members. It
should also be remembered that the members of the
State Wages Committee will gradually acquire the

---

of positions to higher levels, together with the
question of submitting such disputes to the State
Wages Committee. Both professors concluded by
stating that the bill must be considered reconcil-
able with the constitution.

expert insight that is the precondition for an all-round appraisal of the difficult and delicate questions involved.

Conversely, it is to be hoped that the arrangement with arbitration will not result in the organizations' submitting too many cases to the State Wages Committee but, instead, as previously, causing them to concentrate as much as possible on actual negotiations. Indeed, it is primarily through negotiations that the proper confidential relationship is created between employer and employee.

The new arrangement brought about by the Act of July 18, 1958, respecting public service disputes presupposes making more flexible the provisions of the Civil Servants Act regarding the right of the state to discharge its civil servants. The fact is that a system of collective agreements, combined with the right to collective resort to force, must be said to be practically irreconcilable with the present system with irremovable civil servants.

As previously mentioned, this question has been alluded to in the explanatory statement accompanying the bill of the 1958 act, but the question of an amendment of the provisions relating to discharge is to be discussed in connection with a general revision of the Civil Servants Act.

CHAPTER 1

1. Joseph P. Goldberg, "Changing Policies in Public Employee Labor Relations," <u>Monthly Labor Review</u> (U.S. Department of Labor), July 1970, pp. 8-10.

2. Speech by U.S. Secretary of Labor W. Willard Wirtz before the American Federation of State, County, and Municipal Employees, Washington, D.C., April 27, 1966.

3. <u>Ibid</u>.

4. See Foster R. Dulles, <u>Labor in America</u> (New York: Thomas Y. Crowell, 1968), p. 232.

5. Dorchy v. Kansas, 272 U.S. 306, 47 Sup. Ct. 86 (1926).

6. B. V. H. Schneider, <u>Collective Bargaining and the Federal Service</u> (Berkeley: University of California, 1968). Reprint 235, p. 106.

7. Derek C. Bok and John T. Dunlop, <u>Labor and the American Community</u> (New York: Simon and Schuster, 1970), p. 331.

8. Labor-Management Relations Act (Taft-Hartley Act, June 23, 1947), 61 Stat. 136, 29 U.S.C.A. Supp. 1947.

9. Bok and Dunlop, <u>Labor and the American Community</u>, p. 338.

10. David L. Perlman, "Public Employees: An Emerging Force," in Robert Wash, ed., <u>Sorry. No Government Today</u> (Boston: Beacon Press, 1969), p. 26.

11. Theodore W. Kheel, "Strikes and Public Employment," <u>Michigan Law Review</u>, LXVII (1969), 932-33.

12. New York Civil Service Law, sec. 200-212 (McKinney Supp. 1968).

13. <u>Labor-Management Policies for State and Local Government</u>, Advisory Commission on Intergovernmental Relations (1969), p. 24.

14. "Standards of Conduct for Employe Organization and Code of Fair Labor Practices," <u>Federal Register</u>, May 23, 1963, pp. 6127-32. For a detailed

report and analysis of the federal program, see
American Bar Association, Section on Labor Relations Law, "Report of Committee on Law of Government Employee Relations," July 1966; also see
Wilson R. Hart, "The Impasse in Labor Relations in
the Federal Civil Service," Industrial and Labor
Relations Review, XIX, 2 (January 1966), 175-89;
and a rebuttal by the chairman of the U.S. Civil
Service Commission, John W. Macy, Jr., "The Federal
Employee-Management Co-operation Program," Industrial and Labor Relations Review, XIX, 4 (July 1966),
549-61.

15.   Letter to Arvid Anderson from Louis S.
Wallerstein, Chief, Division of Federal Employee-
Management Relations, U.S. Department of Labor,
July 15, 1966.

16.   John W. Macy, Jr., "Employee-Management
Cooperation in Federal Service," in Kenneth O.
Warner, ed., Management Rights with Organized Public Employees (Chicago: Public Personnel Association, 1963), p. 212.

17.   Cited by Louis S. Wallerstein in an address to the Nineteenth Annual Conference on Labor,
New York University, April 19, 1966.

18.   See Louis S. Wallerstein, ibid.; Davis S.
Barr, in "Government Employee Relations Report"
(GERR), No. N2, p. A-9; and John W. Macy, Jr., in
GERR, No. 140, p. A-1.

19.   Speech by Wirtz.

20.   Address by Assistant Secretary of Labor
James Reynolds, University of Chicago, March 11,
1966.

21.   Hart, "The Impasse in Labor Relations in
the Federal Civil Service," p. 32.

22.   Macy, "The Federal Employee-Management
Co-operation Program."

23.   "Report of Committee on Law of Government Employee Relations," p. 138.

24.   Ibid.

25.   "Analysis of Data and Report on Union
Recognition in the Federal Service," U.S. Civil
Service Commission, Bulletin No. 711-22 (Washington,
D.C., March 3, 1971).

26.   See GERR, No. Rf-21, pp. 1-8.

27.   Postal Reorganizational Act of 1970, Public Law 91-375, August 12, 1970, in GERR, No. Rf-4.

28.   See "Developments in Industrial Relations," Monthly Labor Review, July 1971, p. 65.

29.   Truax v. Corrigan, 257 U.S. 312 (1921).

30.   See, generally, National Governor's Conference, 1970 Supplement to Report of Task Force on State and Local Government Labor Relations (Chicago: Public Personnel Association, 1971).

31.   "Year Three of the Taylor Law--a Time for Reflection," New York State, Public Employment Relations Board, PERB Newsletter, May 1971.

32.   The necessity for exclusion of supervisory personnel, with supportive reasons and description of state treatment is examined by Harry H. Rains, "Collective Bargaining in the Public Section and the Need for Exclusion of Supervisory Personnel," Labor Law Journal, Chicago, May 1972, pp. 275-88.

33.   Wesley Wildman, "Representing the Teachers' Interests," Industrial Relations Research Association, Spring Meeting, May 7, 1966.

34.   See GERR, No. 405, p. B-7.

35.   52 O.A.G. 363 (October 3, 1953).

36.   During the New Hampshire Republican Presidential primary, Richard Nixon backed Mayor John Lindsay's firm position regarding the sanitation strike and supported the mayor's request for National Guard intervention. Nixon advocated strict compliance with state legislation and was disappointed with Governor Nelson Rockefeller's willingness to assist with negotiations during an illegal strike. See The New York Times, February 15, 1968, p. 33.

Senatorial candidate Paul O'Dwyer, counsel for the sanitation union, recommended suitable alternatives to the strike: "You cannot take away a public employee's right to strike unless you give him something in its place." See The New York Times, February 12, 1968, p. 42.

Senator Jacob Javits recommended binding arbitration in public employment labor disputes. See The New York Times, September 9, 1968, p. 39. The New York Times summarized editorials supporting strict compliance with the Taylor Law. This summary

included opinions from the Buffalo Evening News, the
Rochester Democrat & Chronicle, The Chicago Ameri-
can, The New York Daily News, and the Suffolk Sun.
See The New York Times, February 2, 1968, p. 38.

It is said that John DeLury, president of the
New York City Uniformed Sanitation Workers Association, doesn't support strike action by public employees: "He doesn't believe in strikes by public
employees (his union has had only one major strike in
its history, in 1968), but rather that their legitimate objectives should be achieved through political
activity." Edward Costikyan, "Who Runs New York?"
New York Magazine, December 23, 1968, p. 25.

37. This high degree of organization in New
York City reflects a long-standing policy of the
city government to encourage unionization and collective bargaining among its employees. Mayor
Robert Wagner's Executive Order 49, issued in 1953,
encouraged collective bargaining by employees appointed by the mayor. See also New York City Collective Bargaining Law, 53SS1170.0-74.0(b), reproduced in GERR, No. 205, p. E-1.

38. For a list of these statutes, see Russell
Smith, "State and Local Advisory Reports on Public
Employment Labor Legislation: A Comparative Analysis," Michigan Law Review, LXVII (1969), 891 and
892, n. 5.

39. Pa., S.B. 1333, L. 1970, in GERR, No.
Rf-3, 51:4711; and Hawaii, Act, L. 1970, in GERR,
No. Rf-28, 51:2011.

40. Public Employment Relations Act, (Hutchin-
son Act), Mich. Comp. Laws Ann., secs. 423.210-16.
(1967).

41. Roger Rapoport, "Militant Public Employees," Wall Street Journal, August 9, 1966, p. 14.

42. Final Report, New York State, Governor's
Committee on Public Employee Relations (1966), pp.
4711 and 2011.

43. New York Civil Service Law, secs. 200-212
(McKinney Supp. 1968). The present version of this
law, as amended by a bill passed on March 4, 1969
(effective April 1, 1969), appears in GERR, No.
288 (March 17, 1969), p. F-1.

44. Nelson Rockefeller, in The Chief (the New York City Civil Employees' Weekly), January 17, 1969, p. 1.

45. GERR, No. 282 (February 13, 1969), p. B-1.

46. The Citizens Budget Commission, a New York City nonprofit taxpayer group, criticized the $10,000 ceiling on the daily fine that could be imposed against a striking union under the original version of the Taylor Law. The commission also preferred an indeterminate jail sentence to the 30-day maximum sentence then available for union leaders who urged disobedience of an injunction. New York City Citizens Budget Commission, "Is New York Governable?" (mimeo., November 24, 1968).

A spokesman for the Commerce and Industry Association of New York recommended that a union that violates the strike ban loses its dues-deduction privilege for an unlimited period. GERR, No. 274, p. B-5. Under the original Taylor Law a union in violation of the antistrike provision lost the privilege for no more than 18 months. Public Employees' Fair Employment Act, ch. 392, sec. 210(f), NY Laws 1102 (1967).

The amendments call for unlimited fines against striking unions and the loss of check-off privileges for unlimited periods. Another section provides for the loss of two days' pay for each day a public employee is on strike. Moreover, a striking worker is subject to one year's probation, with loss of tenure, for any violation of the strike prohibition. For the text of the law as amended, see GERR, No. 288 (March 17, 1969), p. F-1.

Several other amendments were also pending before the New York legislature. S.1207 was introduced January 14, 1969, by State Senator Rollison to amend the Civil Service Law to repeal the limitation of penalty for a striking union. To replace the provision providing for a fine equal to 1/52d of total annual dues of the organization or $10,000, whichever is the lesser, it provided that the method of calculation of the fine would be equal to $100 multiplied by the number of members or $10,000, whichever is greater.

State Senator Rollison also introduced S.1206, January 14, 1969. Its purpose was to amend the Civil Service Law in order to permit a taxpayers suit in the nature of a special proceeding in the Appellate Division of the New York Supreme Court against a striking public employee organization in cases where the chief legal officer fails, within 10 days after the commencement of such strike, to apply to that court for an injunction. It might be asked whether the N.Y. Civ. Prac. secs. 7801-06 (McKinney, 1963) proceeding in the nature of mandamus is not an adequate remedy.

S.2168, introduced January 26, 1969, would amend the Civil Service Law to require a no-strike pledge of every public employee and a penalty for violation consisting of forfeiture of all rights of tenure, accumulated sick leave and vacation time, and the portion of the pension fund that has been paid by the employer. Furthermore, dismissal of striking public employees would be mandatory.

On the same date, State Senators Balletta and Jonas also introduced S.2170 to provide for the appointment by the governor of seven public-spirited citizens to act as arbitrators. S.2170 would also resolve impasses by final referral to compulsory arbitration by the governor's named panel. Any person found guilty of refusing to implement or obey the panel's decision could be found in contempt, fined $500, imprisoned 60 days, or both.

In addition, the second interim report on the governor's "Taylor Panel" recommended that limits on fines for the contempt convictions of public employee union leaders be repealed. Second Interim Report, New York State, Governor's Committee on Public Employee Relations, January 23, 1969, p. 18.

47. More than 100 agreements were negotiated in 1968 between the City of New York and its municipal unions. The Chief, January 17, 1969, p. 4.

48. For the text of the statute, see GERR, No. 205 (August 14, 1967), p. E-1.

49. Supra note 3, p. 7.

50. But see Kheel, "Strikes and Public Employment," pp. 931 and 941.

51. See, e.g., ibid., pp. 940-41.

52.   See, e.g., _ibid_., pp. 941-42.

53.   E.g., Pub. L. No. 90-54, 81 Stat. 122 (1967, special resolution and mediation of dispute under Railway Labor Act).

54.   City of New York v. DeLury, 23 N.Y.S. 2d 175, 243 N.E. 2d 128, 295 N.Y.S. 2d 901 (1968), appeal dismissed, 37 U.S.L.W. 3363 (U.S., March 31, 1969).

55.   23 N.Y. 2d, p. 186; 243 N.E. 2d, pp. 133-34; and 295 N.Y. 2d, p. 909.

56.   _Ibid_.

57.   "The Public Interest in Collective Negotiations in Education" (address delivered at University of Pennsylvania, mimeo, June 1968).

58.   Board of Education v. Redding, 32 Ill. 2d 567, 207 N.E. 2d 427 (1965).

59.   E.g., Public Service Staff Relations Act, ch. 72, sec. 101 (1) (c) (1966-1967), Can. Stat.; see Arthurs, "Collective Bargaining in the Public Service of Canada: Bold Experiment or Act of Folly," _Michigan Law Review_, LXVII (1969), 971 and 988-89.

60.   Quebec Civil Service Act, ch. 14, sec. 75, 1 Que. Stat. 157 (1965). Albert Shanker, president of the United Federation of Teachers, in proposing an end to the blanket New York City strike ban, suggested that it would be the best public policy to make a determination of essentiality only after a strike revealed the essential nature of the public service involved. See GERR, No. 276, p. B-5 (December 23, 1968). See also pp. 25-26, above.

61.   _Report and Recommendations_, Pennsylvania, Governor's Commission to Revise the Public Employee Law of Pennsylvania (1968), p. 14.

62.   This proposal was subsequently embodied in Pa. Stat. Ann., tit. 43, sec. 217 (Supp. 1969). The increase in the incidence of public employee strikes affecting essential services has made the idea of compulsory arbitration seem more attractive--or at least less objectionable--as an alternative method of dispute resolution in the public sector. For instance, virtually no one would suggest that policemen should have the right to strike, and arbitration has been accepted as an alternative in

an increasing number of states. See Ill. Rev.
Stat., ch. 24, secs. 10-3-8 to 11 (1967) (advisory
arbitration of municipal firemen disputes); Ill.
Rev. Stat., ch. 11-213, secs. 301-44 (1967) (Chicago
Transit Authority Employees); La. Rev. Stat. Ann.,
sec. 23:890 (Supp. 1969) (public transportation and
municipal employees); Me. Rev. Stat. Ann., tit. 26,
secs. 980-92 (Supp. 1968) (fire fighters); Pa. Stat.
Ann., tit. 43, secs. 123.1-.16 (1947) (arbitration
of public utility disputes); Fire Fighters Arbitration Act, R.I. Gen. Laws Ann., secs. 28-9.1-1 to -14
(1969); Policemen's Arbitration Act, R.I. Gen. Laws
Ann., secs. 28-92-1 to -14 (1969); and School Teachers' Arbitration Act, R.I. Gen. Laws Ann., secs.
28-9.3 to -16 (1969).

63. The experience under Taft-Hartley and
under the Railway Labor Act has been critically examined in H. Northrup, Compulsory Arbitration and
Government Intervention in Labor Disputes: An
Analysis of Experience (Washington, D.C., 1966).
Northrup notes that between 1934 and June 30, 1964,
159 cases (35 of them involving airlines) were
handled by emergency boards and 58 additional boards
were selected from the National Railway Labor Panel.

Northrup's three major conclusions from this
experience were that the appointment of emergency
boards had become commonplace; recommendations of
emergency boards at critical times have been handled
with political expediency; and the procedure has
severely inhibited collective bargaining (p. 64).

The criticisms of the Taft-Hartley emergency
procedures at least recognize the problems associated with the administration of any emergency provisions. But it is doubtful that the problem is
intrinsic to the procedure as a whole. Society is
filled with all kinds of complex administrative
problems, and consideration of emergency procedures
should not be discarded merely because their administration is difficult.

64. Ida Klaus, "The Evolution of a Collective
Bargaining Relationship in Public Education: New
York City's Changing Seven Year History," Michigan
Law Review, LXVII (1969), 1033; and Donald Wollett,
"The Coming Revolution in Public School Management,"
Michigan Law Review, LXVII (1969), 1017.

65. Rankin v. Shanker, 23 N.Y.S. 2d 111, 242 N.E. 2d 802, 295 N.Y.S. 2d 625 (1968).

66. Law of March 27, 1947, ch. 391 (1947), N.Y. 842, as amended, Law of April 23, 1963, ch. 702 (1963), N.Y. Laws 2432 (repealed 1967).

67. GERR, No. 277, p. B-2 (December 30, 1968).

68. Report and Recommendations, p. 14.

69. A. H. Raskin, "How to Avoid Strikes by Garbagemen, Nurses, Teachers, Subwaymen, Welfare Workers, Etc.," The New York Times, February 25, 1968, sec. 6 (Magazine), p. 34.

70. See Smith, "State and Local Advisory Reports on Public Employment Labor Legislation," p. 891, n. 5.

71. E.g., Mich. Comp. Laws Ann., sec. 423.25 (1967); and Wis. Stat., sec. 111.88 (1969).

72. E.g., Alaska Stat., sec. 23.40.010 (1962) (compulsory); Ill. Rev. Stat., ch. 24-1/2, sec. 38b3(3) (1964) (compulsory); Minn. Stat., secs. 179.36-.38 (1965) (compulsory); Neb. Rev. Stat., secs. 48-801 to -823 (1960) (advisory).

73. Wall Street Journal, January 28, 1969, p. 1.

74. Ibid.

75. N.Y. City Admin. Code, ch. 54, Local Law 53, sec. 1173-3.0 (g), reproduced in GERR, No. 205, p. E-3.

76. Third Annual Report, New York City, Office of Collective Bargaining (1971).

77. Similar patterns of successful prior mediation and reference to arbitration have been observed in other jurisdictions. The combined data compiled by Edward Krinsky of the Research Staff of the University of Wisconsin Department of Labor Relations for the states of Wisconsin, New York, Connecticut, Michigan, and Massachusetts show that between 60 and 80 percent of mediation cases were resolved without resort to fact-finding; approximately 50 percent of the cases in which fact-finding was initiated were settled prior to the issuance of recommendations.

Krinsky also found that, in the great majority of completed fact-finding cases, work stoppages have been avoided and the recommendations accepted. (Data supplied by Edward Krinsky from an unpublished

and incomplete doctoral thesis on fact-finding in
public employment, February 1969, University of
Wisconsin).

78. George Hildebrand, "The Neutral in Public
Employment Disputes," in Bureau of National Affairs,
Washington, D.C., Proceedings of the 20th Annual
Meeting (1967), pp. 287 and 292.

79. A recently proposed Taylor Law amendment
that would make fact-finding binding would, according to its proponents, "achieve the benefits arbitration invariably imposes. In addition it should
tend to motivate both parties to more effective and
realistic good faith negotiation and earlier
achievement of agreement." "Hearings on the Taylor
Law," Before the New York State Legislature, Joint
Legislative Committee on Industrial and Labor Conditions, December 1968; statement of R. Rowley reproduced in GERR, No. 277, p. B-1.

80. Tobriner, "An Appellate Judge's View of
the Labor Arbitration Process: Due Process and the
Arbitration Process," in Proceedings of the 20th
Annual Meeting, pp. 37-38.

81. See Lloyd Reynolds, Labor Economics and
Labor Relations (Englewood Cliffs, N.J.: Prentice-
Hall, 3d ed., 1959), pp. 280-82.

82. State of Wyoming v. City of Laramie, 68
LRRM 2038 (1968); Erie Fire Fighters Local 293 v.
Gardner, 406 Pa. 395, 178, A2d 691; Harvey v. Russo,
435 Pa. 182, 255 A2d 560 (1969); and Warwicls v.
Regular Fireman's Association, 256 A2d 206 (S. Ct.
of Rhode Island, 1969).

83. State of Wyoming v. City of Laramie.

84. Harvey v. Russo.

85. Ontario Fire Department Act, ch. 149, Rev.
Stat. Ont. (1960); and Police Act, ch. 298, Rev.
Stat. Ont. (1960).

86. Public Service Staff Relations Act, ch.
22, Can. Stat.

87. Robert Howlett, in Proceedings of the
Southwestern Legal Foundation (1969).

88. William E. Simpkin, "Mediation and the
Dynamics of Collective Bargaining," Bureau of National Affairs (1971), pp. 331-55.

CHAPTER 2

1.   Louis Paul Suetens, "Le droit de grève,"
Revue du travail (Brussels, 1966), p. 1633.

2.   Annales parlementaires, Sénat, January 16,
1969.

3.   Conseil d'Etat, December 16, 1955, in
Recueil des arrêts et avis du conseil d'Etat, section d'administration siégeant au contentieux
(Courtrai, Belgium, 1955), p. 963. Hereafter cited
as RAACE.

4.   "Aperçu des effectifs du secteur public,
Situation au 30 Juin 1969," Fonction publique
(mimeo.).

5.   "Rapport," Institut national d'assurance
maladie-invalidité (mimeo., Brussels, 1970), p. 107.

6.   Conseil d'Etat, January 28, 1954, in RAACE,
1954, p. 121.

7.   Conseil d'Etat, November 6, 1969, in RAACE,
1969, p. 940.

8.   Conseil d'Etat, October 16, 1959, in RAACE,
1959, p. 615.

9.   Conseil d'Etat, December 19, 1969, in RAACE,
1969, p. 1097.

10.   Conseil d'Etat, October 12, 1956, in RAACE,
1956, p. 653.

11.   Cour de cassation, November 23, 1967, in
Journal des tribunaux (Brussels, 1968), p. 41.

12.   Louis Camu, Premier rapport sur la réforme
administrative, Le statut des agents de l'Etat
(Brussels: IMIFI, 1937), p. 26.

13.   Annales parlementaires, Sénat, 1960-61
session, p. 588.

14.   Folke Schmidt, "Collective Negotiations
Between the State and Its Officials," Revue inter-
nationale des sciences administratives (Brussels,
1962), p. 300.

15.   Adalbert Brandt, Das Beamtenrecht (Berlin:
Goetz, 1926), p. 427.

16.   Herman Finer, Theory and Practice of Modern
Government (rev. ed.; New York: Henry Holt & Co.,
n.d.), p. 571.

17.   Conseil d'Etat, June 8, 1966, in RAACE,
1966, p. 533.

18. Cour de cassation, December 8, 1932, in Pasicrisie (Bruylant, Brussels, 1933), I, 44.

19. Cour de cassation, October 22, 1942, in Pasicrisie (1942), I, 249.

20. Conseil d'Etat, April 6th?, 1951, in RAACE, 1951, p. 127.

21. Conseil d'Etat, February 3, 1950, in RAACE, 1950, p. 41.

22. Cour de cassation, April 29, 1960, in Pasicrisie (1960), I, 1000.

23. Paul Horion, Nouveau précis de droit social (The Hague: Martinus Nyhoff, 1965), p. 7.

24. Conseil d'Etat, November 3, 1961, RAACE, 1961, p. 893.

25. Cour de cassation, November 23, 1967, in Journal des tribunaux (1968), p. 41.

26. Conseil d'Etat, January 9, 1964, in RAACE, 1964, p. 15.

27. Tijdschrift voor Gemeenterecht (Brussels, 1965), p. 234.

28. Conseil d'Etat, April 27, 1967, in RAACE, 1967, p. 430.

29. Paul De Visscher et al., L'exercice de la fonction disciplinaire dans les administrations des pays du Marché commun (Brussels: Larcier, 1965).

30. Chambre des Représentants, Document 889, No. 1, 1970-71 Session.

CHAPTER 3

1. The Committee on Relations Between Employers and Employed, chaired by J. H. Whitley, Chairman of the Ways and Means Committee of the House of Commons and later the Speaker of that body. Whitleyism has been an important influence in British industrial relations for more than half a century; see Roger Charles, "National Consultation and Co-operation between Trade Unions and Employers in Britain, 1911-1939" (unpublished Ph.D. dissertation, Oxford University, 1970).

2. Report of the National Provisional Joint Committee on the Application of the Whitley Report to the Administrative Department, Cmnd. 198, 1919.

3. Her Majesty's Treasury, Staff Relations in the Civil Service (London: Her Majesty's Stationery Office, 1965), p. 5.

4. George Sayers Bain, <u>Trade Union Growth and Recognition</u>, Royal Commission on Trade Unions and Employers' Associations, Research Papers, No. 6 (1968). This commission was set up by the Wilson Administration to advise on the reform of British industrial relations in 1965; it reported in June 1968. Cmnd. 3623, 1968.

5. Bain, <u>Trade Union Growth and Recognition</u>, p. 67.

6. A similar influence has been exercised by the Treasury in agreeing in July 1965 to offer check-off (or deduction of trade union dues at the source by the employer) to all recognized staff associations, although in this case the effect has been felt almost entirely in the public sector, where check-off is now generally applied. See A. I. Marsh and J. W. Staples, <u>Check-off Agreements in Britain</u>, Royal Commission on Trade Unions and Employers' Associations, London, Research Papers, No. 8 (1968).

7. See, for example, F. J. Lynch of the Confederation of Health Service Employees, in <u>Post Donovan Conferences on Collective Bargaining and Trade Union Development, Public Sector</u> (Trade Union Congress, 1969), pp. 29-33.

8. Association of Scientific Workers, "Evidence to the Donovan Commission," RC/WE/62, September 9, 1965. Since that time the Commission on Industrial Relations has made recommendations on recognition at one of the councils concerned, <u>Medical Research Council</u>, Report No. 12, Cmnd. 4531, November 1970.

9. Most recently in K. W. Wedderburn and P. L. Davies, <u>Employment Grievances and Disputes Procedures in Britain</u> (Berkeley: University of California Press, 1969).

10. A situation excellently described by Roy Lewis, "The Legal Enforceability of Collective Agreements," <u>British Journal of Industrial Relations</u>, VIII, 3 (November 1970).

11. See <u>Staff Relations in the Civil Service</u>, pars. 46, 73, and 93.

12. <u>Report of a Court of Inquiry into a Dispute between the Parties Represented on the National Joint Industrial Council</u> (Wilberforce Report), Cmnd. 4594, February 1971.

13. See Post Donovan Conferences, Public Sector.

14. Ibid., p. 72.

15. See B. V. Humphreys, Clerical Unions in the Civil Service (London: Blackwell and Mott, 1958), pp. 94ff.

16. Marjorie McIntosh, "The Negotiation of Wages and Conditions for Local Authority Employees in England and Wales," Public Administration, Autumn 1955.

17. The object of the National Dock Labour Board was not only to assume management of the labor force of the industry but also to achieve decasualization, an objective further advanced in the 1960s as a result of the report of the Devlin Committee (Final Report, Cmnd. 2734, August 1965).

18. Agreement of May 3, 1921, reproduced as an appendix to the "Memorandum on the Railways Bill," 1921.

19. The original papers of the Whitley Committee, mislaid for many years and not rediscovered until 1969, establish this point beyond any doubt; see Charles, "National Consultation and Co-operation bwtween Trade Unions and Employers in Britain, 1911-1939," chs. 4 and 5.

20. The decline of formal consultation has been associated with the growth of the bargaining role of the shop stewards; see W. E. J. McCarthy, The Role of Shop Stewards in British Industrial Relations, Royal Commission on Trade Unions and Employers' Associations, Research Papers, No. 1 (1966), pp. 32ff. It is significant that editions of the official Industrial Relations Handbook contained a chapter on joint consultation until 1961; in the edition of that year the chapter was reheaded "Industrial Relations at the Place of Work" and gave shop stewards pride of place, joint consultation appearing only as part of the text.

21. As, for example, in the report of the Fulton Committee on The Civil Service, Vol. I, Cmnd. 3638, June 1968, p. 90. It is difficult not to believe that the wish was not, at least in part, the father of the thought, and that the Fulton Committee would have preferred to forget the negotiating element in Whitleyism; see pp. 166-67, above.

22. See Richard Hayward, Whitley Councils in the United Kingdom Civil Service, Civil Service National Whitley Council, Staff Side, June 1963, p. 10.

23. A development of the local advisory committees toward primary working groups is discussed by H. Sallis, "Joint Consultation and Meetings of Primary Working Groups in Power Stations," British Journal of Industrial Relations, III, pp. 326-44.

24. The relevant agreement contains the words "to consider and decide," claimed by some unions in the industry to infer that local panels are empowered to make joint decisions and, hence, to negotiate; see Richard Coates, "An Analysis of Joint Consultation in Terms of Political Democracy in Particular Reference to British European Airways" (unpublished B.Litt. thesis, Oxford University, 1970), for an interesting view of these panels as exercising constraints on airline "government."

25. T. L. Johnston, in D. J. Robertson and L. C. Hunter, eds., Labour Market Issues of the 1970s (London: Oliver and Boyd, 1970), p. 52.

26. Robert Carr, Secretary of State for Employment, as reported in The Times, November 3, 1970, announced that some of the review body functions operated for some years by the terminated National Board for Prices and Incomes (on Armed Forces pay, for example) and those of the Kindersley Committee (set up in 1960 to review the pay of doctors and dentists employed in the National Health Service) would in the future fall under three new review bodies, serviced by a new Office of Manpower Economics. University teachers obtained an ingenious piece of negotiating machinery reconciling the interests of themselves, the university authorities, the University Grants Committee (which advises the government on university financial needs), and the Secretary of State in May 1970.

27. For an account of the system, see A. I. Marsh and W. E. J. McCarthy, Disputes Procedures in Britain, Royal Commission on Trade Unions and Employers' Associations, Research Papers, No. 2, Part 2, London (1968), ch. 6.

28. Until 1969 the awards of the tribunal were not formally recognized as binding, although

they were generally accepted by management. Since
1969 a joint agreement to refer an issue, on agreed
terms of reference, makes the ensuing decision binding. See Charles McLeod, All Change; Railway Industrial Relations in the Sixties (London: Gower Press,
1970).

   29. Post Donovan Conferences, Public Sector,
pp. 32-33. Public-sector unions have often found
arbitration useful as a means of developing and con-
solidating membership and collective bargaining machinery, and particularly compulsory arbitration--
that is, arbitration at the request of either party.
Such arbitration was provided for in Orders 1305 and
1376, which established the National Arbitration
Tribunal (1940-51) and the Industrial Disputes Tribunal (1951-59), together with a condition that
awards would be legally enforceable in the sense of
becoming an implied term of contract of the workers
concerned. Health service unions found it conve-
nient to have binding rulings on the application of
existing agreements, useful on occasion in advancing
the cause of particular groups and sometimes even in
resisting government wishes over wage restraint.
See H. A. Clegg and T. E. Chester, Wage Policy and
the Health Service (1957).

   Alec Spoor, the historian of the national and
local government officers, records that the National
Arbitration Tribunal was regarded as a charter for
trade unionism and was used to force wages and conditions negotiated by provincial Whitley councils
on many reluctant local authorities. See Alec
Spoor, White Collar Union (1967). Such unions were
fiercely opposed to the abolition of the Industrial
Disputes Tribunal in 1959.

   30. Final Report, Royal Commission on the
Civil Service, 1930-31, Cmnd. 3909, 1931, par. 308.

   31. Royal Commission on the Civil Service,
1953-55, Cmnd. 9631, 1955, pars. 95, 116, 133-44,
and 157-85.

   32. The highest grades of civil servants in
the administrative, executive, professional, and
scientific classes have since 1957 been subject to
an independent Standing Advisory Committee, which
reviews their pay either on its own initiative or

at the request of the government; the committee
also collects information on salaries in comparable
employment outside. See Pay of Higher Civil Servants, National Board for Prices and Incomes, Report
No. 11, Cmnd. 2882, 1966.

33. Royal Commission on the Civil Service,
Cmnd. 3638, June 1968.

34. Pay of Industrial Civil Servants, National
Board for Prices and Incomes, Report No. 18, Cmnd.
3034, June 1966.

35. The phrase "productivity agreement" was
coined by Allan Flanders to describe the result of
a negotiation in which higher pay was agreed to in
return for better use of manpower--for example, in
manning practices, abandonment of systematic overtime, use of shift working, and so forth. See The
Fawley Productivity Agreements (London: Faber and
Faber, 1964). Since that time, the de facto definition of the phrase has widened. Some of the productivity agreements for industrial civil servants
(for example, those employed on public building and
works) have been akin to the Fawley type; others
(for example, in Army Department engineering workshops) have been of a different type, based on the
acceptance of the introduction of method study and
work measurement.

36. Report of the Royal Commission on the
Police, Cmnd. 1222, 1960.

37. Royal Commission on Doctors' and Dentists'
Remuneration, Cmnd. 939, 1960.

38. Prices and Incomes Policy, Cmnd. 2639,
1965.

39. Pay and Conditions of British Railways
Staff, National Board for Prices and Incomes, Report No. 8, Cmnd. 2873, January 1966.

40. Pay of Nurses and Midwives in the National
Health Service, National Board for Prices and Incomes, Report No. 60, Cmnd. 3585, 1968.

41. Remuneration of Academic Staff in Universities and Colleges of Advanced Technology, National
Incomes Commission, Report No. 3, Cmnd. 2317, 1964,
p. 17.

42. Standing Reference on the Pay of University Teachers in Great Britain, National Board for

Prices and Incomes, First Report, Report No. 98, Cmnd. 3866, 1968.

43. _Ibid._, Second Report, No. 99, Cmnd. 4334, 1970.

44. Pay and Conditions of Manual Workers in Local Authorities, the National Health Service, Gas and Water Supply, National Board for Prices and Incomes, Report No. 29, Cmnd. 3230, March 1967.

45. Report of a Court of Inquiry into a Dispute (Wilberforce Report).

46. George Hildebrand, "The Public Sector," in John T. Dunlop and Neil W. Chamberlain, eds., Frontiers of Collective Bargaining (New York: Harper & Row, 1967).

47. For a brief account see H. A. Clegg, The System of Industrial Relations in Great Britain (London: Basil Blackwell, 1970), ch. 11.

48. Now the Civil and Public Services Association. See CSCA Strike Policy, Civil Service Clerical Association (1969).

49. _Ibid._, pp. 7, 8, and 17.

50. C. J. Margerison and C. K. Elliott, "A Predictive Study of the Development of Teacher Militancy," British Journal of Industrial Relations, VIII, 3 (November 1970).

51. Productivity Agreements, National Board for Prices and Incomes, Report No. 36, Cmnd. 3311, June 1967.

52. Remuneration of Administrative and Clerical Staff in the Electricity Supply Industry, National Board for Prices and Incomes, Report No. 5, Cmnd. 2801, October 1965.

53. Pay and Conditions of British Railway Staff.

54. Pay and Conditions of Busmen, National Board for Prices and Incomes, Report No. 16, Cmnd. 3012, May 1966; Pay of Industrial Civil Servants; Pay and Conditions of Manual Workers in Local Authorities, the National Health Service, Gas and Water Supply; and National Board for Prices and Incomes, Report No. 51, Cmnd. 3499, January 1968.

55. Whether this prediction is justified remains to be seen, but it is certainly true that local authority productivity schemes are patchy,

that centralized authority in some utilities (electricity, for example) may inhibit their development,
and that in others substantially no progress has
been made, In this last category can be placed an-
cillary staff in the National Health Service. See
National Board for Prices and Incomes, Cmnd. 4644,
April 1971.

56. A manpower committee reporting in 1950
and 1951 recommended its extension to local authority work. See Cmnd. 7870, January 1950, and Cmnd.
8421, December 1951.

57. W. L. Wilding, "The Post-Fulton Programme:
Strategy and Tactics," Public Administration, XLVIII
(Winter 1970), 397.

CHAPTER 4

1. Paul Bobrowski and Dieter Gaul, Das Arbeitsrecht im Betrieb (Labor law in business) (6th
ed.; Heidelberg: Recht und Wirtschaft, 1970), p.
M I 3.

2. Alfred Hueck and Hans Carl Nipperdey,
Lehrbuch des Arbeitsrechts (Reader of labor law),
Vol. II (7th ed.; Berlin: Franz Vahlen, 1963,
1967, 1970), I, II (Part 1), II (Part 2), sec. 7,
p. III 1.

3. Dieter Gaul, Betriebsinhaberwechsel und
Arbeitsverhältnis (Change of owner of an establish-
ment and employment), Arbeitsrecht 3 (Labor law 3)
(Munich: Moderne Industrie, 1966), s. 25.

4. Rolf Dietz, Personalvertretungsgesetz mit
Wahlordnung (Right of acting for the personnel with
regulation of voting rights) (Munich: C. H. Beck,
1956), Part B, Introduction.

5. Galperin, Die Stellung der Gewerkschaften
im Staatsgefüge (The position of the trade unions
within the state), pp. 30ff.

6. Bobrowski and Gaul, Das Arbeitsrecht, p.
M II.

7. Ibid., p. H III; and Hueck and Nipperdey,
Lehrbuch des Arbeitsrechts, sec. 47, p. A II 2.

8. Hans Carl Nipperdey and Franz-Jürgen
Säcker, "Suspendierende und losende Arbeitskampf-
mittel" (Means of suspending and solving labor

combats), Der Betriebsberater (Heidelberg), 1st
semivolume (1969), p. 321.
    9. Bobrowski and Gaul, Das Arbeitsrecht, pp.
D II and F I.
    10. Oskar Georg Fischbach, Kommentar zum
Bundesbeamtengesetz (Commentary to the Civil Servant Law) (3d ed.; 2 vols.; Cologne: Carl Hagemann,
1964, 1965), I, II, Introduction, p. III; and Her-
mann von Mangoldt and Friedrich Klein, Kommentar--
Das Bonner Grundgesetz (Commentary--The Bonn Constitution) (2d ed.; 3 vols.; Berlin: Franz Vahlen,
1966), art. 33.
    11. Bobrowski and Gaul, Das Arbeitsrecht, pp.
A V 7 and 8.
    12. Dieter Gaul, Die Arbeitsbewertung und
ihre Rechtliche Bedeutung (Valuation of work and
its legal importance), p. B 1.
    13. Zander, Gehaltsfestsetzung in Wirtschaft
und Verwaltung (Fixing of salaries in industry and
administration), Heidelberger Fachbücher (Readers
of Heidelberg) (2d ed.; Heidelberg: I. H. Sauer,
1968), p. 67.

CHAPTER 5
    1. Morone, "Impiego pubblico," Novissimo
Digesto Italiano (Turin), VIII (1962), 266. Sul
pubblico impiego in generale v. anche: Zanobini,
Corso di diritto amministrativo (Milan, 1958), III,
258 ss.; Landi-Potenza, Manuale di diritto amministrativo (Milan, 1967), p. 413 ss.; Virga, Il pubblico
impiego (Palermo, 1957).
    2. Ministero del Tesoro, Ragioneria generale
dello Stato, Dipendenti delle Amministrazioni
Statali (Rome: Istituto Poligrafico dello Stato,
1968).
    3. Ibid., p. 5.
    4. Istat, "Bollettino Mensile di Statistica,"
No. 4 (April 1968), p. 102.
    5. See Pergolesi, Istituzioni di Diritto
Corporativo (Bologna, 1938); and Fantini, Legis-
lazione Corporativa del Lavoro (Milan, 1938).
    6. Ross, "Prosperity and Labor Relations in
Western Europe: Italy and France," Industrial Labor
Relations Review, XVI (October 1962).

7. See Bocca, "Il Sindacato Povero," <u>Il Giorno</u>, September 26, 1965.

8. See Istat, "Bollettino Mensile di Statistica," p. 102.

9. CISL, "La Questione del Sindacalismo Autonomo" (Rome, 1967), p. 11.

10. See Pera, <u>Problemi Costituzionali dei Diritti Sindacali Italiani</u> (Milan, 1960), p. 258.

11. D'Eufemia, <u>Diritto Sindacale</u> (Naples, 1967), p. 83; Di Narcantonio, <u>Appunti di Diritto del Lavoro</u> (Milan, 1958), p. 275; and Riva Sanseverino, <u>Diritto Sindacale</u> (Turin, 1964), p. 169.

12. Contrary to registration are D'Eufemia, <u>Diritto Sindacale</u>, p. 83; and Ghidini, <u>Labor Law</u> (Padua, 1969), p. 55. In favor are Carullo, <u>Diritto Sindacale Transitorio</u> (Milan, 1960), p. 71; and Napoletano, <u>Nozioni di Diritto Sindacale</u> (Naples, 1966), p. 41.

13. The decision can be found in <u>Labor Law</u>, II (1967), 76ff.

14. See Pera, "Una Grave Decisione sul Diritto di Associazione Sindacale del Personale della Pubblica Sicurezza," in <u>Boll. scuola perfez.</u> (Trieste, 1966), pp. 3ff., nn. 35-36; Napoletano, <u>Nozioni di Diritto Sindacale</u>, p. 26, n. 1; and D'Eufemia, <u>Diritto Sindacale</u>, pp. 84-85. In favor of the above-mentioned decision, although disagreeing with the grounds of the decree, see Audau, "La Funzione di Tutela della Sicurezza Pubblica Quale Limite Soggettivo del Diritto di Sciopero," in <u>Massimario Giurisprudenza del Lavoro</u> (1966), pp. 227ff.; and Acciarini, "Divieto per il Personale di P.S. di Appartenere a Organizzazioni Sindacali," <u>Labor Law</u>, II (1967), 82ff.

15. Napoletano, <u>Nozioni di Diritto Sindacale</u>, p. 26, n. 1.

16. CISL, "La Questione del Sindacalismo Autonomo."

17. <u>Ibid</u>.

18. For all figures quoted see table attached to Presidential Decree No. 749 of June 5, 1965.

19. <u>Ibid</u>.

20. See <u>Dipendenti delle Amministrazioni Statali</u>, p. 33.

21. <u>Ibid</u>., p. 74.

22. See Report of the State Administrative Reform Commission (Rome, 1966), p. 52.

23. Simi, Il diritto di sciopero (Milan, 1956), p. 192; Ardau, "Lo Sciopero ed i Servizi Pubblici," Il Diritto del Lavoro, I (1955), 177; and Mazzoni, I Rapporti Collecttivi di Lavoro (Milan, 1967), p. 333.

24. Simi, Il diritto di sciopero, p. 194.

25. Mazzoni, I Rapporti Collecttivi di Lavoro, p. 331; Branca, "Libertà e Diritto di Sciopero," in Rilevanza dell'Interesse Pubblico nel Diritto del Lavoro con Particolare Riguardo al Diritto di Sciopero (Padua, 1968), pp. 86-87; and Simonetto, "Spunti sul Diritto di Sciopero," in Rilevanza dell'Interesse Pubblico, p. 95.

26. Mengoni, "Lo Sciopero e la Serrata nel Diritto Italiano," in CECA, Sciopero e Serrata (Luxembourg, 1961).

27. Branca, "Libertà e Diritto di Sciopero," p. 87.

28. Scotto, op. cit., pp. 94ff.

29. Simonetto, "Spunti sul Diritto di Sciopero," p. 99.

30. Branca, "Libertà e Diritto di Sciopero," p. 87.

31. Scotto, op. cit., p. 93.

32. D'Eufemia, Diritto Sindacale, p. 119.

33. Stendardi, "I Dipendenti dell'Amministrazione dello Stato e lo Sciopero," Foro Padano, IV (1954), 142ff; and Scotto, op. cit., p. 92.

34. Simi, Il diritto di sciopero, p. 197; and Scotto, op. cit., p. 92.

35. Miele, "Lo Sciopero dei Pubblici Dipendenti e degli Esercenti Servizi Pubblici," in L'Esercizio del Diritto di Sciopero (Milan, 1968), p. 169.

36. See, for example, State Council, October 16, 1956, No. 95, in Il Consiglio di Stato, I (1956), 1180; and State Council, November 6, 1957, in ivi, I (1957), 1458.

37. Constitutional Court, December 28, 1962, No. 123, in Giustizia Civile, III (1963), 49ff.

38. See, for example, State Council, October 16, 1956, No. 95, in Il Consiglio di Stato, I (1956),

1180; and State Council, November 6, 1957, in _ivi_,
I (1957), 1458.

39. See, for example, State Council, July 27,
1964, No. 930, in Il Consiglio del Stato, I (1964),
1242.

40. State Council, April 28, 1965, in Massimario Giuridico del Lavoro (1966), p. 300.

41. State Council, June 16, 1966, in Il Consiglio di Stato, I (1966), 2077-2078.

42. Riva Sanseverino, Diritto Sindacale, p.
440.

43. See Smuraglia, La Costituzione e il Sis-
tema del Diritto del Lavoro (Milan, 1958), p. 224.

44. Constitutional Court, December 28, 1962,
No. 123, in Giustizia Civile, III (1963), 52.

45. Ibid., p. 49.

46. Constitutional Court, March 17, 1969, No.
31, in Foro Italiano, I (1969), 795.

47. Ibid.

48. Miele, "Lo Sciopero dei Pubblici Dipen-
denti," p. 184; Pace, "Spunti per una Delimitazione
Costituzionale dello Sciopero," Giurisprodenza
Costituzionale (1964), pp. 1447-48; and Zaccaria,
"In Tema di Legittimità dello Sciopero dei Vigili
urbani," Foro Italiano, II (1968), col. 419.

49. Supreme Court, February 25, 1967, No. 339,
in Massimario di Giurisprudenza del Lavoro (1967),
p. 150.

50. Appellate Court of Bologna, April 26,
1962, in Rivista di Diritto del Lavoro, II (1962),
339; Tribunal of Genoa, March 30, 1966, in Foro
Italiano, II (1966), col. 368; and Tribunal of Leghorn, March 29, 1968, in Foro Italiano, II (1968),
col. 416.

51. Tribunal of Genoa, March 30, 1966.

52. Tribunal of Leghorn, March 29, 1968.

53. See article dated February 21, 1967, in
La Magistratura, Nos. 1-2 (1967).

CHAPTER 6

1. See, for example, T. L. Johnson, Collective
Bargaining in Sweden (London: George Allen and Un-
win, 1962); and S. D. Anderman, "Central Wage

Negotiation in Sweden: Recent Problems and Developments," British Journal of Industrial Relations,
V (1968), 322.

2. The State Officials Act, 1965 (Statstjänste-
mann a Lagen den 3 juni 1966, nr. 274). For a summary of the related legislation, see K.M. prop. nr.
60, 12 mars 1966.

3. The findings of these labor force surveys
must be treated with some caution, given the small
size of the sample (18,000-60,000 out of 3.7 million) and the method of survey (95 percent telephone interview). See The Labour Force Surveys,
1961-69, National Central Bureau of Statistics,
Statistical Reports, Am 1969:57.

4. F. Schmidt, The Law of Labor Relations in
Sweden (Cambridge, Mass.: Harvard University Press,
1962), pp. 154-55.

5. In addition, some public employees may be
listed as officials but not hold positions of public responsibility under the penal code; see ibid.,
pp. 155-56.

6. There are five sectoral groups in SF:
railways; defense; education and welfare; and post
office, telecommunications and radio; roadworks;
power and electricity. See Statsunställdus Forbund,
Organizationskommittens forslag (Stockholm, 1968).

7. See A. Nilstein's chapter in A. Sturmthal,
White Collar Trade Unions (Urbana: University of
Illinois Press, 1966).

8. Lag om förenings och förhandlingsrätt, den
11 September 1936 (nr. 506).

9. See Schmidt, The Law of Labor Relations in
Sweden, p. 154; and Johnson, Collective Bargaining
in Sweden, p. 132.

10. Kungörelse angående förhandlingsrätt for
statens tjaustemän den 4 juni 1937 (nr. 292). The
position of municipal officials was regulated by a
1940 act, Lag om förhandingsrätt för kommunala
tjaustemän den 17 mai 1940 (nr. 331).

11. Johnson, Collective Bargaining in Sweden,
pp. 135-36.

12. An excellent summary of this legislation
is contained in ibid. and in Schmidt, The Law of
Labor Relations in Sweden.

13. *Lag om medling i arbetstviste* den 28 maj 1920 (nr. 245).

14. See Johnson, *Collective Bargaining in Sweden*, pp. 169ff.

15. See Nilstein, in Sturmthal, *White Collar Trade Unionism*, p. 284.

16. See, for example, E. Kassalow, "Professional Unionism in Sweden."

17. Thus, it suggests the creation of a special working committee within the NCBO consisting of four members--including the head of the NCBO, a representative from the finance department, and two other members of the governing board--to coordinate between government departments and the parliamentary Wage and Salary Delegation. See Forhandlings Utredningen: Stencil Fi. 1970:2.

18. *Fackforeningsrörelsen och den fulla sysselsältringen*, p. 152.

19. *Ibid*.

CHAPTER 7

1. Remark attributed to Victor Gotbaum, executive director of District Council 37, American Federation of State, County, and Municipal Employees Union, AFL-CIO.

2. Emmet John Hughes, "Politics of the Sixties--from the New Frontier to the New Revolution," *The New York Times Magazine*, April 4, 1971, p. 70.

3. John V. Lindsay, in *The New York Times*, June 21, 1971, p. 13.

4. ILO, International Labor Office, Joint Committee on the Public Service, *Freedom of Association and Procedures for Staff Participation in Determining Conditions of Employment in the Public Service* (Geneva, 1970), pp. 6-7.

5. *Time Magazine*, March 15, 1971, p. 26.

6. *The New York Times*, November 30, 1971, p. 41.

7. Theodore W. Kheel, "Strikes and Public Employment," *Michigan Law Review*, LXVII (March 1969), 941-42.

8. Public Services International, *Negotiating Rights of Public Servants and the Right to Strike in the Public Service* (London, 1966), p. 2.

9. *Ibid*.

10. Hughes, "Politics of the Sixties."

SEYMOUR P. KAYE, counsel to the law firm of Rains, Pogrebin, and Scher, is a lecturer in labor legislation at Hofstra University and adjunct professor of Labor-Management Relations at Pace College Graduate School. He serves as an arbitrator, mediator, and fact-finder on panels of the American Arbitration Association in New York, and on the Jersey State Boards of Mediation, the Federal Mediation and Conciliation Service, the New York and New Jersey Public Employment Relations Boards, and is a member of the permanent panel of the New York City brewery industry.

Mr. Kaye formerly was counsel for the New York City Mayor's Office of Labor Relations, and Director of Staff Relations for the New York City Off-Track Betting Corporation. At one time he was Vice President of Industrial Relations of the Olivetti Underwood Corporation and Director of Industrial Relations of ITT in Europe. He has also contributed many articles to professional journals.

He received his B.A. degree from the University of Pennsylvania, his J.D. from Columbia, and an LL.M. from NYU Law School.

ARTHUR I. MARSH is a Senior Research Fellow at St. Edmund College, Oxford University. He also serves as arbitrator of disputes for the Department of Employment and Productivity and is a member of the Local Employment Committee of the same department. While Staff Tutor from 1949-64 at Oxford University Mr. Marsh specialized in the development of trade union education. Since 1964 he has been concerned with research projects in teaching disputes procedures of the check-off in Britain, in disputes procedures in British industry in general, and in trade union welfare benefits and earnings drift.

Mr. Marsh is the author of several research papers for the Royal Commission on Trade Unions and Employers Associations including "Industrial Relations in the Engineering Industry," "Disputes

Procedures in Britain," parts I and II, and "The Check-off in British Industry." He has also authored Contrasts in Agricultural Price Policies, Shop Steward Organization in the Engineering Industry, and Industrial Relations in the Engineering Industry.

At present Mr. Marsh is studying workplace relations in the engineering industry, while also studying trends of workplace bargaining in a number of British industries.

He received honors degrees, (M.A.) in Modern History and Philosophy, and Politics and Economics from Hertford College, Oxford.